MATHEMATICS AND SCIENCE FOR EXERCISE AND SPORT

Mathematics and Science for Exercise and Sport introduces students to the basic mathematical and scientific principles underpinning exercise and sport science. It is an invaluable course companion for students who have little prior experience of maths or science, and an ideal revision aid for higher level undergraduate students.

The book explains the basic scientific principles that help us to understand sport, exercise and human movement, using a wide range of well-illustrated practical examples. Written by three leading sport scientists with many years' experience teaching introductory courses, the book guides beginning students through those difficult to grasp areas of basic maths and science, and identifies the common problems and misconceptions that students often experience. It includes coverage of key areas such as:

- Science of physical states – gas, liquid and solid
- Science of biomechanics, motion and energy
- Mathematical formulae, calculus and differential equations
- Statistics
- Scientific report writing
- Key concepts such as pressure, torque and velocity
- Self-test features and highlighted key points throughout each chapter

Fully referenced, with guides to further reading, this book is an essential companion for all students on foundation or undergraduate courses in sport and exercise science, kinesiology and the human movement sciences.

Craig A. Williams is Associate Professor and Director of Teaching at the School of Sport and Exercise Science, and Co-director of the Children's Health and Exercise Research Centre, both part of the University of Exeter, UK.

David V.B. James is Associate Dean (Research) in the Faculty of Sport, Health and Social Care at the University of Gloucestershire, UK.

Cassie Wilson is Senior Lecturer in Sports Biomechanics and Programme Leader for the Sport and Exercise Science degree programme at the University of Bath, UK.

MATHEMATICS AND SCIENCE FOR EXERCISE AND SPORT

The Basics

CRAIG A. WILLIAMS, DAVID V.B. JAMES AND CASSIE WILSON

 Routledge
Taylor & Francis Group

LONDON AND NEW YORK

First published 2008
by Routledge
2 Park Square, Milton Park, Abingdon, Oxon, OX14 4RN

Simultaneously published in the USA and Canada
by Routledge
270 Madison Avenue, New York, NY 10016

Routledge is an imprint of the Taylor & Francis Group, an informa business

Typeset in Zapf Humanist and Eras by
Keystroke, 28 High Street, Tettenhall, Wolverhampton
Printed and bound in Great Britain by
TJ International Ltd, Padstow, Cornwall

British Library Cataloguing in Publication Data
A catalogue record for this book is available from the British Library

Library of Congress Cataloging-in-Publication Data
Williams, Craig A.
   Mathematics and science for sport and exercise : the basics / by Craig A. Williams,
D.V.B. James and Cassie Wilson.
      p. cm.
   Includes index.
   1. Sports sciences–Textbooks. 2. Physical sciences–Textbooks. 3. Mathematics–Textbooks.
I. James, David V. B., 1971– II. Wilson, Cassie. III. Title.
   GV557.5.W55 2008
   502.4'796—dc22   2007050667

ISBN10 0–415–44169–2 pbk
ISBN13 978–0–415–44169–8 pbk

ISBN10 0–415–44168–4 hbk
ISBN13 978–0–415–44168–1 hbk

CONTENTS

V

contents

FIGURES

ix

figures

TABLES

PREFACE

The number of universities in the United Kingdom which offer undergraduate courses in sport and exercise has increased considerably since the 1980s. There are over 100 different institutions around the country offering a combination of single or joint honours degrees in sport and exercise science, coaching science, exercise and health science, sport engineering, sport development, physical education, sport and management, sport and business or sport and computing, to name a few. The increase in courses related to sport and exercise reflects not only the interest students have in the subject, but also the expanding career opportunities in the exercise and sport industry.

The idea for this book has grown out of our experiences as lecturers in sport and exercise science at our respective academic institutions. We are aware that during the first year of undergraduate studies the range of knowledge and skills brought to the lecture theatre or laboratory is very varied, particularly in relation to the student's experiences in science. For example, at some high schools the science subjects are taught through the separate disciplines of chemistry, physics and biology. In other schools it is common practice to combine the science disciplines and students obtain an award in combined sciences. For some students this is their last exposure to the subject before embarking on their undergraduate programme. Our concern as lecturers was therefore how best to facilitate students' learning in the sciences when there is an absence of core knowledge. At the time of writing this book, there are very few texts written for the first-year undergraduate in exercise and sport. Although there are many quality texts devoted to single disciplines within exercise and sport (e.g. biomechanics, psychology, physiology, sociology), there is a gap in texts that cover material which would provide a base of science knowledge for the subjects of exercise and sport.

It is not uncommon for a first-year undergraduate student on a sport and exercise degree course to take laboratory-based sport and exercise science modules. This would certainly be the case for a student studying sport and exercise science as a single honours subject, but might also be common for students on a joint honours course who can opt for laboratory-based modules. One of the difficulties of teaching a laboratory-based module is the diverse scientific background of the students. This book was written to help students who enrol for laboratory-based scientific modules in sport and exercise who may not possess a post-16 years science qualification. A knowledge of science at the level taught up to 16 years has been assumed as the starting point, and, as with all good learning and teaching strategies, it is hoped that enthusiasm for the subject will allow the student to overcome initial weaknesses.

The material covered in the text might be considered typical for a first-year undergraduate, although this will vary between courses depending on the specific aims and objectives of the course. It is possible that certain sections of the book might be useful for second- or third-year students, and skills such as report writing will always be in demand at all levels.

The philosophy behind the book centres on the fact that the student will have a willingness, because of their interest in exercise and sport, to increase their understanding of the science underpinning this subject. We recognise that no single book could replace a post-16 years education in sciences. We have tried not to assume core knowledge, and have concentrated on areas of science that students might experience in a sport and exercise course.

We have approached each topic by initially covering the science that underpins it. It is our belief that in order to improve the understanding of exercise and sport, the scientific knowledge base must be increased prior to application. Once these underpinning scientific principles have been covered, they are then related to an exercise or sport situation. In this respect, students can see the role science has to play in an applied setting, and are encouraged to think of further applications.

It should also be stressed that this textbook is not a 'catch-all' science book. There are many more principles that we could have covered, but instead we hope that the student will be motivated to go on to read other specialist science books. Our goal has been to make the book as 'user friendly' as possible. To that end we have included a number of common features throughout the book:

- In each chapter, scientific facts are presented first, followed by their application to exercise and sport.
- Each chapter covers a separate topic, but related chapters are grouped into three sections to promote cross-referencing.
- Key words are highlighted (in bold) throughout the text and definitions are provided in a list of key terms at the back of the textbook.
- Stop and think boxes and self-test questions are included to assist the student in developing their science knowledge and its application.
- Towards the end of each chapter, key points are provided for quick reference.
- At the end of all chapters, a bibliography and further reading list are provided. Both lists include textbooks and journals.
- The book is accompanied by additional electronic resources available via a website.

In Part 1, the three physical states of matter (gases, liquids and solids) are considered in three separate chapters. In Chapter 2, the defining features of gases are discussed,

XiV

preface

followed by laws which apply to gases. In the application section, reference is made to the atmospheric gas inspired and the issues surrounding the collection and analysis of expired gas. The various methods that can be used to examine pulmonary gas exchange are also examined.

In Chapter 3 the properties of liquids are considered. Although it is possible to consider gases and liquids under the banner of 'fluids', we have chosen to consider each state separately. The liquid laws are considered, followed by the application of these laws to exercise and sport. The concepts of pressure, buoyancy and flow are examined, and the laws of Archimedes, Pascal and Bernoulli are provided. This scientific basis is then applied to blood pressure and cardiovascular health examples.

Chapter 4 focuses on the properties of solids. The internal energy of solids is examined along with the way in which solids are affected by temperature. Additionally, heat transfer, and factors such as thermal conductivity and radiation, are explained. Heat transfer from a solid object and the structure of bone provide relevant exercise and sport examples.

In Part 2 the forces, energy and electricity are considered in three chapters (5, 6 and 7 respectively). In Chapter 5 the effect of application of force is discussed in relation to Newton's laws of motion. The relationship between force and pressure is examined, followed by a definition of each term. Different types of forces are discussed, and the measurement of both force and pressure is considered. Applications examine the concept of torque, and the relationship between torque about a joint and joint angle, and torque about a joint and joint angular velocity.

In Chapter 6 the concepts of energy, work and power are defined. Rather than concentrate on energy transfer in the body, a subject that is covered in many physiology and nutrition texts, the chapter focuses on the application of energy, work and power principles to exercise and sport. Examples of pole-vaulting, running and cycling are provided.

Chapter 7 focuses on electricity, including considerations of static electricity, Coulomb's law, the flow of electricity, and how electricity relates to power. The applications to exercise and sport include examples such as an electrocardiogram, a defibrillator and bioelectrical impedance analysis.

Part 3 concentrates on data analysis, numerical calculations and report writing, which are examined in three chapters (8, 9 and 10 respectively). In Chapter 8 the process of analysing data is covered, in conjunction with related issues such as hypothesis testing, experimental design, reliability and validity. Throughout the chapter, exercise and sport examples are used. To a large extent the chapter examines the concepts of data analysis rather than the derivation of complex formulae. Most students of exercise and sport have to embark on an independent study, project or dissertation at some stage during their course, so this chapter will be useful not only for first years, but also for other years as well.

Chapter 9 examines numerical calculations and how an understanding of numeracy underpins learning in exercise and sport disciplines. In addition to presenting and working through typical equations, the equations are applied to a range of exercise and sport

XV
preface

examples. Numerical skills are crucial to exercise and sport students and, more importantly, numerical competence is highly sought after by employers.

Chapter 10 focuses on report writing. Laboratory reports are commonly used as a method of dissemination of information from experiments. The ability to write succinctly and conventionally is an important skill. All areas of a report are addressed; from the abstract through to the references. Once again, this chapter will be useful not only for first-year students unaccustomed to scientific report writing, but also for second- and third-year students producing a dissertation.

Craig A. Williams
David V.B. James
Cassie Wilson
November 2007

ACKNOWLEDGEMENTS

We would like to acknowledge the inspiration provided by colleagues at the Universities of Exeter, Gloucestershire, Brighton and the University of Wales Institute of Cardiff. We are also grateful to the students we have taught over the years who have also provided the inspiration for this book.

PART 1

PHYSICAL STATES

CHAPTER ONE

INTRODUCTION

AIMS OF THE CHAPTER

This chapter aims to introduce science as applied to exercise and sport. After reading this chapter you should be able to:

- Understand the basis for maths and science in exercise and sport.
- Recognise the Système Internationale for units of measurement.
- Understand the importance of accuracy of measurement.
- Recognise scientific notation.
- Recognise issues relating to measurements on human participants.

INTRODUCTION

The study of exercise and sport draws upon many disciplines, including biomechanics, medicine, nutrition, philosophy, physiology, psychology and sociology, to name a few. In the sport performance area, biomechanists, physiologists, psychologists, medics and nutritionists often work alongside athletes and coaches with the aim of improving performance. In the exercise and health area, these scientists work alongside patients/healthy clients and exercise and health practitioners with the aim of improving health. Whatever the aim of the interdisciplinary team, the quality of the science underpinning practice is critical to reaching the ultimate goals. In turn, many scientific approaches require a sound appreciation of basic mathematics.

Much of the work of members of an exercise or sport team should have a sound scientific basis. It is a key responsibility of the exercise or sport scientist to ensure that the approach has a scientific basis. In practice, this might be evident through a systematic approach to solving problems, or ensuring that high-quality evidence exists for implemented strategies.

It has been said that, 'there is no such thing as applied science only the application of science' (Huxley). This quotation applies to the area of exercise and sport science in that, to investigate an exercise or sport problem, scientific principles are often applied to the problem. In this respect, appreciating what a scientific approach may bring to a situation is of benefit to all members of an exercise or sport team.

SCIENCE AND MATHS IN EXERCISE AND SPORT

A scientific approach to the study of exercise and sport is often considered useful, particularly when the benefits of exercise or sport participation must be maximised. The scientific body of evidence that should underpin practice is based on a set of principles that are widely understood by the scientific community. A scientific approach involves posing a problem, often in the form of a question, which can then be investigated. Once the question has been investigated, the results may be used to develop a **theory**. The theory may then be applied to similar problems in the future. However, theories evolve as they are challenged. If it is found that the theory does not apply to a certain situation, the theory must be modified to account for that situation. It is the responsibility of scientists to continually challenge theories so that they can be either modified or discarded. It is these principles that guide work in science. Williams and Wragg (2004) provide a brief overview of the development of scientific theory, and consider alternative paradigms.

Existing knowledge in exercise and sport science is often challenged through the collection of new factual information. Prior to the collection of such information, it is necessary to formulate a precise question. The question is normally posed in the form of **hypotheses** that can be tested through the collection of information. Two hypotheses are normally formulated, based on two possible outcomes. One hypothesis is known as the **null hypothesis**, and relates to a theory remaining unchanged. The other hypothesis is known

4

physical states

as the **alternative hypothesis**, and relates to a need for modification of a theory. At the end of the investigation, one hypothesis is rejected and one is accepted.

The information that is collected in order to test the hypotheses is normally referred to as **data**. In Chapter 8 the close relationship between data collection, data analysis and hypothesis testing is examined in more detail.

MEASUREMENT

The collection of data often involves the measurement of some related phenomenon. Measurement might appear an easy task, but on closer inspection it is considered to be an involved process. The quality of measurement is critical in science, so the remainder of this chapter will examine aspects of measurement. Measurement concepts will underpin many of the following chapters, hence their inclusion at this early stage of the book.

A student of exercise and sport should have a good understanding of measurement issues. A common problem related to the understanding of measurement is described by Paulos (1988). In an attempt to familiarise students with numbers and what their quantity means, Paulos asked a student how fast (in miles per hour) human hair grows, to which the student replied, human hair doesn't grow in miles per hour! The answer is actually 10^{-8} miles per hour or 0.00000001 miles per hour. In this example, the student failed to realise that hair growth, albeit very slow, could be expressed as miles per hour as a unit of speed.

To understand measurement units, it is necessary to learn about **Système Internationale (SI) units**. The SI units are an abbreviation of 'le Système Internationale d'Unités'. These standardised units have been developed to promote international co-operation and to provide a universally accepted system of measurement. The system not only allows information from different countries to be easily exchanged and understood, but also offers a standardised form for presentation of measurement outcomes. The seven base units of the SI are found in Table 1.1. It is important that the fundamental units are learnt because other units are subsequently derived from these seven.

Table 1.1 The seven base SI units

Physical quantity	Base unit	Symbol
length	metre	m
mass	kilogramme	kg
time	second	s
amount of substance	mole	mol
thermodynamic temperature	kelvin	K
electric current	ampere	A
luminous intensity	candela	Cd

The symbols are a mixture of lower-case and upper-case letters, which can be confusing. All symbols are written in lower-case roman letters except when the name of a unit is derived from the name of a person; for example, (W) to symbolise power in watts. When the unit has a proper name and is written in full, the whole word is in lower case. For example, the unit of measure for pressure is 'Pa', named after the scientist Blaise Pascal (1623–1662); when written out in full, it should be written as 'pascal'. A common mistake made by students is the symbol representing kilogramme (for measurement of mass), often writing it as 'Kg'; this is incorrect as it should appear as 'kg'. Recall, from Table 1.1, that the upper-case 'K' is the symbol for temperature, named after Lord Kelvin (1824–1907). All symbols should be lower case, except where the unit is derived from a proper name. An exception to the rule is the litre, where it is now common practice to accept it as 'L'. This exception is partly to avoid confusion between the lower-case 'l' and the numeral '1'.

Other rules include never following a period after a symbol unless at the end of a sentence, as well as never pluralising any symbols. Another common mistake is to mix names and symbols together; for example, newton·metre·s^{-1}. The correct style should be N·m·s^{-1}. Students are also sometimes confused as to when to use the solidus symbol (/). With personal computers it should be possible to learn how to use the symbol period instead, that is, · raised above the line when there is a product of two units. The solidus can be used but is not considered to be as clear for scientific work, especially when multiple symbols are combined. If the solidus symbol is used then only one per expression should be included, that is, kg·m/s^2, this is because the division is not associative. When two or more units are formed by multiplication or division in text, a multiplication of two units is indicated by a space between two words and never by a hyphen; for example, newton-metre would be incorrect; rather, newton metre is the correct style. To indicate in text a division of several units we would write 'per', rather than use the solidus; for example, litres per minute rather than litres/minute. When units are reported, it is preferable to use symbols rather than writing out the full name. Whenever numbers are reported with symbols, a space between the two should be left, that is, 400 W rather than 400W. There is, however, an exception to the rule, that is, the use of the symbol for degree (°). In this instance, there is no space left between the numerical value and the symbol: 40° not 40 ° and 30°C not 30 °C.

When reporting measurement quantities, a zero should always be placed before a decimal, that is, 0.01 not .01. Decimals are preferable to fractions, that is, 0.75 is preferable to ¾. If possible, long numbers should be separated with the use of a space, so 1,300,000 becomes 1 300 000. It is, however, optional with four digits; for example, 1000 or 1 000.

Derivatives of units in Table 1.1 are included in Table 1.2. Students should be aware that there are a number of other non-SI units associated with time. Although the SI unit for time is the second (s), day (d) is sometimes accepted for long periods of time. In Table 1.3 are the non-SI units for time, commonly used in science journals.

Other derivatives from the original seven base units (Table 1.1) such as energy, power and force will be dealt with in greater detail in Chapters 5 and 6.

physical states

Table 1.2 Units derived from the seven base SI units

Derived unit	Name and symbol	Derivation from base units
area	square metre	m^2
volume	cubic metre	m^3 *
force	newton (N)	$kg \cdot m \cdot s^{-2}$
pressure	pascal (Pa)	$kg \cdot m^{-1} \cdot s^{-2}$ ($N \cdot m^{-2}$)
work, energy	joule (J)	$kg \cdot m^2 \cdot s^{-2}$ ($N \cdot m$)
mass density	kilogramme per cubic metre	$kg \cdot m^{-3}$
frequency	hertz (Hz)	s^{-1}

* Although the cubic metre is the correct derivative for volume, the litre (L), or cubic decimetre (dm^3) has been accepted as the reference for volume.

Table 1.3 Symbols for the non-SI units for time .

minute	m
hour	h
day	d
week	wk
month	mo
year	y

One of the reasons why the SI was devised was to help to report data that was numerically very large or very small. Therefore, a number of prefixes are used to form multiples and sub-multiples of the base units. These prefixes usually change the quantity by a factor of 10^3 or 10^{-3}, but other smaller or larger increments are used (see Table 1.4). The prefix is written without a space and the symbols are as shown in Table 1.4. Therefore, a megagram (Mg) is a kilogramme (kg) multiplied by a thousand.

It is often impractical to write a number with several zeros if you are dealing with very large or small numbers. To overcome this issue, scientific notation, or powers of ten, can be used. It is common practice to shift the decimal place between the number one and ten and then multiply by the appropriate number. For example, if you wanted to write the number of thin filaments in a single muscle fibre, which may be about 64 000 000 000, on several occasions, it would become very tedious to constantly write this expression. By using notation, you can convert this number by placing a decimal place between the first two digits 6 and 4, making 6.4, and then counting the number of places the decimal point has moved. This conversion is now 6.4×10^{10}. Similarly, 0.00000159 becomes 1.59×10^{-6}. The decimal place has been inserted between the 1 and 5 to create a number lower than 10, and this is normal practice. Because we are dealing with a small number below 1 in this example, the superscript 6 is preceded by a negative symbol (–).

Now that the correct units of measurement and scientific notation have been discussed, it is important to consider the accuracy of measurement. The first point to bear in mind

Table 1.4 Unit multiples

Prefix	Factor	Equivalent	Symbol
atto	10^{-18}	= 1/1 000 000 000 000 000 000	a
femto	10^{-15}	= 1/1 000 000 000 000 000	f
pico	10^{-12}	= 1/1 000 000 000 000	p
nano	10^{-9}	= 1/1 000 000 000	n
micro	10^{-6}	= 1/1 000 000	μ
milli	10^{-3}	= 1/1 000	m
centi	10^{-2}	= 1/100	c
deci	10^{-1}	= 1/10	d
deka	10^{1}	= 10	da
hekto	10^{2}	= 100	h
kilo	10^{3}	= 1000	k
mega	10^{6}	= 1 000 000	M
giga	10^{9}	= 1 000 000 00	G
tera	10^{12}	= 1 000 000 000 000	T
peta	10^{15}	= 1 000 000 000 000 000	P
exa	10^{18}	= 1 000 000 000 000 000 000	E

about accuracy is that invariably there is some error in the measurement. No matter how careful the experimenter is, the measurement is never exact. In other words, the measured value is rarely the same as the true value, so there is normally some measurement error. It is the job of the scientist not only to minimise the error, but also to be aware of the range of potential error. If a stadiometer measures a person's stature as 1.05 m, it is assumed that the stadiometer can measure between 1.0 and 1.1 m. If a third digit is unlikely to be accurate, then it would be sensible to record the measure as 1.1 m. If the stadiometer was poorly calibrated and there was uncertainty in the measurement at the level of ± 0.1 m, it would be concluded that the stadiometer cannot be trusted to give an accurate reading. The best guidance is to use the following advice: the outcome value recorded should not have more digits than the number of digits that can accurately be measured. This is akin to saying that a racing team is only as fast as the slowest runner. If betting how fast a team would complete a race, the speed of the slowest runner would be worked into the equation, rather than ignoring the slowest runner and banking on the fastest runners.

It is common for students to 'blindly' trust all figures that a computerised instrument churns out: the so-called 'black-box syndrome'. It is not uncommon for students, therefore, to frantically write down all the figures produced by a computer. For example, a computerised programme is often used to calculate the oxygen uptake. Invariably a figure produced by the computer reads something like 2.7654384 L·min^{-1}, which many students then write down. If the student truly understood the nature of the measurement, they would realise that writing down the figure to that many decimal places would imply the instrument could measure sub-atomic levels. Quite clearly the instrument could not measure with that precision and the correct written form would have been 2.77 L·min^{-1}. Unfortunately, in

physical states

one laboratory demonstration a student had written down -2.34529 L·min^{-1}, not only demonstrating their lack of appreciation of numerical concepts but also their belief that the person they had been measuring was photosynthesising rather than respiring!

MAKING MEASUREMENTS ON HUMANS

In the area of exercise and sport, most measurements are made with human participants. Very strict guidelines exist about the treatment of human participants when they are involved in a scientific investigation. When measurements are made on human participants, the research is often referred to as clinical research. Such strict guidelines have arisen because of the potential harm that may be caused to a participant during such investigations. A subject may be harmed in a variety of ways, ranging from the use of procedures which damage health to disclosure of sensitive or confidential information.

Guidelines or codes of practice are published in a number of sources, and are generally based on the **Declaration of Helsinki**. This declaration states:

1. Clinical research should be based on the principles of medical research, and should be based on scientifically established facts from laboratory experiments;
2. Clinical research should only be conducted by scientifically qualified persons;
3. Importance of the objective should be in proportion to the inherent risk;
4. Clinical research should be preceded by careful assessment of inherent risk;
5. Clinical research should be approached particularly cautiously when drugs or experimental procedures may affect the personality of the subject.

Most scientific **journals** in the area of exercise and sport provide guidelines that must be adhered to by researchers who conduct investigations which they intend to publish in such journals. For example, the official journal of the British Association of Sport and Exercise Sciences (BASES), the *Journal of Sports Sciences*, requires all researchers to work within the principles of the Declaration of Helsinki. The participation of human subjects in experimental research, and particularly the process of gaining **informed consent** from participants, is normally a key part of gaining approval for research from a local **research ethics committee**. Such approval is normally a prerequisite for publication of findings from experimental research.

When undertaking investigations in exercise and sport, again approval is normally required from a local research ethics committee prior to the investigation taking place (see Chapter 10). When measurements are made on human participants, prior **health screening** is essential to establish whether physical activity may cause harm to the participant. Such health screening is normally carried out with a **health questionnaire**, an example of which is included in Appendix 1. In addition to health screening, it is normal practice to obtain informed consent from a participant (see Appendix 2). Informed consent simply means that the participant has given consent to take part in an investigation about which they have been fully informed. To be fully informed, the participant must be told about the inherent risks and benefits of participation in the investigation. Whilst verbal or written consent may be obtained, written consent is generally preferred. For investigations undertaken as part of an undergraduate programme in exercise and sport, ethical approval will normally be sought by the tutor. Nevertheless, it is important that students are aware of the issues when making measurements on human subjects. For further detail in this area, Olivier (2007) provides a brief overview of the key issues.

CONCLUSION

Science is an important aspect of practice in exercise and sport. Scientific research often provides a sound evidence base for interventions. Furthermore, a systematic approach to problem solving often requires a scientific way of thinking. Scientific approaches normally require an understanding of basic mathematics principles, and we have presented many basic principles that underpin science in this chapter. In particular, the importance of measurement has been examined, including the units of measurement and their representation. Since scientific research in exercise and sport normally involves human participants, we have also drawn attention to the important principles of the Declaration of Helsinki.

KEY POINTS

- The common SI units from Table 1.1 used in exercise and sport situations are length (m), mass (kg), time (s), amount of a substance (mol) and thermodynamic temperature (K).
- The process of communicating understanding through written text is an important feature of scientific work. Both SI symbols and numbers used should be correct and accurate.
- An instrument is only as accurate as the divisions on its measuring scale. The number of decimal places recorded implies confidence in the accuracy of the instrument.
- When dealing with human participants, informed consent should be provided by the participant before measurements are made.
- When measurements are made on human participants, the risks should be carefully considered.
- When making measurements on human participants, the risk may be lessened by prior health screening, often through a pre-activity health questionnaire.

10

physical states

BIBLIOGRAPHY

Olivier, S. (2007) Ethics and physiological testing. In E.M. Winter, A.M. Jones, R.C.R. Davison, P.D. Bromley, T. Mercer (eds), *Sport & Exercise Physiology Testing Guidelines: The British Association of Sport & Exercise Sciences Guide*. Oxon: Routledge.

Paulos, J.A. (1988) *Innumeracy. Mathematical Illiteracy and its Consequences*. London: Penguin Books.

Williams, C. and Wragg, C. (2004) *Data Analysis and Research for Sport and Exercise Science*. London: Routledge.

FURTHER READING

Morrison, P., Morrison, P., The Office of Eames, C. and Eames, R. (1982) *Powers of Ten. About the Relative Size of Things in the Universe*. New York: Scientific American Library.

Young, D.S. (1987) Implementation of SI units for clinical laboratory data. *Annals of Internal Medicine*, 106: 114–129.

CHAPTER TWO

GASES

AIMS OF THE CHAPTER

This chapter is designed to provide an understanding of the scientific principles of gases as applied to the theory which underpins exercise and sport. After reading this chapter you should be able to:

- Describe the properties of gases.
- Explain how gases are affected by temperature and pressure.
- Express the ideal gas laws.
- Understand partial pressure.
- Relate diffusion of gases to pressure gradients.
- Conceptualise the flow of gases in the human body.
- Appreciate the terms ATPS, BTPS and STPD.
- Apply the scientific principles of gases to laboratory experimentation.

INTRODUCTION

The property of gases is such that they will not occupy a fixed shape nor a fixed volume unless contained. Gases will always fill a container completely. Hence, a container of gas may not be described as half full or three-quarters full; a gas container is always full. The property of a gas contrasts with that of a liquid, which takes the shape of a container and the container may be described as being half full (see Chapter 3). With regard to a solid, both shape and volume are fixed at a constant temperature and pressure (see Chapter 4). In Chapters 3 and 4, the relationship with pressure, which does not alter the volume of a liquid or a solid, is discussed in detail. The pressure–volume relationship of liquids and solids contrasts to that of a gas, where the gas volume does depend on the applied pressure.

KEY APPLICATIONS TO EXERCISE AND SPORT

An understanding of the properties of gases is important for a student of exercise and sport, since gas exchange supports the continuing conversion of energy in the human body through aerobic metabolism. Energy conversion is ultimately dependent upon respiration, which is the term used to represent both oxygen utilisation and carbon dioxide production. Respiration is constantly taking place within the human body, and the rate of respiration is markedly increased during and immediately following exercise to support the increased rate of energy turnover. The importance of adequate respiration is clearly evident when climbers attempt to reach the summit of Mount Everest. The low pressure environment at the 8,840 m summit results in severely compromised oxygen uptake and utilisation, which in turn results in compromised exercise performance.

13

SCIENTIFIC PRINCIPLES OF GASES

The behaviour of liquids is relatively difficult to explain and predict when compared to the behaviour of gases. Gases possess a number of properties, such as being easily expanded, and this can be explained by their weak attraction between molecules. The absence of strong bonds between adjacent molecules allows gases to easily expand. However, gas molecules do not strongly repel each other either. In fact, there is very irregular spacing between gas molecules, unlike the spacing between molecules of solids. Gas molecules are in constant motion and it is for this reason that a gas will completely fill any container in which it is placed. Gases also differ to liquids and solids in their density (volume per unit mass), such that the density of a gas is approximately 1/1000 of a liquid or solid; a fact which highlights the capability of gas molecules to move further apart. The great distances which gas molecules travel, and their speed, are impossible to calculate on an individual molecule basis, hence an average value of velocity according to the kinetic theory of gases has been formulated. The kinetic theory of gases relates the pressure to the resulting forces of collisions between molecules where any factors which increase the number of collisions will increase the pressure of the gas.

The temperature of a gas can be used as a measure of the energy of motion and although the gas movement is random, the overall behaviour of the gas can be observed. For example, a gas which is much hotter than a neighbouring gas will leak faster than the colder gas when both are leaking through similar-sized holes in a container. Hence the hotter the gas, the faster the molecules appear to move.

A gas whose molecules possess high speeds, and move randomly, can be described as an **ideal gas**. To understand the behaviour of ideal gases, only four properties need to be understood (note that, despite convention, SI units are not always used):

1. Pressure symbolised as P; units of measurement: atmosphere (A), torr (T), pascal (Pa).
2. Volume symbolised as V; units of measurement: Litre (L), centimetre cubed (cm³), metre cubed (m³).
3. Temperature symbolised as T; units of measurement: kelvin (K).
4. **Moles** symbolised as n; units of measurement: moles (mol).

The four properties can be represented in Equation 2.1, which is known as the ideal gas law:

$$PV = nRT \quad\quad .. \quad .. \quad .. \quad .. \quad .. \quad .. \quad .. \quad .. \quad\quad (2.1)$$

where:

P = absolute pressure
V = volume
n = number of moles of the gas (equivalent to the atomic mass unit)

14

R = gas constant (equivalent to 8.32 J.mol^{-1}.K^{-1})
T = absolute temperature.

It should be emphasised that from the ideal gas law two important factors must be acknowledged. First, note the explicit use of absolute pressure. This refers to the fact that atmospheric pressure must be added to the pressure reading measured on a pressure gauge. Therefore, the pressure gauge reading plus atmospheric pressure (760 mmHg) equals the absolute pressure. Second, this is also similar for the absolute temperature (in kelvins). Hence, absolute zero is equal to zero kelvins. Note zero degree Celsius is 273.15 kelvins. Therefore, in all gas calculations the temperature must be in kelvins not Celsius. Note that to make the equation PV = nRT formula work, SI units should be used for P and V, that is, Pa for pressure, m^3 for V, unless everything is changed for use with other units.

Fortunately there is an abundance of historical evidence from scientific experimentation which has firmly established the three most common laws related to gas, known as the Gas Laws. These are:

- Boyle's law (for use with constant temperature or isothermal conditions)
- Charles' law (for use with constant pressure or isobaric conditions)
- The pressure law (for use with constant volume or isovolumetric conditions).

Boyle's law

Boyle's law states that 'the pressure of a fixed mass of gas is inversely proportional to its volume if the temperature is constant' (see Equation 2.2).

$$P \quad \alpha \quad \frac{1}{V} \qquad \qquad \qquad \qquad \qquad \qquad \qquad (2.2)$$

When applied to gas molecules this law means that as the volume decreases, and a smaller space is being occupied by the gas molecules, there are a greater number of collisions, hence the pressure will increase. Or conversely, as the volume of a gas increases, and occupies a larger amount of space, less collisions occur, hence the pressure will decrease. This scenario assumes that the temperature and mass of the gas are constant.

From the ideal gas law equation (Equation 2.1), if the molar mass (n) and temperature (T) are constant, the following relationship is revealed in Equation 2.3:

$$P_1 V_1 = P_2 V_2 \qquad \qquad \qquad \qquad \qquad \qquad \qquad \qquad (2.3)$$

where:

P_1 V_1 are the initial pressure and volume, and
P_2 V_2 are the final pressure and volume.

Equation 2.3 can be used to calculate the pressure and volume of a gas and what the consequences are should either of these two factors change. So, as an example, if a gas has a volume of 10 mL and absolute pressure of 760 mmHg and the volume is suddenly increased to 30 mL, what is the resulting absolute pressure?

$$P_1 V_1 \quad = \quad P_2 V_2$$

$$10 \times 760 \quad = \quad P_2 \times 30$$

$$\frac{7600}{30} \quad = \quad P_2$$

$$P_2 \quad = \quad 253.3 \text{ mmHg}$$

In the above example it can be seen that for a factor of three increase in volume, there is a corresponding proportional factor of three decrease in the pressure. Manipulating the numbers in the opposite direction would show that for a factor of three decrease in volume, there would be a factor of three increase in pressure.

The law only holds true for gas densities which are low, such as those observed during human respiration. Gases such as Hydrogen (H_2), Oxygen (O_2), Nitrogen (N_2) and Helium (He), also known as the permanent gases, will follow this law at normal pressure but will deviate at high pressure when their density is high.

In the sport of sub-aqua, a scuba diver's exhaled bubbles will expand as the surface of the water is reached. This is because the pressure exerted by the weight of water decreases as depth decreases, so the volume increases as the air bubbles rise towards the surface. An understanding of the gas laws is critical for the scuba diver. For example, divers are told not to ascend from a depth of as little as 10 m (33 feet) without exhaling, because the air in the diver's lungs will expand to about double its volume during the ascent. Failure to exhale on ascent can lead to debilitating conditions such as the bends because of the expansion of nitrogen gas bubbles within the blood.

STOP AND THINK

If an inflated balloon rose up from sea level to the height of Mount Everest, how would its size change?

Charles' law

Charles' law applies to volume and temperature, whilst pressure is held constant, and was formulated by Charles in 1787. Charles' law states that 'a volume at a fixed mass and constant pressure is directly proportional to temperature', as shown in Equation 2.4.

$$V \alpha T \qquad .. \quad .. \quad .. \quad .. \quad .. \quad .. \quad .. \quad .. \quad .. \qquad (2.4)$$

In practice, this relationship means that as the temperature increases so too will the number of collisions of the gas molecules, hence the volume will increase for a constant pressure. For example, a rugby ball which is inflated indoors and is then left outdoors in the warm sunshine will increase in volume as the temperature of the gas inside the bladder of the rugby ball swells. This is a direct result of the sun's heat energy.

In order to calculate changes in volume and temperature, Charles' law may be re-written as in Equation 2.5:

$$\frac{V_1}{T_1} = \frac{V_2}{T_2} \qquad .. \quad .. \quad .. \quad .. \quad .. \quad .. \quad .. \quad .. \qquad (2.5)$$

Therefore, to determine the change in temperature if a gas had an initial gas volume of 25 mL and absolute temperature of 298 K and the final volume was 50 mL, the following calculation is performed:

$$\frac{V_1}{T_1} = \frac{V_2}{T_2}$$

$$\frac{25}{298} = \frac{50}{T_2}$$

$$0.0838 = \frac{50}{T_2}$$

$$\frac{50}{0.0838} = T_2$$

$$596 \text{ K} = T_2$$

In the above equation it can be shown that a doubling of the volume is associated with a doubling of the temperature.

The pressure law

This law applies to temperature and pressure of a gas if the volume and amount of that gas remain constant. It can be shown that doubling the temperature will double the pressure (see Equation 2.6).

$$\frac{P_1}{T_1} = \frac{P_2}{T_2} \quad .. \quad .. \quad .. \quad .. \quad .. \quad .. \quad .. \quad .. \qquad (2.6)$$

$$\frac{750}{300} = \frac{P_2}{600}$$

$$2.5 = \frac{P_2}{600}$$

$$2.5 \times 600 = P_2$$

$$1500 = P_2$$

An application of this law is the fact that gas bottles which are often used in laboratories must not be left in exposed hot environments. The increase in temperature of the gas inside the gas bottles could become critical were they to reach a high enough temperature for the gas bottle to explode!

THE MOVEMENT OF A GAS FROM AIR INTO A SOLUTION

Air flow is very similar to blood flow, as discussed in Chapter 3. The gas from the air must be transported through the respiratory tracts to the alveoli of the lungs whereby a small fraction of the gas will move into a solution: blood. The movement of gas molecules is directly proportional to three factors:

1. The pressure gradient of the individual gas.
2. The solubility of the gas in the given liquid.
3. The temperature.

Air flow, similar to blood flow, moves from an area of high pressure to areas of low pressure. Therefore, for air to flow from the atmosphere to the lungs means that there is higher pressure in the atmosphere in comparison to the pressure within the lungs. It should also be pointed out that the movement caused by the pressure gradient also applies to the constituent gases such as O_2 or CO_2 forming the air. The simple diffusion of O_2 and CO_2 in and out of the lungs is a reflection of the pressure gradients; the larger the gradient the

physical states

greater the gas diffusion. As air consists primarily of O_2, CO_2, N_2 and water vapour, each of these will exert their own pressure. A law, known as Dalton's law, states that 'the total pressure of a mixture of gases is a result of the pressures of the individual gases' which are known as partial pressures. Hence, on a typical day, air at sea level has a total gas pressure of 760 mmHg which is a reflection of the sum of the individual gas pressures, as shown in Equation 2.7.

$$\text{Partial pressure} = \text{\% concentration} / 100 \times \text{total pressure} \quad (2.7)$$
$$\text{of gas mixture}$$

Oxygen:
$$159 \text{ mmHg} = 20.93 / 100 \times 760$$

Carbon dioxide
$$0.23 \text{ mmHg} = 0.03 / 100 \times 760$$

Nitrogen
$$600.7 \text{ mmHg} = 79.04 / 100 \times 760$$

Hence, the **partial pressures** (denoted as P or p) for air at sea level are: $pO_2 = 159$ mmHg, $pCO_2 = 0.2$ mmHg and $pN_2 = 601$ mmHg. There will be slight variations of the actual partial pressures because of the effect of the water vapour. However, the movement of O_2 and CO_2 from a gaseous state to blood will be dependent on the partial pressure gradients existing between the two mediums.

STOP AND THINK

If ambient pressure is 600 mmHg and the percentage of O_2 is 20.93, what is the partial pressure of oxygen in the gas mixture?

The solubility of a gas is the ease at which the gas will dissolve in a solution. Carbon dioxide is about 20 times more soluble in water than O_2. This means that CO_2 molecules more readily move into a solution at very low partial pressures. Oxygen on the other hand is not very soluble in water solutions, hence at high partial pressures only a few molecules may dissolve. A clear example of the lack of solubility of O_2 is the fact that the majority of O_2 must be transported in a form bound to haemoglobin in the blood rather than dissolved in the watery solution (the plasma) of the blood. This is a clear example of how the body has evolved in order to account for the low solubility of O_2.

Scuba diving is an ideal example of how the gas laws can apply when the human body is exposed to increasing pressure as a diver descends deeper and deeper. The exposure of the diver's body to increased pressure is known as **hyperbaria**. The pressure on the body will increase 760 mmHg (1 atmosphere) every 10 metres in sea water (there is a slight difference with fresh water because of the difference in water density, such that 1 atmosphere is equal to every 10.4 m). Applying Boyle's law to this scenario means that the increasing pressure will decrease the gas volume in the diver's body. At the same time, the increasing pressure will increase the total gas pressures in the lung in proportion to the gas fractions in the inspired air (Dalton's law). When ascending, a diver must be careful because as the pressure decreases the alveolar gas partial pressure can suddenly decrease, which may cause a loss of consciousness.

The above scenario of scuba diving has allowed discussion of the term hyperbaria; the opposite of this term being **hypobaria** (decreased barometric pressure). Hypobaric conditions present a challenge for mountaineers when climbing at high altitudes. A working knowledge of Dalton's law will assist in understanding the implications of decreasing pressure found with increasing altitude and its effect on the availability of O_2. For example, at an altitude of 3800 m, the barometric pressure is ~460 mmHg and the partial pressures of oxygen, carbon dioxide and nitrogen are:

$$p_IO_2 \quad = \quad 460 \quad \times \quad 0.2093 \quad = \quad 96.3$$

$$p_ICO_2 \quad = \quad 460 \quad \times \quad 0.0003 \quad = \quad 0.14$$

$$p_IN_2 \quad = \quad 460 \quad \times \quad 0.7904 \quad = \quad 363.6$$

$$\text{Total pressure of mixed gas} \quad = \quad 460 \text{ mmHg}$$

AVOGADRO'S LAW

This law states that if different gases have the same volume, temperature and pressure then they also contain the same number of molecules. If this number of molecules is 6.02×10^{23} (which is Avogadro's number), then the gases are said to have a quantity of 'one mole' of the gas molecules. The result of this law implies that the volume of a mole of gas is independent of the type of gas. When two samples of gas have the same volume, pressure and temperature, they contain the same number of moles and therefore the same number of molecules.

APPLICATION OF SCIENCE TO EXERCISE AND SPORT

CORRECTING GAS VOLUMES

The rate of ventilation and the volume of a particular gas uptake or output by the body are important measurements in the study of exercise and sport. Often in such study, the volume of gas contained in the lungs is also examined. The volume of gas exhaled per minute is known as expired minute ventilation ($\dot{V}_E$). The volume of oxygen uptake by the body each minute is known as oxygen uptake ($\dot{V}O_2$). The volume of carbon dioxide output by the body each minute is known as the carbon dioxide output ($\dot{V}CO_2$). Whilst the total volume of gas in the lungs can never be exhaled, the total volume which can be forced from the lungs following an inspiration is often measured, and termed vital capacity (VC).

In exercise physiology, an understanding of the gas laws is important when expressing volumes of gas. Gas within the lungs is at the temperature of the body (usually 273 + 37 K), the pressure the body is under (i.e. atmospheric or ambient pressure; usually about 760 mmHg at sea level) and is fully saturated with water vapour ($pH_2O = 47$ mmHg). These sets of conditions are known as **BTPS**, which stands for **b**ody **t**emperature, ambient **p**ressure and **s**aturated with water vapour. Once gas is expired, it quickly changes to ambient temperature. Usually the ambient temperature is lower than body temperature and therefore the gas cools. The result of the gas cooling is a decrease in volume and a condensation of water vapour. Under these conditions the gas is said to be at **ATPS**, which stands for **a**mbient **t**emperature, ambient **p**ressure and **s**aturated with water vapour. In order to compare gas volumes, a volume may be reported in the **STPD** form, which stands for **s**tandard **t**emperature (273 K or 0°C), standard **p**ressure (760 mmHg) and completely **d**ry of any water vapour ($pH_2O = 0$ mmHg). This standardised form allows comparison of gas volumes under diverse conditions. Since the barometric pressure, temperature and humidity will vary considerably with time, and throughout the world, a standard form is essential for comparative purposes. However, when gas volumes are used to express either minute ventilation or vital capacity (VC), gas volumes are normally reported in a BTPS form. The reason for this is that it is the absolute volume, rather than a standardised volume, that is important when examining ventilation and lung function.

As already mentioned, gas volumes are also used to express the quantity of oxygen uptake ($\dot{V}O_2$) by the body each minute, and the quantity of carbon dioxide output ($\dot{V}CO_2$) by the body each minute. These quantities are always expressed in a standardised (i.e. STPD) form to aid comparisons over time and between laboratories around the world.

Using the equations from the ideal gas laws, it is possible to standardise a volume of gas collected under ATPS conditions (see Equation 2.8). For example, resting oxygen uptake under ATPS conditions can range from 250–400 mL·min^{-1}. If a gas volume of 250 mL·min^{-1} was collected and it is assumed that the barometric pressure that was exerted on the gas is 770 mmHg, and the temperature was 25°C, then using the ideal gas laws, the standardised or STPD volume would be:

$$\text{since} \quad \frac{P_1 V_1}{T_1} = \frac{P_2 V_2}{T_2} \quad .. \quad .. \quad .. \quad .. \quad .. \quad .. \quad \quad (2.8)$$

Where: P = pressure, V = volume and T = temperature, the subscripts $_1$ and $_2$ represent ATPS and STPD values respectively. Rearranging equation 2.8 becomes:

$$\frac{P_1 V_1 T_2}{T_1 P_2} = V_2$$

$$\frac{(760 + 10) \times 250 \times (273 + 0)}{(273 + 25) \times (760 - 0)} = V_2$$

$$232.04 \text{ mL·min}^{-1} = V_2$$

Therefore, the new volume under STPD conditions is 232.04 or rounded down 232 mL·min^{-1}. Because the body temperature is greater than the ambient temperature the correction to STPD has lowered the volume.

MEASURING GAS VOLUMES DURING VENTILATION

One method of measuring gas involves collection of a relatively large quantity of expired gas in a special type of bag (known as a Douglas bag) or meteorological balloon for subsequent measurement. Douglas bags or meteorological balloons are used to collect several expired breaths, and can normally hold at least 150 L of gas. Once a collection has been made, the volume measurement can take place at the experimenter's leisure, since the bags are not permeable to the gas contained within. Normally, a series of collections would be made during an experiment, and the measurement of the gas takes place at the end. The analysis of the gas at the end of the experiment includes the collection of all the required information needed to derive the **pulmonary** gas exchange variables. Such information includes the concentration of O_2 and CO_2 in the expired gas, the temperature of the gas, and the volume of the gas. In addition, the ambient temperature and pressure must be determined. The concentration of O_2 and CO_2 in the expired gas is determined with O_2 and CO_2 gas analysers from a small sample from the bag. The temperature and volume of the gas is determined as the gas passes into a spirometer or volume meter. The measurement of gas temperature at this point is important, since the temperature of the gas is measured in order to convert the volume of gas from ATPS to BTPS. The method of correction into a BTPS form has been discussed earlier. The collection of this data allows determination of a range of pulmonary gas exchange variables, including expired minute ventilation ($\dot{V}_E$), oxygen uptake ($\dot{V}O_2$) and carbon dioxide output ($\dot{V}CO_2$) for the time over which the gas was collected.

Various devices are available to measure volume of expired gas, including a range of spirometers and gas meters. Spirometers are simply a container of fixed volume, which moves relative to a stable surrounding area, depending upon the volume of gas added to or removed from the container. The output from such a device is interpreted by knowing the output from a fixed input volume. More sophisticated spirometers have an output in litres, so no correction has to be performed. An example of a spirometer used extensively for determination of expired gas volumes is the Tissot spirometer. Gas meters are often referred to as dry gas meters. This is simply a result of the use which they are usually put to. However, with expired gas, the term is misleading, since the volume of gas is saturated with water vapour.

What has been described above is known as an off-line gas collection and analysis system. It is, however, possible to determine gas volumes and other respiratory variables on-line, where outcome variables are derived almost instantaneously. With an on-line system, the mouthpiece is usually extended in the direction away from the subject's mouth to house the device for measuring flow rates of gas (i.e. volume per unit time). Various devices have been put to this use, including turbines, hot wires, pneumotachographs and ultrasonic flow meters. All such devices can measure flow rates of expired gas from the mouth continuously and can rapidly detect changes in gas flow.

A turbine is like a small propeller that rotates at various speeds depending upon the flow of gas past it. Turbines have developed greatly over the past few years in terms of reductions in mass, and now provide a practical method of determining rapidly changing bi-directional gas flow rates. In the past, turbines have been relatively heavy, and consequently have a large amount of inertia. This inertia led to inaccuracies in results, particularly when the turbine was used to measure inspired and expired flow. The previously heavy turbines also resulted in resistance to gas flow, which was undesirable, particularly when athletes are ventilating heavily during intense exercise.

Hot wires utilise the cooling effect of gas flowing past an object. If a wire is kept at a constant temperature, regardless of the gas flow rate past it, the energy put into the wire to keep it at that temperature can be constantly monitored. The energy put into the wire is then proportional to the flow rate of gas past the wire.

Pneumotachographs are pressure-measuring devices, utilising the potential of gas to exert a pressure over an object. The pneumotachograph looks like a grid of thin wire mesh, and presents a fixed surface area perpendicular to the gas flow direction. Since the surface area is fixed, the pressure exerted against the pneumotachograph is proportional to the velocity of gas flow. It is inherent with such a device that the method of detection of gas flow presents a resistance to flow.

Ultrasonic flow meters are based on the distortion of an ultrasonic beam. The beam is presented perpendicular to the direction of flow, and the gas is capable of distorting the beam according to the velocity of flow. The magnitude of distortion is related to the velocity of flow. The advantage of such a device is the lack of resistance to flow. It has been suggested, however, that such devices are better for measuring a larger range of flow rates than would typically be encountered during human ventilation.

MEASURING GAS CONCENTRATIONS

A large proportion of the gas inspired from the surrounding air (inspirate) and the gas expired from the lungs (expirate) consists of three gases: oxygen (O_2), carbon dioxide (CO_2) and nitrogen (N_2). Whilst the three primary gases do not change in the air that is

23

inspired and expired, the relative proportion of each gas does change. Inspirate normally consists of 20.95 % O_2, 0.04 % CO_2 and 79.01 % N_2. The relative proportion of each gas in the expirate depends upon a number of factors, especially whether the individual is at rest or not. During exercise, for example, the faster rate of oxygen utilisation by the body for energy transfer results in lower O_2 values in expirate compared with values at rest. Conversely, the faster rate of carbon dioxide production by the body caused by energy transfer, results in higher CO_2 values in expirate compared with values at rest. Nitrogen is known as an inert gas, and is not normally utilised or produced during exercise. In the study of exercise and sport, when the rate of O_2 utilisation and CO_2 production is increased to support rapid energy utilisation, it is necessary to rapidly determine changes in the relative proportions of expirate gas constituents.

Three types of analyser are commonly used for determination of O_2 concentration. Mass spectrometers are used to determine O_2 concentration, often in conjunction with breath-by-breath on-line systems. The mass spectrometer is based on the principle of determination of the relative quantity of molecules with specific atomic masses. The other two types of analyser, more commonly employed in mixing chamber-based on-line systems and off-line systems, are paramagnetic and fuel cell analysers. Paramagnetic analysers make use of the magnetic properties of O_2 in determination of the relative partial pressure in the gas. Such analysers are the least rapidly responding. Fuel cell analysers are commonly used in all types of gas analysis systems. The relative amount of O_2 in the gas determines the rate of combustion, and consequently the output from the analyser reflects the relative partial pressure of O_2 in the gas sample.

The concentration of CO_2 in expired gas is usually determined via the infrared absorbance method or mass spectrometry. The latter is a direct determination of the relative number of molecules with specific atomic masses, as was the case with O_2. A property of CO_2 is the ability to absorb infrared light, unlike O_2 or N_2. The intensity of infrared light once it has passed through the expired gas containing CO_2, determines the relative partial pressure of the CO_2 within the expired gas. Both methods are rapidly responding, and have been used in all types of gas concentration measurement systems.

Breath-by-breath systems are dependent on gas analysers with a very fast response time, such as the mass spectrometer. A response time is the time it takes an analyser to reach the true value from the value it started at. For example, if an analyser is measuring the concentration of O_2 in air, the analyser would be reading 20.95 %. If the analyser is then suddenly presented with expired gas with a hypothetical O_2 concentration of 15.12 %, the response time would be the time it takes the reading on the analyser to move from 20.95 % to 15.12 %. Usually, however, the 95 % response time is required, which is the time taken for the analyser to reach 95 % of the total change between 20.95 % and 15.12 %. So, this difference is 5.83 %, and 95 % of this value is 5.54 %. By subtracting 5.54 % from 20.95 % we get the 95 % value of 15.41 %. Once the time is determined for the analyser to reach 15.41 % from 20.95 %, the 95 % response time is known. The 95 % response time is used in preference to the 100 % response time because the 95 % response time is significantly less.

24

physical states

THE EFFECT OF TEMPERATURE ON GAS VOLUMES

Even though the total number of gas molecules remains constant with changes in temperature, gas temperature is directly related to gas volume since an increase in temperature results in faster movement of gas molecules (i.e. Charles' law). Therefore, gas temperature should always be measured when determining respiratory variables. The temperature of a gas is determined in different ways depending on the system used. For off-line systems, the temperature is usually determined before the gas enters the volume meter, usually by a small temperature probe inserted into the gas flow. For on-line systems, the temperature of the gas is usually estimated based on the short time that the gas has been outside the body. As the gas leaves the body, the temperature will be similar to that of the body (i.e. 37°C).

THE EFFECT OF AMBIENT PRESSURE ON GAS VOLUMES

Again, even though the total number of gas molecules remains constant with changes in pressure, the pressure acting on a gas is directly related to gas volume since an increase in pressure forces the molecules closer together (i.e. Boyle's law). Therefore, ambient pressure should always be measured when determining respiratory variables. Generally ambient pressure does not change rapidly, so a measurement at the start of an expirate collection period is adequate. If the weather conditions are changing rapidly, it may be necessary to make more frequent pressure measurements; perhaps one in the morning and one in the afternoon. Ambient pressure is normally measured with a calibrated mercury barometer, hence the common unit of ambient pressure, mm of mercury (mmHg). For further discussion of pressure see Chapter 5.

THE EFFECT OF GAS HUMIDITY ON GAS VOLUMES AND CONCENTRATIONS

Again, even though the total number of gas molecules remains constant with changes in gas humidity, the amount of water vapour (i.e. humidity) in a gas is directly related to gas volume since an increase in humidity adds an extra constituent to the gas. Therefore, humidity of the gas should always be measured when determining respiratory variables. Normally, gas expired from the human body (i.e. expirate) is saturated with water vapour. Evidence of this fact is seen as expirate cools in a Douglas bag, and condensation forms on the inside of the bag. The water vapour has come from the moist airways between the nose and mouth and the lungs. Inspirate normally contains some water vapour but is rarely saturated, which is why participants sometimes complain of a dry throat following exercise. The water in the saturated expirate has come from the participant's airways. The absolute amount of water vapour in a gas is a function of temperature. For example, air at a temperature of 26°C can hold 25.2 mmHg of water vapour pressure, whilst air at a temperature of 39°C can hold 52.4 mmHg of water vapour pressure. In most physiology textbooks, tables are provided which indicate the water vapour pressure of a saturated gas for a given temperature (i.e. Robergs and Roberts, 1996: 794–795). When the volume of gas is measured, water vapour is corrected for in the conversion from ATPS to either STPD or BTPS.

Gas humidity has an effect on the constituent gas concentrations in addition to overall gas volume. If it is assumed that water vapour is simply another gas in the expirate, the other constituent gas proportions will be distorted. When gas analysis techniques are used which measure a total amount of gas (i.e. mass spectrometry), water vapour is not a problem. However, many gas analysis techniques are based on partial pressures of the constituent gases (e.g. paramagnetic analysers), so distortion caused by water vapour is a problem. To overcome such a problem, when the concentration of gases in expirate are measured, rather than attempt to correct for the water vapour, the gas should be dried prior to measurement. The gas is normally dried with a condensing unit. Although the condensing unit will not remove all the water vapour, the important factor is that all gas enters the analysers with the same humidity. James et al. (2007) provides further reading on determination of pulmonary gas exchange variables.

SELF-TEST

1. What is the effect of temperature on a squash ball during a squash match?

2. If the pressure experienced by a scuba diver at 10 m (33 feet) is approximately 2 atmospheres (1520 mmHg) and 79 % of the gas mixture is Helium and 21 % is O_2, what are the partial pressures of the two gases?

3. At the summit of Mount Everest (8,840 m), the ambient pressure may be as low as 230 mmHg. What is the partial pressure of O_2, and how does this compare with the partial pressure of O_2 at sea level?

4. Hypoxic (reduced pO_2) gas is often inspired in order to simulate altitude in a normobaric (i.e. sea level) environment. In order to simulate a partial pressure of 474 mmHg (i.e. an altitude of 3,500 m), what percentage of the gas should be comprised of O_2?

CONCLUSION

The study of gases is underpinned by more than 300 hundred years of scientific investigation. Gases do not occupy a fixed shape or volume unless enclosed and are easily expandable because of the weak attraction of the bonds between gas molecules. Gases are less dense than solids or liquids. The low density allows gas molecules to travel at high speeds, which does not enable calculation of individual gas molecule speeds; rather an average velocity is considered, according to the kinetic theory of gases. Three gas laws, known as Charles', Boyle's and the pressure law, are particularly applicable to physiology. All three laws involve manipulating the variables of pressure, volume and temperature. A fourth factor, a mole, denoting the amount of a substance, is also represented in an equation known as the ideal gas law. Other laws which have relevance to work in physiology laboratories are Dalton's law, which states the relationship between total pressure and the pressure of individual gases, and Avogadro's law, which states the relationship between different gases and volume. Under conditions of the same pressure, volume and temperature, gases will possess the same number of molecules.

The determination of pulmonary gas exchange variables in physiology is so common that the gas laws should form an integral part of a student's understanding about gas volumes. Since gas volumes are collected under varying conditions of pressure and temperature, such outcomes must be carefully expressed. There are a number of different procedures for determining pulmonary gas exchange variables and these range from standard off-line systems to highly automated on-line systems.

KEY POINTS

1. Temperature, pressure and volume have significant impact on the behaviour of gases.
2. Gas molecules possess little molecular attraction or repulsion between one another compared with liquids and solids.
3. Charles' law relates to constant pressure conditions for which volume is directly proportional to the temperature.
4. Boyle's states that pressure is inversely proportional to the volume under constant temperature conditions.
5. The pressure law states that temperature is directly proportional to the pressure under constant volume conditions.
6. The flow of a gas is dependent on pressure gradients, such that a gas will move from a region of high pressure to one of low pressure.
7. For a gas to flow from the environment into a liquid, three factors are directly linked to its flow: a) pressure gradient; b) solubility of the gas; c) temperature.
8. Dalton's law refers to the pressures of the individual gases which form a mixed gas, such that the total pressure of a mixed gas is the sum of the pressures of the individual gases.
9. Diffusion, as applied to a mixed gas, is influenced by the total pressure but is also applicable to an individual gas and its partial pressure.
10. Appropriate respiratory gas volume representation is dependent on such factors as the temperature of the gas, the barometric pressure and the relative humidity of the gas.
11. The classic technique for the determination of gas exchange variables is via expirate collections in Douglas bags, but there are also many semi-automated systems available.

BIBLIOGRAPHY

Robergs, R.A. and Roberts, S.O. (1996) *Exercise Physiology: Exercise, Performance, and Clinical Applications*. St Louis, MS: Mosby. Appendix B, pp. 794–795.
Scratcherd, T. (1992) *Aids to Physiology*. Singapore: Churchill Livingstone, Longmans.

FURTHER READING

James, D.V.B., Sandals, L.E., Wood, D.M. and Jones, A.M. (2007) Pulmonary gas exchange. In E.M. Winter, A.M. Jones, R.C.R. Davison, P.D. Bromley, T. Mercer (eds), *Sport & Exercise Physiology Testing Guidelines: The British Association of Sport & Exercise Sciences Guide*. Oxon: Routledge.
McConnell, A. (2007) Lung and respiratory muscle function. In E.M. Winter, A.M. Jones, R.C.R. Davison, P.D. Bromley, T. Mercer (eds), *Sport & Exercise Physiology Testing Guidelines: The British Association of Sport & Exercise Sciences Guide*. Oxon: Routledge.
Wilber, R.L. (2004) *Altitude Training and Athletic Performance*. Leeds: Human Kinetics.

CHAPTER THREE

LIQUIDS

AIMS OF THE CHAPTER

This chapter is designed to provide an understanding of the scientific principles of liquids which are relevant to the theory which underpins exercise and sport. After reading this chapter, you should be able to:

- State the properties of liquids.
- Understand how liquids are affected by temperature and pressure.
- State the concept of buoyant force and Archimedes' principle.
- State Pascal's principle.
- Understand the key concepts in relation to pressure in flowing liquids.
- Understand the terms 'viscosity', 'laminar flow' and 'turbulent flow'.
- Understand the terms 'moles', 'equivalents', 'percent solution' and 'pH'.
- Apply the scientific principles of liquids to situations in exercise and sport.

INTRODUCTION

The term 'fluid' can be defined as 'a substance that flows', which by definition could include gases as well as liquids. There are many examples of exercise and sport activities taking place in a fluid environment, such as swimming, water aerobics, sailing and trampolining. This chapter will, however, refer to fluids only in the context of liquids (see Chapter 2 for discussion of gases), although there will be times when the laws/principles apply equally to gases. To appreciate the laws and principles as applied to gases it is advisable to read this chapter in conjunction with Chapter 2. In instances whereby laws/principles apply not only to a liquid but also a gas, the text will refer to the dual application.

The majority of the earth's surface is covered by water. It is also the main constituent within the human body and accounts for the largest proportion of total body mass. On average, the percentage of water in relation to total body mass for males is 60 per cent and 51 per cent for females. There are of course many other liquids in the body such as synovial fluid, cerebrospinal fluid, mucus and saliva, all of which are water-based solutions. The chemical formula for water is H_2O. The hydrogen bond with oxygen is the result of a weak interaction between a positive region of the hydrogen and the negative region of an oxygen atom. It is the hydrogen bonding in the water molecule that is responsible for water **surface tension** (defined as the cohesive force between liquid molecules which create a surface film). As water is such an important property within the human body, it is worth noting some of its characteristics:

- It is liquid at standard temperature.
- It has a large heat of fusion.
- It has a large heat capacity.
- It has a large heat of vaporisation.
- Its **density** at 4°C is 1 g·cm^{-3}.

30

physical states

KEY APPLICATIONS TO EXERCISE AND SPORT

The measurement of liquids as applied to exercise and sport sciences has greatest application to such disciplines as biomechanics and physiology. In biomechanics, certain aspects of the curriculum might be devoted to studying the dynamic effects of water on its surroundings. The study of water is known as hydrology. It should not be forgotten that such structures as cartilage and synovial sacs whilst containing elements of solids are also comprised of watery materials. In physiology, an understanding of water balance and the effects of blood flow are important considerations during sport performance or physical activity. The list below contains some specific examples of how details from this chapter can be applied to exercise and sport examples:

■ When analysing a swimmer's technique, biomechanists will need to understand the interaction of the flow of water over the swimmer's body and its effect on performance.
■ Biomechanists who study injury will need to understand the properties of liquids within human tissue; for example, the lumbar discs and cartilage and the effects of exercise on these structures.
■ Physiologists interested in cardiovascular disease need to understand the effects of flow, volume and pressure of blood, particularly concerning hypertension (high blood pressure) and stroke.
■ Physiologists working with athletes in hot climates need to understand the effects of exercise or sports competition on water balance. The process of dehydration and its consequences affects the water balance of the body and has ramifications for an athlete's drinking strategy.

SCIENTIFIC PRINCIPLES OF LIQUIDS

The molecular structure of gases and solids is covered in Chapters 2 and 4 respectively. Liquids, like solids, have a very strong bond holding their atoms together. This strong bonding is termed **cohesion**, which implies that there is an attraction of like molecules for one another. The cohesiveness of a liquid has implications for such concepts as surface tension and **viscosity** (defined as resistance to flow). Liquids, unlike solids, are able to move more freely and hence will take the shape of any container in which they are placed. The molecules within a liquid move more slowly than those of a gas. The molecules do, however, continue to vibrate and collide. There is also less space between the molecules of a liquid so they occupy much less space than the same number of molecules as a gas. These rapidly moving molecules cannot be observed with the human eye. However, if a very fine particle of dust is dropped into a beaker of liquid, its random movement through the liquid can be observed using a microscope. The movements of the particles are random because the fast-moving molecules are continually colliding. Indeed, a botanist, Robert Brown (1773–1858), observed this type of movement, hence its name, Brownian motion. As the molecules rapidly move around inside the beaker, some of the fastest moving molecules free themselves from the attractive forces of nearby molecules and escape from the liquid into the gas above it. This process is known as evaporation, and it is those molecules with the greatest energy that escape. The overall effect is a reduction in the average energy of the remaining molecules, resulting in a decrease in the temperature of the liquid.

A further property of a liquid is incompressibility, as it is extremely difficult to force a liquid to occupy a smaller volume than it is already currently occupying. Therefore, two distinguishing features of liquids are:

- At a particular temperature, a liquid has a fixed volume but will take the shape of any container.
- Pressure applied to a liquid will not change the volume (unlike a gas).

Hence, the state of a liquid will vary according to the surrounding temperature and pressure. Clearly, the addition of heat energy will change a liquid to a gas, known as vaporising. Cooling a gas into a liquid is known as condensation. The changing of a liquid to a solid is a process known as freezing.

PRESSURE IN STATIONARY LIQUIDS

The definition of **pressure** is given as force per unit area (the SI unit is the pascal, Pa), which is equal to a pressure of 1 newton per square metre (1 N·m^{-2}). The definition and the units of measurement of force and pressure are all covered in Chapters 1 and 5. The pressure in a stationary liquid is a function of the depth of the liquid and its density. If a swimmer dives into water, the deeper the dive, the greater the pressure upon the body. This pressure is directly proportional to the depth of the liquid and the density of the liquid (see Figure 3.1).

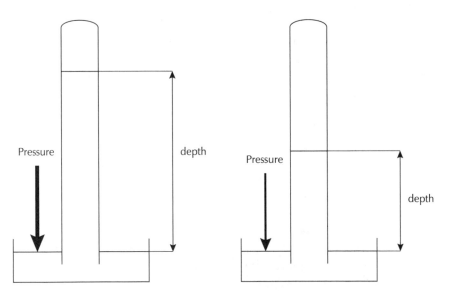

Figure 3.1 The relationship between depth and pressure in a stationary liquid

The exerted pressure by the liquid is a consequence of the contact it has with the container and the fact that the liquid has weight.

The relationship between the depth of the liquid and the pressure of the liquid can be described as follows:

$$P = \rho.g.h \qquad .. \qquad .. \qquad .. \qquad .. \qquad .. \qquad .. \qquad .. \qquad .. \qquad (3.1)$$

Where P is pressure of the liquid, ρ is density, g is acceleration caused by gravity, and h is depth of the liquid.

For example, if a container held a liquid with a depth of 5 m and the liquid within the container had a density of 1 $g \cdot cm^{-3}$ (1 $g \cdot cm^{-3}$ = 1000 $kg \cdot m^{-3}$), the pressure exerted by the liquid at the base of the container would be:

$$
\begin{aligned}
P &= \rho.g.h \\
&= 1000 \text{ kg·m}^{-3} \times 9.8 \text{ m·s}^{-2} \times 5 \text{ m} \\
&= 49\,000 \text{ N·m}^{-2} = 49\,000 \text{ Pa} \\
&= 49.0 \text{ kPa}
\end{aligned}
$$

(Note that the density measure has been multiplied up to ensure SI units in the calculation.) Note that the pressure at any point within the liquid acts in all directions.

The simplest example of pressure exerted on a stationary liquid is that used in a barometer such as those used in laboratories to record atmospheric pressure (see Figure 3.2). In a

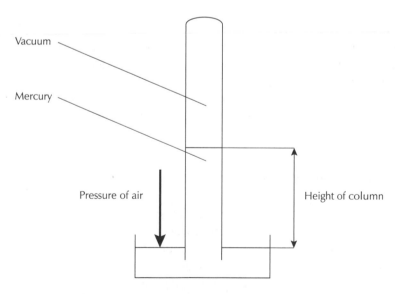

Vacuum

Mercury

Pressure of air

Height of column

Figure 3.2 The principle of a barometer

barometer, one of the ends of the tube is closed and evacuated, creating a vacuum. In this arrangement, the absolute pressure can be measured. In laboratory barometers mercury is typically used. As mercury has a density of 13.6 g·cm³, it will require 13.6 times the pressure to push mercury to the same height as water. In laboratory experiments that involve collecting respiratory gases (oxygen and carbon dioxide), it is important to know the barometric pressure under which the gases are collected (see Chapter 2). Typically, at sea level the barometric pressure is 101 kPa. Using a mercury barometer and equation 3.1, if a column of mercury were raised 760 mm high, the atmospheric pressure could be calculated as follows:

$$P = \rho.g.h$$
$$= 13600 \text{ kg·m}^{-3} \times 9.8 \text{ m·s}^{-2} \times 0.76 \text{ m}$$
$$= 101396.2 \text{ N·m}^{-2} = 101396.2 \text{ Pa}$$
$$= 101 \text{ kPa *}$$

(* Note that because there is some rounding of the number, it does not add up exactly to 760 mm of mercury raised.)

For various reasons, although kPa is the correct SI unit for pressure, another unit is more commonly used in the literature. At sea level an atmospheric pressure of 101 kPa, which is also known as standard pressure or 1 atmosphere, is defined as the pressure exerted at the foot of a column of mercury, with a specific density of 13.6 g·cm⁻³ and at a specific gravity value sufficient to raise the mercury 760 mm high.

STOP AND THINK

1. Although it is possible to measure pressure in mmH$_2$O, what is the most common unit used to measure pressure? Consider also what units weather forecasters usually use for their pressure readings.
2. Consider how you could use some tubing and water to measure the force exerted by the respiratory muscles during either inspiration or expiration.

BUOYANCY FORCE AND ARCHIMEDES' PRINCIPLE

The effects of buoyancy are clearly seen when an object floats in water. The object appears to lose its weight and to be supported within the water. The effect of buoyancy is a result of an upward lift or upthrust of water, which is in turn a result of the pressure exerted by the water being greater on the lower parts of the submerged object than on the top of the object (remember pressure increases with depth). This application also applies to gases, as can be seen when a hot air balloon floats into the air. Hence:

physical states

- If the buoyant force is equal to the weight of the object, it will float.
- If the buoyant force is less than the weight of the object, it will sink.

Therefore, the buoyant force can be described as the difference between the liquid pressure above and below the object. The law that describes this phenomenon was discovered by Archimedes (287–212 BC) and is known as Archimedes' principle:

> The buoyant force on a completely or partially submerged object is equal to the weight of the fluid displaced.

Note the use of the word 'fluid'; this principle applies equally to both gases and liquids.

The upthrust on the object will be equal to the weight of the displaced liquid. By weighing objects in air and in water, and calculating the difference, Archimedes was able to determine the buoyancy force. In this way the volume of an object, and also its density (by dividing mass in air by volume), can be determined.

It is often common practice in the study of exercise and sport to estimate percentage body fat. In order to calculate percentage body fat, underwater weighing is often used to determine the density of the human body by using the principles of buoyancy force and Archimedes' principle. The density of a human body can then be converted, using standard equations, into a percentage body fat score. If a human body has a mass of 75 kg in air and a mass of 6 kg when submerged in water, 69 kg of water must have been displaced (i.e. 75 kg – 6 kg = 69 kg). If the density of the water is 1 g·cm^{-3} (the density of water at 4°C), then the specific volume of the body will be 0.069 m^3 (69 kg / 1000 kg·m^{-3}). Next, the body density is calculated as 75 kg / 0.069 m^3 = 1086.9 kg·m^{-3} = 1.087 g·cm^{-3}. Since the water is only 0.92 times as dense as the body, the resulting buoyancy force of 69 kg will not overcome the weight of the body and therefore it will sink (i.e. a mass of 6 kg when submerged).

If the same example as above is examined again, but this time the human body only has a submerged mass of 3 kg, the resulting displacement of water will be 72 kg. The specific volume of the body is 0.072 m^3, which results in a body density of 1.041g·cm^{-3}. Similarly, the resulting buoyancy force will not overcome the weight of the body and it will sink. Although there are a number of other factors which must be considered during underwater weighing – for example, the amount of air remaining in the gastrointestinal tract and the residual volume left in the lungs after maximally exhaling during the submersion – the procedure is common practice in exercise and sport science.

The above observation is known as the 'principle of flotation':

> A floating object will displace its own weight of fluid.

The Archimedes' principle is routinely employed in the use of hydrodensitometry, or underwater weighing, where a human body is immersed in a tank of water and the weight of the submerged body is recorded in order to calculate the density of the body. Another

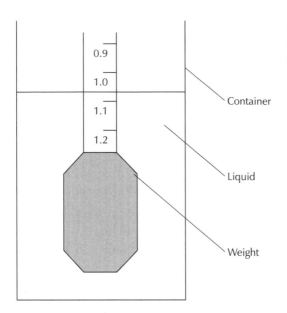

Figure 3.3 A hydrometer, an instrument used for measuring the specific gravity of a liquid

Container

Liquid

Weight

instrument, which uses the same flotation principle is a hydrometer, used to determine the specific gravity of a liquid (see Figure. 3.3). A hydrometer is floated in the liquid and a reading may be made off the scale inside the stem, level with the liquid's surface. In certain occupations, such as nursing, an urinometer is used to measure the specific gravity of urine. The progression of some diseases is monitored by examining the specific gravity of urine.

PASCAL'S PRINCIPLE

Pascal's principle refers to the transmission of pressure to all parts of a liquid:

Any change of pressure in an enclosed fluid is transmitted to all parts of the fluid.

Earlier in the chapter it was shown that the density of the liquid multiplied by the depth determined static pressure within a liquid, and that the exerted pressure was equal in all directions. In order to calculate the total pressure on the liquid, any other external pressure must also be taken into consideration. For example, the atmosphere exerts a pressure of approximately 101.3 kPa (760 mmHg) at sea level. This external pressure is transmitted throughout the whole of the liquid (i.e. Pascal's principle). Pascal's principle is applied in such devices as hydraulic presses: a small amount of pressure is applied to an enclosed fluid and because of the incompressibility and transmission of the pressure, very large forces can be generated. Other examples of such devices are hydraulic lifts, car brake systems, cutters used by the emergency services, and even barbers' chairs.

PRESSURE IN FLOWING LIQUIDS

The previous examples demonstrate that the pressure within a static liquid is a direct function of the depth and density of the liquid. Likewise, as there is no flow in a stationary liquid, there is equally no change in pressure. The pressure is therefore equal in all directions (see Figure 3.4). However, pressure within a flowing liquid means that further variables need to be considered. To understand the principles of pressure in flowing liquids it is important to consider four points:

- For a liquid to flow through a tube, there must be a drop in pressure (see Figure 3.4).
- The pressure will be lower at the exit of the tube than at the entrance to the tube.
- If there are equally spaced vertical tubes placed in succession to one another, the amount of pressure drop will be the same.
- It is conventional to use the term '**pressure gradient**' rather than 'pressure changes' to describe the pressure in flowing liquids.

The pressure gradient can be defined as the pressure drop per unit length:

$$\text{pressure gradient} \quad = \quad \text{pressure drop} / \text{length} \quad .. \quad .. \quad (3.2)$$
$$= \quad P_1 - P_2 / L$$

Where P_1 is pressure at point 2, and L is the length between point 1 and point 2.

As can be seen from Equation 3.2, the variable L (length) is introduced as the denominator of the pressure drop. Several other variables affect the rate of flow through a tube (see Figure 3.5). The volume flow rate (F) is the volume of flow per unit of time and is dependent not only upon the drop in pressure but also the resistance to the flow within the tube. The volume flow rate may be calculated as follows:

$$F \quad = \quad P_1 - P_2 / R \quad .. \quad .. \quad .. \quad .. \quad .. \quad (3.3)$$

where F is flow rate and R is the resistance to flow.

Pressure = 120 mmHg   No flow   Pressure = 120 mmHg

No flow since the pressure gradient equals 0 (i.e. 120 – 120 = 0 mmHg)

Pressure = 120 mmHg   Flow ⟶ Pressure = 70 mmHg

Flow occurs since the pressure gradient is 50 mmHg (i.e. 120 – 70 = 50 mmHg)

Figure 3.4 The relationship between pressure in a flowing liquid and the pressure gradient

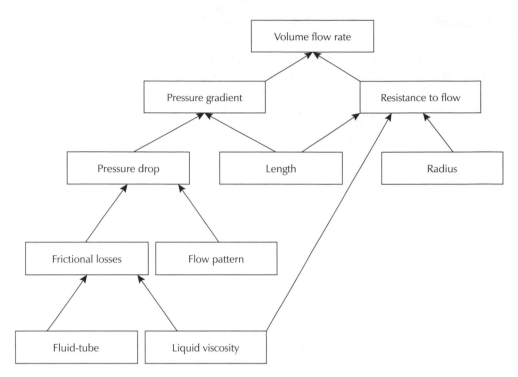

Figure 3.5 Schematic showing the variables that affect the rate of flow of a liquid through a tube

Figure 3.5 shows that the pressure drop is characterised as representing losses of energy, principally through frictional losses of the tubing, the fluid or the pattern of liquid flow. We will consider each of these in turn.

When the wall of a piece of tubing comes into contact with the fluid flowing through it, the friction will depend on the material of the wall. For example, rubber tubing causes greater **friction** between the fluid and the wall than plastic tubing, and for this reason the latter is more frequently used nowadays.

There can also be friction within the liquid itself. The force that opposes flow within a liquid is known as viscosity (symbol η). The viscosity of a liquid is a result of the collective cohesive forces of the molecules in the liquid. The stronger the cohesive force, the greater is the resistance to flow. For example, human blood can be up to five times as viscous as water. As blood becomes more viscous, more pressure will be required for it to flow at the same rate, which will naturally have consequences for the amount of stress placed on the heart. Therefore, providing the pressure gradient is constant, flow rate is inversely proportional to viscosity.

Loss of energy is related to the type of flow pattern, which can be categorised as either **laminar** or **turbulent**. Laminar flow represents the minimum loss of energy and is representative of a tube which might be straight and have smooth walls, so the flow will tend to be in smooth layers. In fact, if it were possible to look at the flow of the liquid through smooth tubes, it could be seen that the liquid next to the walls is at rest whilst the maximum speed of the liquid is found at the centre of the vessel. As some parts of the liquid are at rest while other parts are travelling quickly, the mean speed of flow is approximately half the maximum speed found at the centre. Problems in fluid dynamics occur when the speed of the flow exceeds a critical value or if the liquid collides with an obstruction. Both of these situations create eddies, which results in the laminar flows being transformed into turbulent flow. Although there are a number of equations for calculating pressure gradients and flow rate, accurate prediction of the dynamics of turbulent flow has proved very difficult. This area continues to be a subject of extensive research by scientists around the world.

The study of liquids through cylindrical tubes was greatly influenced by the work of a French scientist, Poiseuille, who in 1844 investigated steady flows of liquid through a pipe. Poiseuille was interested in the relationships of steady flow so he could apply it to blood flow through veins and arteries. Poiseuille devised an equation to gauge the resistance to flow of a pure liquid under laminar flow conditions:

$$R = 8.\eta.L / \Pi.r^4 \qquad .. \qquad .. \qquad .. \qquad (3.4)$$

Where η is the viscosity of fluid, L is the length of the tube, and r is the radius of the tube.

Equation 3.4 shows the resistance to flow. However, for flow rate to be determined, the pressure gradient needs to be introduced. Therefore, by substituting Equation 3.4 into Equation 3.3, Equation 3.5 is derived:

$$F = (P_1 - P_2) / (8.\eta.L / \Pi.r^4) = (\Pi (P_1 - P_2) r^4) / 8.\eta.L \qquad .. \qquad (3.5)$$

Equation 3.5 is known as Poiseuille's law and it can be seen from this equation that the radius is raised to the fourth power. This factor is an important determinant in volume flow rate calculations. In fact, the equation and the resulting calculations show that volume flow rate depends more on the size of the radius than on the fluid pressure.

Although water as a pure liquid follows Poiseuille's law fairly well, some liquids such as blood do not behave precisely as expected. This is thought to be because of the many different types of substances that are found in blood in solution or suspension. For example, red blood cells may accumulate in the faster axial part of the flow, hence there are fewer red blood cells to create friction against the vessel walls. The practicalities of this law will be discussed later in the section on applications to exercise and sport.

STOP AND THINK

1. Why might it be suggested that somebody weighs less underwater when clearly their mass has not changed?

BERNOULLI'S PRINCIPLE

Another consideration relating to pressure and velocity in a moving fluid is Bernoulli's principle. Daniel Bernoulli (1700–1782) was an Italian scientist who found that the pressure in a flowing liquid is at its lowest where the speed is greatest. The principle states that faster flowing fluids exert lower pressures than slower flowing fluids. Note the use of the word 'fluid': once again this principle applies equally to both gases and liquids. The equation for this principle can be expressed as follows:

$$p + \rho.g.h + \tfrac{1}{2}\,\rho.v^2 = constant \qquad .. \qquad .. \qquad .. \qquad (3.6)$$

where P is pressure, ρ is density of the fluid, g is gravity, h is height and v is mean fluid velocity across the section.

The relationship between the variables in Equation 3.6 shows that an increase in speed is directly related to a drop in pressure. For example, for a liquid in a tube to flow there must be a pressure drop. If a tube is reduced in diameter in its middle section, the liquid would flow more quickly through the constricted area in order to transport the same volume of fluid in a given time. Bernoulli's principle can be applied to gases under certain conditions, including air travelling at moderate speeds. However, the principle is based on an incompressible fluid and as gases are compressible, caution should be taken if applying the principle to them. In fact, care must be taken with many of these fundamental laws when applying them to real-life conditions because the laws have often been constructed under 'ideal' conditions. Therefore, although Bernoulli's principle is a straightforward one, fluids, such as blood, water and oil, do not strictly obey the principle outlined by Bernoulli.

SOLUTES, SOLUTIONS AND CONCENTRATION

As already mentioned, a major component of the human body is water. Substances such as starch which enter the body will ultimately dissolve into watery cells. The substances which dissolve are known as **solutes** and the liquids into which they dissolve are known as **solvents**; the combination of a solute and a solvent results in a solution. If a solvent is described as being highly soluble, it means that molecules are easily dissolved in it, but if the solvent possesses a low solubility, this means the molecules are not easily dissolved into it.

Solutions are often described as having a **concentration**, and this relates to the amount of solute per unit volume of the solution. In physiology, there are a number of different ways in which the concentration of a solution may be expressed. These include:

- Moles per unit volume ($mol \cdot L^{-1}$)
- Equivalents (equiv.)
- Mass/volume ($g \cdot L^{-1}$)
- Percentage of solution (%).

Moles

A mole can be defined as 6.02×10^{23} atoms, ions or molecules of a substance. Therefore, one mole of one substance has exactly the same number of atoms as one mole of any other substance. The weight of a mole of a substance is, however, different for different substances. Therefore, we can use the term 'molecular weight', which is the equivalent of the combined atomic mass of the substance expressed in grams. For example, glucose has a chemical formula of $C_6H_{12}O_6$, and the atomic mass of carbon is 12 g, hydrogen is 1 g and oxygen is 16 g (check the periodic table to confirm the atomic masses), resulting in a molecular weight of 180 g (6 C $\times$ 12 g + 12 H $\times$ 1 g + 6 O $\times$ 16 g).

In biology it is often common to refer to concentration as **molarity**, which is the number of moles of solute in 1 litre of solution, and often signified as $mol \cdot L^{-1}$ or M. Therefore, a 1 M solution of glucose is made by dissolving 1 mole or 180 g of glucose into 1 litre of water. A derivative of a mole is the millimole (mmol), which is 1/1000 of a mole. The mmol is commonly used because often solutions are very dilute.

Equivalents

Another method of expressing concentration is to refer to the concentration of ions and this is represented as equivalents per litre. An equivalent is the sum of the molarity of the ion multiplied by the number of charges the ion carries. A sodium ion, often written as Na^+, has a single charge of +1 and is therefore one equivalent per mole. The same rule is followed for negatively charged ions; for example, the hydrogenphosphate ion, HPO_4^{-2}, which has two equivalents per mole. As with mmol, a milliequivalent (meq) is 1/1000 of an equivalent.

Weight by volume and percentage of solution

On many occasions it is not possible to use solutes by the mole and so the more conventional measure of weight is used instead. The solute concentration can be expressed as a percentage of the total solution. A 25 per cent solution means that there are 25 parts of solute per 100 parts of the total solution. However, if the solute represents a solid, then weight per unit volume must be used to represent the percentage solution. Hence, an 8 per cent glucose solution would be made by weighing out 8 g and adding enough water to make a total solution volume of 100 mL. If the solute is already a liquid, the solution uses a volume per unit volume measure. Further information on fluids and sports performance can be found in Maughan et al. (2004).

HYDROGEN IONS

One of the most important solutes in the human body is the hydrogen ion, H^+. As indicated by the symbol, the hydrogen ion has a positive charge because of the loss of an electron, and therefore consists of only a single proton. These positively charged ions are called cations. In the same manner, an ion symbolised as negatively charged, for example a chloride ion, denoted by Cl^-, has an extra electron. Negatively charged ions are called anions. Thus a calcium ion (Ca^{2+}) has lost two electrons and a sulphate ion (SO_4^{2-}) has gained two electrons.

The concentration of H^+ in the human body has important consequences for physiological function, particularly in relation to acidity. Hydrogen ions are constantly produced in the body via H_2O when it separates into H^+ and OH^- or from ionised molecules that release H^+ when dissolved in water. A molecule donating a hydrogen ion to a solution is known as an acid. Molecules that decrease the concentration of H^+ in a solution, by combining with the free H^+, are known as bases. The H^+ ion concentration within the body is measured as pH, which stands for power of hydrogen. The pH is calculated as the negative log of the hydrogen ion concentration:

$$pH \quad = \quad -\log [H^+] \qquad .. \qquad .. \qquad .. \qquad .. \qquad .. \qquad \qquad (3.7)$$

Note the use of the square brackets [ ] which symbolise concentration.

Equation 3.7 can be re-written as:

$$pH \quad = \quad \log(1/[H^+]) \qquad .. \qquad .. \qquad .. \qquad .. \qquad .. \qquad \qquad (3.8)$$

Equation 3.8 states that the pH is inversely related to the concentration of the H^+ ions: as pH goes up, H^+ concentration goes down. Figure 3.6 shows a pH scale, which runs on a scale of 0 to 14. Pure water has a $[H^+]$ equal to 1×10^{-7} M and is therefore classified as having a pH value of 7 or 'neutral'. Solutions that have gained H^+ from an acid will have a higher $[H^+]$. Thus acidic substances such as vinegar have a pH score of 3 and have a H^+ concentration of 1×10^{-3} M. What is not obvious from the scale is that the pH scale is actually based on a logarithmic interval, such that a 1 unit increase, for example from 6 to 7, will represent a tenfold decrease in the H^+ concentration (remember the closer pH moves towards 14 the more alkaline the solution is becoming). Similarly, if the pH values move from 7 to 4, there has been a 1000-fold ($10 \times 10 \times 10$) increase in the H^+ concen-

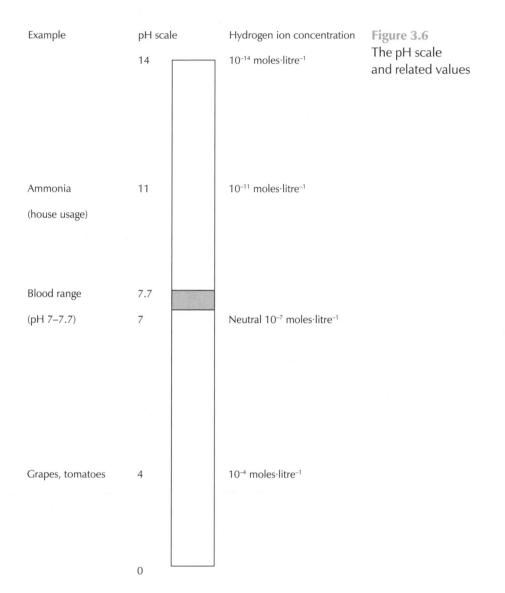

Example	pH scale	Hydrogen ion concentration
	14	10^{-14} moles·litre^{-1}
Ammonia (house usage)	11	10^{-11} moles·litre^{-1}
Blood range (pH 7–7.7)	7.7	
	7	Neutral 10^{-7} moles·litre^{-1}
Grapes, tomatoes	4	10^{-4} moles·litre^{-1}
	0	

Figure 3.6
The pH scale
and related values

tration. During increasing, moderate or heavy intensity exercise, increasing acidity within cells and the blood has to be dealt with by the body. Exercise and sport physiologists have for a long time known that acidity is strongly associated with muscle fatigue during exercise.

APPLICATION OF SCIENCE TO EXERCISE AND SPORT

The preceding discussion on the principles and laws of liquids has given some examples of their application in an exercise and sport context. Other useful examples to note at this stage are:

43

- Working out solutions for sports drinks, and how concentrated the glucose should be in relation to water (see section on solutes, solutions and concentration, p. 40).
- The use of a water manometer to examine lung function (see section on pressure in stationary liquids, p. 32).
- The relationship between blood lactate concentration ($[La^-]_B$) and the H^+ concentration $[H^+]$ in the body. In exercise physiology, $[La^-]_B$ is often used as a measure of how hard an individual is working during a specific exercise test or sports event (see section on pH, p. 42).

BLOOD PRESSURE

Blood pressure is often determined during a routine medical examination, and used in an exercise and sport context prior to a fitness test. Blood pressure could also be taken during a laboratory experiment to investigate the blood pressure response to exercise. An athlete or patient who is diagnosed as being hypertensive (i.e. high blood pressure) would have to undergo a more thorough medical examination before being allowed to undertake an exercise test.

Blood pressure is a reflection of the driving pressure created by the ventricular contraction of the heart (i.e. in systole) and the residual pressure in the circulatory system (i.e. in diastole). As the blood which leaves the left ventricle is under the greatest pressure, systolic blood pressure is a reflection of the highest pressure exerted by the left ventricle during a cardiac cycle. Diastolic blood pressure is the lowest pressure recorded during a cardiac cycle, whilst the ventricles are relaxing. Blood pressure is very difficult to measure directly from the ventricles, hence it is often estimated indirectly from the brachial artery of the arm. This method is assumed to be indicative of the driving pressure for blood flow. During ventricular contraction, the reading is on average 120 mmHg and this falls to 80 mmHg during ventricular relaxation. One of the important considerations for blood pressure is the ability of the aorta and arterioles to expand and store the energy in their elastic walls. The elastic properties of the walls that enables them to expand and store energy results in a flow to the arterial side that is pulsatile (in rhythmical oscillations).

The pulse that a person can feel in their arm or through their chest is a result of the rapid contraction of the ventricles forcing blood through the aorta. The result of this pulse is to create a pressure wave that transmits itself through the blood and travels through the arteries and arterioles. This pressure wave is actually travelling faster than the blood, in fact about ten times as fast. Therefore, the pulse that is felt in the arm occurs after the contraction of the ventricle that created the pressure wave. Depending upon the distance the wave has travelled and the resulting friction, the size of the pulse wave will decrease and the flow of the blood will become smoother rather than pulsatile.

In physiology there is a parameter called pulse pressure that is an index of the amplitude of the pulse pressure wave. Pulse pressure is calculated as follows:

physical states

$$\text{Pulse pressure} \quad = \quad \text{systolic pressure} - \text{diastolic pressure} \qquad (3.9)$$

e.g. 40 $\qquad$ = $\qquad$ 125 − 85

Because of the distance the blood has had to travel to pass through the veins, the pressure decreases dramatically. The veins channelling blood back to the heart are therefore known as low pressure capacitors (remember that the pulse wave disappeared because of friction). The blood in the veins below the level of the heart must be returned back in circulatory fashion to the heart. Although a pressure gradient does not exist to help the blood travel towards the right atrium, the blood does get help from two other types of pump: the respiratory muscle pump and the skeletal muscle pump. For example, during exercise that involves the lower limbs, the action of muscle contractions in the calf or upper leg result in the constriction of the veins and the blood is squeezed back towards the heart. To assist this flow, which is known as venous flow, veins have valves that prevent the blood flowing backwards, similar to the valves in the heart. This ensures that blood is forced upwards against gravity during upright exercise. One of the main reasons why soldiers on parade faint or collapse is because of venous pooling of the blood in the lower legs. As there is very little muscle contraction of the lower legs during the long hours some soldiers have to stand, less blood is forced upward to the heart and more blood is left pooling in the veins. This action results in less blood circulating and transporting oxygen around the body, particularly to the brain, and when a critical point is reached the body's natural response is to faint, and the victim is brought crashing to the ground. As a result, the pooled blood in the legs will begin to re-circulate and, providing there are no other serious injuries from the fall, the soldier should quickly regain consciousness.

As described previously, arterial blood pressure is estimated from the brachial artery in the arm. To measure blood pressure directly, an indwelling catheter would have to be placed directly into an artery. The sphygmomanometer (from sphygmus – pulse, and manometer – instrument for measuring fluid pressure) uses an inflatable cuff device strapped around the upper arm (usually the left arm). The cuff is inflated to a higher pressure than the systolic pressure and as a result of this the blood flow into the lower arm is stopped. As the cuff is slowly deflated, the cuff pressure approaches the systolic pressure. Eventually the cuff pressure drops just below the systolic pressure and blood begins to squeeze through the constricted artery. Blood flow is turbulent at this point, and causes what is known as a Korotkoff sound. This sound can only be heard through a stethoscope placed just below the cuff. For the sound to be heard the artery has to be compressed, and each Korotkoff sound is heard with each heart beat. It is at this point that the reading on the sphygmomanometer is recorded. As the cuff pressure continues to fall, the pressure exerted on the artery becomes less until eventually the artery is no longer compressed. It is at this point that the Korotkoff sounds disappear, since blood flow is no longer turbulent and silent, at which point the second reading, the diastolic pressure, is recorded. The two readings which are taken, that is, systolic/diastolic pressure, are 120/80 mmHg in a person with normal blood pressure. For a person to be considered hypertensive (having sustained high blood pressure) a blood pressure reading of 140/90 would have to be found several times, as there is some variation within a single individual from one moment to the next.

Consider the scenario if a student was late for a laboratory practical on blood pressure and had to rush to get to the laboratory. What would be the effect of their anxiety on their blood pressure?

In addition to pulse pressure, mean arterial pressure (MAP) is used to describe blood pressure. The arterial pressure is a wave, and therefore pulsatile, so a single value is thought to be useful to indicate the driving pressure. To calculate the MAP, which typically only applies to a heart rate range between 60 and 80 beats per minute, the following formula is used:

$$MAP \quad = \quad \text{diastolic pressure} + 1/3 \,(\text{systolic pressure} - \text{diastolic pressure})$$

$$= \quad 82 \text{ mmHg} + 1/3 \,(125 - 82)$$

$$= \quad 96 \text{ mmHg} \quad .. \quad .. \quad .. \quad .. \quad .. \quad .. \quad\quad (3.10)$$

The calculation of MAP gives a figure that is closer to the diastolic figure than the systolic one. This is because at rest the heart is in diastole twice as long as it is in systole. This is why the formula will only work for a resting heart rate value. For example, if the heart rate increases, the amount of time spent in diastole (relaxation period of the heart's ventricles) decreases and therefore systole (contraction phase of the heart's ventricles) becomes relatively more important to the contribution of the MAP.

MAP is a major determinant of blood flow and is influenced by four factors:

- Resistance to blood flow within the circulatory system.
- Cardiac Output (Q).
- Relative distribution between blood in arterial and venous vessels.
- Blood volume.

The site of greatest resistance is the arterioles, which contribute over 60 per cent of the total resistance to the flow in the circulatory system. The resistance is principally because of the amount of smooth muscle possessed by the arterioles, and it is the smooth muscle that enables the arterioles to constrict and hence decrease flow or dilate and hence increase flow. As has already been noted, a very small change in radius creates a large change in the resistance (see Equation 3.4). By applying the fundamentals of pressure, flow and resistance, Equation 3.4 may be applied to physiological responses such as blood flow and pressure. For further development of knowledge in this area, topics such as blood volume and how the blood is distributed throughout the body should be examined.

CARDIOVASCULAR HEALTH

Bernoulli's principle is usually illustrated with the application to flight such that the air flow over the top of a curved wing is faster and creates a negative pressure above the wing, hence the generation of lift is greater than the force of gravity and consequently there is upward motion. For liquids, Bernoulli's principle can be applied in the context of cardiovascular health as applied to a patient who has atherosclerosis (a disease which affects the arteries, particularly the heart). In this condition the inside wall of an artery has become coated with fatty deposits known as plaque. If this plaque builds up over time, the artery becomes constricted. As a consequence of the constriction, blood speed is higher than elsewhere through the artery but pressure is lower compared to other regions of the artery. The higher blood speed can result in a collapse of the artery, which interrupts blood flow briefly. At this moment, blood flow is zero and blood pressure increases and the artery regains its shape. If this process is allowed to continue over time, then it can result in a stroke. Although it might surprise students that as the liquid flows more quickly through the constricted section, the pressure drops rather than increases, this well-known principle has been put to good use for many purposes where a liquid is flowing through pipes, tubes or nozzles. Figure 3.7 shows the increase in velocity accompanied by a decrease in pressure for the constricted artery.

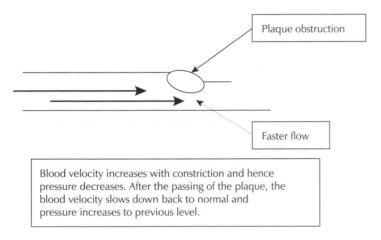

Figure 3.7 Blood speed and pressure in an obstructed artery

SELF-TEST

1. Define pressure at a point in a liquid.

2. Since most of the body is composed of liquids (mostly water) why is there no danger that the body will be crushed or compressed by increasing pressures found with ever-increasing depths from underwater diving?

3. Select a volume flow rate using Poiseuille's equation and then individually double one parameter at a time to examine the effects on the flow rate.

4. One of the consequences of ageing is that arteries become stiffer. What would the consequences be for blood flow and pressure?

CONCLUSION

Although the behaviour of some aspects of liquids is difficult to predict, an extensive amount of research findings have been amassed. In the third century BC work by Archimedes established a principle which stated the buoyant force on a submerged or partially submerged object was equal to the weight of the fluid displaced. If the volume of fluid can be calculated, and if an object's mass were known, the density of an object could be determined. These principles have been put into practice to determine such variables as body fat estimations by using the technique known as hydrodensitometry (underwater weighing).

A property of liquids is their fixed volume. It is known that in liquids the bonding between molecules is strong and this accounts for their incompressibility. This incompressibility under pressure has been verified from work by Pascal, who found that pressure within an enclosed liquid was transmitted equally. Pascal's principle has lead to devices such as hydraulic presses and braking systems. Pressure affects not only stationary liquids but also flowing ones. Many physiological responses in the body involve flowing liquids. For a liquid to flow there must be a drop in pressure, and this is often referred to as the pressure gradient. A number of other factors influence flowing liquids, such as length of the vessel through which the liquid flows, the resistance offered by the vessel to the flow of the liquid, plus the internal resistance of the liquid itself. Such scientific facts allow investigation of conditions such as hypertension (high blood pressure).

Besides the issues discussed in this chapter, there is a whole branch of engineering devoted to the study of mechanical properties of fluids, known as hydraulics. A subdivision of hydraulics is hydrostatics, which deals with the study of liquids at rest. Another subdivision is hydrokinetics, which deals with liquids in motion and is particularly concerned with friction and turbulence generated by the flowing liquids.

KEY POINTS

- Pressure is defined as force per unit area.
- Liquids are essentially incompressible.

- In a stationary liquid the pressure is proportional to the density of the liquid multiplied by the height of the liquid.
- Pascal's principle states that any change in pressure in an enclosed liquid will be transmitted evenly to all parts of the liquid.
- Any submerged object will have an upward buoyant force equal to the weight of the liquid displaced.
- If the density of an object is less than that of the liquid, it will float.
- The percentage of the floating object which is submerged gives an indication of the specific gravity for the liquid.
- When a liquid flows there is a pressure drop.
- Poiseuille's law states that the pressure drop divided by the resistance is equal to the flow rate.
- The resistance to flow is most strongly influenced by the radius of the tube through which the liquid flows.
- Although blood is not an ideal liquid, unlike water, Poiseuille's law can usefully be used to describe some aspects of the dynamics of blood flow.
- It is more accurate to use the term 'pressure gradient' than 'pressure change'. If there is no pressure gradient, there is no flow of liquid.
- Flow rate is most affected by radius of the vessel through which the liquid travels.
- Obstructions to the flow of a liquid are likely to cause disturbances in laminar flow and possibly lead to turbulent flow.
- Bernoulli's principle states that in an incompressible fluid, the sum of its pressure and velocity is always constant.
- A solute plus a solvent equals a solution. The solute is the dissolved substance and the solvent is the liquid into which the solute was dissolved.
- A concentration describes the ratio of the solute and solution. It can be expressed in moles (mol), equivalents (equiv.), weight per unit volume (g·L^{-1}) or percentage of solution (%).
- Blood pressure represents the driving force of the ventricles during systole and the residual pressure within the circulatory system during diastole.
- The resistance to blood flow is an important factor in the physiology of the circulation.

BIBLIOGRAPHY

Bender, D.A. (2002) *Introduction to Nutrition and Metabolism*, 3rd edition. London: Taylor & Francis.

Duncan, T. (1994) *Advanced Physics*, 4th edition. London: John Murray Publishers.

Green, J.H. (1972) *An Introduction to Human Physiology*, 3rd edition. London: Oxford University Press.

Maughan, R.J., Burke, L.M. and Coyle, E.F. (2004) *Food, Nutrition and Sports Performance II, The International Olympic Committee Consensus on Sports Performance*. London: Routledge.

Nave, C.R. and Nave, B.C. (1985) *Physics for the Health Sciences*, 3rd edition. Philadelphia, PA: W.B. Saunders.

Silverthorn, D.U. (1998) *Human Physiology. An Integrated Approach*. New Jersey: Prentice Hall.

Uvarov, E.B. and Isaacs, A. (1986) *The Penguin Dictionary of Science*, 6th edition. London: Penguin Group.

FURTHER READING

Rose, S. and Mileusnic, R. (1999) *The Chemistry of Life*, 4th edition. London: Penguin Books.

CHAPTER FOUR

SOLIDS

AIMS OF THE CHAPTER

This chapter is designed to provide an understanding of the scientific principles of solids when applied to the practical issues, which underpin exercise and sport. After reading this chapter, you should be able to:

- State the properties of solids.
- Appreciate the term 'internal energy'.
- Understand how solids are affected by temperature.
- Understand the terms 'conduction', 'thermal conductivity' and 'radiation'.
- Apply the scientific principles of solids to exercise and sport.

INTRODUCTION

A solid is defined as 'the physical state of matter in which the constituent molecules, atoms or ions have no translatory motion although they vibrate about the fixed positions that they occupy in a crystal lattice' (Uvarov and Isaacs, 1986: 376). A solid, such as metal, possesses the property of stiffness or rigidity. This is because of the atoms possessing order and being held in approximately fixed positions. Molecules forming a solid are typically arranged in an orderly fashion known as a lattice. Most solids will thus keep their shape and, unlike a liquid, a solid will not take the shape of a container that it is placed into. Although the human eye sees a solid as a fixed state of matter, on a molecular scale the picture is very different. The atoms of a solid are in fact moving continuously and rapidly. Solids cannot move as quickly as gases because the movement of the molecules is limited by the attraction between molecules. Unlike gases, this means that there is limited distance over which the molecules move. There is a large amount of kinetic energy in a solid.

KEY APPLICATIONS TO EXERCISE AND SPORT

There are many examples of where knowledge about solids can be applied to exercise and sport. Many of these examples relate to the materials that performers and exercisers interact with, such as rackets, bats, boats or the objects that are struck, such as cricket balls, squash balls or shuttlecocks. The interest in these materials has lead to many degree programmes which focus on sport and technology, and clearly elements of engineering, physics and chemistry contribute to our understanding of materials used in exercise and sport. Within the sub-disciplines of a sport and exercise science degree programme it is probably biomechanics that will feature the properties of solids in the curriculum. Investigation of the effect of different pitch surfaces and how different training shoes interact with these surfaces are relevant to some sports. The evolving technology related to the surfaces for gymnastic floors has seen dramatic changes in the performance of floor routines. The motor racing industry has always spent large sums of money on research and development, particularly related to safety, and developments such as better car cockpit design and better crash helmets have undoubtedly saved lives. The impact of carbon fibre frames in track cycling in the mid-1990s also had a dramatic impact on improving performance for cyclists. In relation to health, bone is one of the tissues that may be considered as a solid. Although the body does not strictly conform to rules related to solids, application of some of the principles applied to a solid can help scientists understand more about bone dynamics. Osteoporosis is a bone-related disease currently causing many health problems for younger people as well as the elderly. How exercise can reduce the debilitating effects of this disease is a major topic of current research.

SCIENTIFIC PRINCIPLES OF SOLIDS

Solids can possess all or some of the following characteristics:

1. Thermal conductivity
2. Electrical conductivity
3. Mechanical conductivity.

In terms of mechanical properties, solids can have four different characteristics. First, the strength of a solid refers to how much applied force a material can endure before breaking. Second, stiffness refers to the opposition a material presents against being distorted by having its shape and size altered. Third, ductility is the ability of a material to be hammered, rolled and stretched into a useful shape. Fourth, toughness relates to a material that is not brittle. Some solids, such as steel, will possess all these properties whereas others possess only some. Glass for example is strong and stiff but not ductile or tough.

As stated in the introduction, the atoms of a solid are alternating between attracting and repelling one another whilst vibrating around an equilibrium point. This movement energy is known as **internal energy** and is a result of both the kinetic and the potential energy of the atoms in the solid. In a solid there is approximately equal division between these two energies. This is similar to a spring, which coils and recoils when pressed and released; the energy stored in the bonds of the atoms as they compress and extend is known as potential energy. The kinetic energy is caused by the motion of the atoms and is dependent on temperature. In gases (see Chapter 2) much of the internal energy is a result of kinetic energy as there is little storage of energy between gas atoms.

The kinetic energy in a solid can be increased if heat is applied. The definition of heat is, 'the energy which is transferred from a body of higher temperature to one of lower temperature by conduction, convection or radiation' (Duncan, 1997: 78). The schematic in Figure 4.1 shows what occurs when a solid is heated.

The transference of heat makes the atoms of a solid oscillate over a larger distance and with a faster speed. The larger range of motion of the atoms causes a greater mean distance

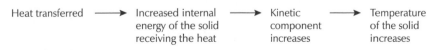

Heat transferred ⟶ Increased internal energy of the solid receiving the heat ⟶ Kinetic component increases ⟶ Temperature of the solid increases

Figure 4.1 Increased internal energy of a solid through heating

between atoms, resulting in the solid expanding. The temperature increase also results in an increased vibration of the molecules because of their faster speed of movement.

However, for the internal energy of a solid to increase it is not solely a matter of heat application. It is also possible for work done on the solid to increase its internal energy. The internal energy of a solid can be increased either by increasing the temperature and/or by the application of work. Therefore, the use of the term 'heating' should be applied carefully, as it might be that the term 'internal energy' as applied to a solid, liquid or gas is more appropriate.

The specific heat capacity is 'the quantity of heat required to produce a unit rise of temperature in unit mass' (Duncan, 1997: 79). The units of measurement for specific heat capacity are joule per kilogram per kelvin. The mean specific heat capacity for aluminium is 910 $J \cdot kg^{-1} \cdot K^{-1}$, lead 130 $J \cdot kg^{-1} \cdot K^{-1}$, and water at room temperature 4200 $J \cdot kg^{-1} \cdot K^{-1}$. In textbooks it is also common to read about the heat (or thermal) capacity of a solid. This is defined as 'the quantity of heat needed to produce one unit rise of temperature in a body' (Duncan, 1997: 79). The term 'specific' preceding heat capacity denotes a quantity that is standardised as 'per unit mass'. The specific heat of the human body is very close to that of water because of the body's very high water content (~60 %).

TRANSFER OF HEAT IN A SOLID

A further characteristic of a solid is the ability to transfer heat in the form of **conduction**. Conduction occurs when molecules of two surfaces contact one another. Conduction allows for the direct transfer of the motion of molecules in a hot area to molecules in a cooler area. Hence, a thermal gradient is created, such that heat will move from a hotter region to a cooler region. At the molecular level, the hotter molecules, which are moving more rapidly because of the increased temperature, are also resulting in more collisions. As a consequence, the rapidly moving hotter molecules are giving internal energy to the molecules of the cooler regions. Many people are aware that metals are better conductors of heat than non-metals but are not necessarily aware of the reason why. A simple experiment such as heating a piece of metal and a piece of wood to the same temperature (e.g. 70°C) will help to elucidate the process of conduction in solids. In a piece of heated metal some of its electrons are freer to move around, in contrast to the more rigidly fixed electrons in a piece of wood. In the metal, the electrons will be moving at great speeds and will transfer energy by colliding with other electrons in the lattice. When a hand touches the metal, heat is transferred to the hand. When a hand touches the wood, although it is heated to the same temperature as the metal, it does not feel as hot. The number of collisions and the amount of energy transferred during each collision is less for the heated piece of wood. The relationship between the number of collisions and the amount of energy transferred is known as the **thermal conductivity**. Metals have a higher thermal conductivity than non-metals because they are more efficient during their energy transference as a result of the number of collisions of atoms. The thermal conductivity of water is about 25 times greater than air; hence it provides a greater transfer of heat. If the simple example with a piece of metal and wood was changed, so that the wood and metal were cooled to the same temperature (e.g. 5°C), what would be the conclusion? When the metal is touched it feels much colder than the wood. For the same reason that the metal felt hotter than the wood, the metal conducts heat more rapidly away from the hand compared with the wood. This example highlights an interesting fact about the human perception of heat; despite the fact that both the metal and wood were heated to the same temperature, the human perception is that the metal felt both hotter and colder respectively. The conduction of heat is dependent on a number of other factors that include the relative masses of the two bodies, the thermal resistance of the contacting surfaces, the thickness of the conductor, the temperature differences between the surfaces and the area of contacting surfaces. The conduction of heat can be represented by an equation known as Fourier's law of heat flow (Equation 4.1) measured in $W \cdot m^{-2}$:

$$H_k = \frac{k}{d} \cdot (T_1 - T_2) \cdot A \qquad \qquad \qquad \qquad \qquad \qquad \qquad (4.1)$$

$H_k =$ Specific heat of substances
$k =$ relative mass of the two bodies and thermal resistance between the two contacting surfaces
$d =$ the thickness of the conductor
$T_1 - T_2 =$ temperature difference between the two surfaces
$A =$ area of contacting surfaces

Another possibility for heat transfer by a solid is **radiation**. Whereas in conduction internal energy is transferred from one molecule to another and requires contact to transfer the energy, in radiation this does not happen, as radiation is not caused by the temperature of the medium. An example would be solar radiation. The energy that the earth receives from the sun is a clear example of radiation. Radiation is independent of air temperature and the presence of air. Hence, it is still possible to become sun-tanned on a cool cloudy day in summer. Equation 4.2 gives the equation for radiation in a human body:

$$R = \sigma \cdot \varepsilon \cdot (A_r / A_d) \cdot (T_{sk}^4 - T_r^4) \qquad \qquad \qquad \qquad \qquad (4.2)$$

$\sigma =$ Stephan–Boltzmann constant ($5.67 \times 10^{-8}\ W \cdot m^{-2} \cdot K^{-4}$)
$\varepsilon =$ the emittance of the body surface (typically 0.99)
$A_r / A_d =$ fraction of skin involved in the radioactive heat exchange (typically 0.696 for sitting and 0.725 for standing position)
$T_{sk} =$ mean of skin temperature in kelvins (K)
$T_r =$ mean environmental radiant temperature in kelvins (K)

The emittance of an object depends on how effective that object is as a radiator. An ideal radiator is also an ideal absorber and has a score equal to one, whereas an ideal reflector has a score of zero. The skin is an ideal absorber and radiator absorbing between 97 per cent and 99 per cent of the infrared radiation that strikes it. The smoothness and thickness of the surface influences emission and absorption of radiation. The difference in skin colour does have a bearing on the amount of reflection of the sun's radiation of visible light range, but there is no difference between skin colour and the absorption of infrared heat, with skin absorbing about 97 per cent. The amount of heat lost by radiation will be examined in the application section as it has a major impact for the amount of heat loss whilst the human body is at rest. The processes of conduction and radiation become relatively less important when exercise is taking place in hot environmental conditions. In such conditions, evaporation becomes the major avenue of heat loss.

All solids will radiate heat, but since this heat is in the infrared spectrum, it cannot be seen by the human eye. The technique that allows recording of infrared radiation is known as thermography. The recorded image taken by the thermal camera is known as a thermo-gram. The image distinguishes different temperature zones, known as isotherms, which are characterised through different colours or shading. Special imaging cameras can be used to find lost people in open countryside where undergrowth might restrict visibility, or at night when visibility is poor. In physiology laboratories it is possible to use thermal imaging cameras to investigate the effects of heat on the body whilst exercising.

CATEGORIES OF A SOLID

In total there are three types of solid:

- Crystalline (which can be sub-divided into four structures):
  1. Face centred cubic.
  2. Hexagonal close packing.
  3. Body centred cubic.
  4. Tetrahedral.
- Amorphous.
- Polymers.

Almost all solids are crystalline, including all metals and most minerals. The key features of crystals are the repetitive nature and regularity of the patterning of atoms, ions or molecules (see Figure 4.2). In crystals which are described as face centred cubic (FCC) such as sodium chloride (table salt), the crystal is shaped like a cube. At the centre of each of the six faces of the cube is a particle. Therefore, each chloride ion is surrounded by a sodium ion and similarly every sodium by a chloride ion. In hexagonal close packing (HCP), as the term implies, the structure of the packing is hexagonal, and zinc and magnesium are two examples of such structures. In body centred cubic (BCC), the structure is less tightly packed than that of FCC. Although similar to the cube structure of the FCC crystal, the BCC has only a single particle in the centre of the cube and one particle in each

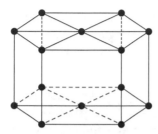

Face centred cubic

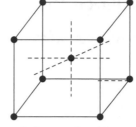

Body centred packing

Figure 4.2
The four types
of crystal

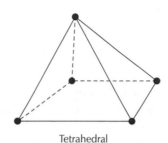

Hexagonal close packing

Tetrahedral

corner. Alkali metals are typically of this structure. The tetrahedral structure is a more open arrangement, and has a particle in the centre and one at each of the four corners of the tetrahedron. Structures like these include carbon in the form of diamonds, silicon and graphite.

The second classification of solids, amorphous structures, does not contain the same organised pattern as crystals. Therefore, it is only for a small volume that there is any order to their pattern, and over large volumes there is a lack of any recognisable regular patterning. Glass is a common amorphous solid. The third type of solid is polymers, which are characterised as having large molecules, ranging from 1000 to 100 000 atoms, and are usually organic (carbon) compounds. Polymers may exist naturally such as cellulose found in plants, or be manufactured such as perspex, nylon or polyester. Natural polymers do possess a repeating and regular patterned structure called monomers. Cellulose, for example, comprises anything from several hundred to several thousand glucose molecules arranged in a long chain. The bicycle used by Chris Boardman to win the gold medal in the 4 km pursuit in the 1992 Barcelona Olympics was carbon fibre reinforced plastic. The bicycle offered greater stiffness and strength than the plastic materials previously used, which were often reinforced with glass, otherwise known as fibre-glass. Although the carbon-reinforced plastic was much lighter than a conventional metal framed bicycle, the material is very costly and therefore its use is not widespread for lower level athletes. Tennis is another sport that has benefited from the use of reinforced plastic. It is very rare for a professional player to compete with a racket made of anything other than carbon fibre plastic. Carbon fibre plastics are extremely strong and resilient, yet are light enough to allow a player control of a powerfully struck tennis ball.

APPLICATION OF SCIENCE TO EXERCISE AND SPORT

RADIATION FROM THE BODY AT REST

The amount of heat gained or lost is important to the survival of the human body. The body maintains temperature within a narrow band: approximately 36°–37.5°C (97°–99.5°F). There will, however, be some variation because of individual differences, such as the effects of the menstrual cycle in women (typically body temperature is 0.5°C higher after ovulation) and time of day (body temperature is lowest in the early hours of the morning and highest in the early evening). Depending on the environmental conditions, the body must therefore regulate the amount of heat lost or heat gained (see Figure 4.3). In actual fact, the body temperature need only experience a 6°C increase and the risk of death from hyperthermia is a very real possibility.

In Chapter 6 it will be seen that the large majority of the chemical processes occurring in the human body result in the release of heat in addition to useful work being done. At rest, the very metabolically active organs (i.e. the heart, kidney, liver and brain) produce the majority of the body's heat, whilst muscle and skin amount to about 20 per cent. The **basal metabolic rate** (BMR) represents the quantity of internal energy that must be used to maintain normal bodily functions during the waking state (i.e. biological maintenance of the body at rest). Typically, the average basal metabolic rate for an adult male is 40 kcal·m^{-2}·h^{-1}. So for a male whose body surface area is 1.8 m^2, this would equate to 72 kcal·hr, and in terms of equivalence to watts this would be equal to approximately 83 W. Females generally have a lower BMR as on average they are smaller than males but the figures are not dissimilar. Hence, for an average person approximately 83 W of heat would be gained every hour, but when heat balance is maintained, the same amount is also lost. If the body could not get rid of the heat, the metabolic processes occurring at rest would increase the body's temperature by about 1°C per hour. Therefore, it only takes a matter of a few hours before the body is in danger from excessive temperature. This situation might occur when the external ambient temperature is very high, particularly when exercise is taking place.

As shown in Equation 4.2 one way the human body can lose heat is through radiation. Radiation is a very effective means of body heat loss. To highlight how much heat can be

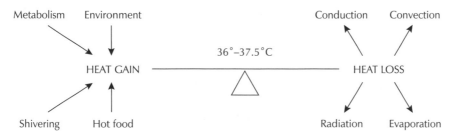

Figure 4.3 The heat balance of the human body through heat gain and heat loss

radiated by a human, take the scenario of an unclothed body with a skin temperature of 32°C and an air temperature of 24°C (for simplicity we are assuming the temperature is uniform around the body). Using Equation 4.2:

$$R = \sigma\varepsilon \, (A_r/A_d) \cdot (T_{sk}{}^4 - T_r{}^4)$$

$\sigma =$	Stephan–Boltzmann constant	$= 5.67 \times 10^{-8}$ W·m^{-2}·K^{-4}
$\varepsilon =$	the emittance of the body surface	$= 0.99$
$A_r/A_d =$	fraction of skin involved in the radioactive heat exchange	$= 0.725$ in standing position
$T_{sk} =$	mean of skin temperature	$= 32$°C *
$T_r =$	mean environmental radiant temperature	$= 22$°C *

* Note temperature data is in kelvin in the equation.

$$R = (5.67 \times 10^{-8}) \times 0.99 \times 0.725 \times (305^4 - 295^4)$$
$$R = (5.67 \times 10^{-8}) \times 0.99 \times 0.725 \times (1.08 \times 10^9)$$
$$R = (5.67 \times 10^{-8}) \times 0.717 \times (1.08 \times 10^9)$$
$$R = 61.25 \times 0.717$$
$$R \approx 44 \text{ W·m}^2$$

If the unclothed body had a surface area of 2 m², then the loss of heat caused by radiation is approximately 88 W. Therefore, it can be seen that the heat gain by the body is effectively being lost by radiation and the body is essentially in thermal balance. If the temperature difference were further widened between skin and air, it can be shown that the heat lost caused by radiation would be greater than the heat gain of the body. In this situation, the body would begin to feel cold. The natural reaction by the body would be to vasoconstrict blood vessels near the surface of the skin so heat would not be lost as readily. In addition, shivering could be initiated to increase the internal energy of the body. For further information on the effects of thermoregulation, and more calculations which include the addition of conductive, convective and evaporative losses, see Eston and Reilly (2001: Chapter 12).

STOP AND THINK

Why are runners sometimes given a silver foil blanket after completing an event such as the marathon?

Why are runners still hot, even an hour after finishing exercise?

BONE AS A SOLID

Bone is not often thought of as an active tissue within the body, however, it is a dynamic tissue. Throughout a human's life, bone is constantly being modelled and remodelled. Bone can be subdivided into two structural types: the cortical and cancellous (trabeculae) bone. The cortical bone is the denser of the two and is found on the external surfaces of bones and in the walls of the diaphyses. The thickness of the bone varies as a function of the mechanical requirements. Bone is therefore strong and resistant to bending. The trabeculae bone is found within the vertebral bodies, in the epiphyses of long bones and in short bones. Irregular spacing found in trabeculae bone reduces the weight of the bone and the orientation of the bone structure is often aligned with the forces impacting on the bone. Bone is a composite of water (25–30 per cent), protein in the form of collagen (25–30 per cent of bone's dry weight) and minerals (mostly calcium phosphate and carbonate which constitute 65–70 per cent of the bone's dry weight). The role of the collagen is to resist tensile loading, that is, loading that stretches the bone along its longitudinal axis. The collagen fibres have limited flexibility, whilst the proteins act to give ductility (i.e. flexibility or ability to deform) and toughness in the form of resistance to shock loading. The minerals calcium and phosphate give resistance to compressive forces and result in hardness and rigidity of the bone. The rigidity is caused by the minerals, calcium phosphate and calcium hydroxide, forming calcium hydroxyapatite ($3Ca_3(PO_4)_2Ca(OH)_2$).

When mechanical force is applied to a bone, it will temporarily bend. This temporary change in shape can be measured as stress, which can be defined as the relative change in length (see Chapter 5). The amount of stress is dependent on several factors, such as the size and direction of the force, the distance between the applied force and the bending point, and the moment of inertia of the bone. Consider the compressive stresses of the tibia as a person walks or runs. The amount of force being absorbed by the body when running can be up to five times the person's body weight. This will be combined with shear stress that is caused by torsional loading associated with lateral and medial rotation of the tibia. In running the tensile stresses are much greater than in walking, but the shear stresses are greater in walking. In all exercise and sport situations mechanical forces will be experienced by bone. In cricket, for example, as a batter goes to play a forward defensive shot, the batter is required to lunge forward quickly onto the front foot. The act of lunging will load the tibia and fibula. In cricket the bowler will also experience large impact forces which must be absorbed by the vertebral bones, so it is of no surprise that many bowlers suffer from bad backs throughout their careers. At present in cricket there is much emphasis being placed on recording a bowler's action to analyse their bowling technique in an effort to correct poor bowling actions and hopefully prevent future back injuries.

Mechanical stress on bone stimulates both cellular and tissue reactions by promoting the activity of such hormones as prostacyclin and prostaglandin E_2 and enzymes such as glucose-6-phosphate dehydrogenase. Without mechanical stress placed on bone, as is the situation for astronauts in space who experience weightlessness, bone mass is lost and optimal conditions for bone modelling and remodelling are reduced. Studies that have investigated athletes such as tennis and baseball players have found that the bones in the arms of the racket holding and throwing arms of these athletes also have a higher bone density than the non-dominant hand. Swimmers have also been shown to have different bone densities, exhibiting a lower vertebral bone mineral density when compared to other athletes and controls (Taaffle et al., 1995). This is one of the reasons why swimming is not promoted as an exercise for optimal bone health. It is still unclear exactly how mechanical stress alters bone density, but the dominant theory at present compares bone to a piezoelectric crystal. The piezoelectric crystal produces a voltage when it is subjected to forces, which deform the crystal. The voltage is then thought to stimulate the osteoclasts that lead to calcium synthesis.

A fracture is one of the most traumatic events to happen to bone. In exercise and sport the chances of this occurring are higher if the sport involves physical contact such as football and rugby. Fractures tend to occur as a result of acute excessive stress, whilst chronic excessive stress results in a stress fracture. Any force acting on a bone in excess of the force limits of the bone can result in a fracture. It is thought that shin splints are often caused by excessive amounts of landing on hard surfaces (e.g. running) and are a result of micro-fractures of the tibia, where the muscle tissue pulls away from the periosteum of the bone. New recruits in the armed forces have been found to suffer from what are termed 'fatigue fractures'. This is as a result of the sudden increases in physical training, which places chronic repetitive forces on the bone.

Fractures can more easily occur if the bone is weak. This is particularly evident in people who may have osteoporosis, a condition which can be described as 'porous bone', or 'brittle bones' or 'too little bone in the bones'. Osteoporosis is a disease related to bone which typically results in low bone mass and a weakened architecture of the bone. The underlying weakened structure of the bone leads to increased risk of fracture. Fractures tend to be most prominent in the vertebrae, distal radius (forearm) and hip bones. The disease affects both males and females but is far more common in women than men. At present the role of physical activity is being promoted as a method to aid bone health, particularly in young teenage girls. This strategy is an attempt to optimise the bone mineral density, which is thought to reach a peak around thirty years of age. For a comprehensive review of osteoporosis, and the impact of physical activity, see Drinkwater et al. (1995). The increasing number of people suffering from osteoporosis has resulted in the American College of Sports Medicine (1995) issuing a position statement about the disease. Four key points were highlighted:

1. Weight-bearing physical activity is essential for normal development and maintenance of a healthy skeleton.
2. Sedentary people may increase bone mass by becoming more active. However, the benefit of becoming active may be one of avoiding further losses of bone through being inactive.
3. Exercise is not a substitute for hormone replacement therapy at the time of the menopause.
4. An optimal programme for the elderly would include strength, flexibility and co-ordination.

1. Go through Equation 4.1 and input a variety of different skin and air temperatures to calculate the effect on heat loss through radiation.

2. What causes rickets and how does it affect bone?

3. Put the following in order of the highest mechanical loading for the promotion of bone health: cycling, running, swimming, weight training.

CONCLUSION

The factors that impact on a solid are simpler than those of a liquid, and a solid's behaviour is more predictable. In a solid, the atoms vibrate around a fixed point and successively repel and attract neighbouring atoms. The alternate movement of atoms creates the internal energy and is associated with the potential and kinetic energy available within the solid. The fixed position of the atoms also gives the solid its characteristic shape and rigidity.

There are three main types of solids: crystalline, amorphous (or glassy) and polymer structures. In subjects such as mechanical engineering, the external forces imposed on the solid and its subsequent behaviour are investigated. Mechanical properties such as strength, stiffness, ductility and toughness are important factors to consider in construction materials. In recent years information from an engineering perspective has been incorporated into exercise and sport. In particular, biomechanists have routinely argued for an engineering approach or model in which to investigate many problems faced in exercise and sport.

An important aspect of solids is the ability to transfer heat and this is achieved in one of two ways: radiation or conduction. At rest, radiation would appear to be the more important mechanism by which heat is lost from the body, although during exercise in humans, radiation or conduction may not be adequate heat loss mechanisms. In this instance, evaporation would be the best method to lose heat from the body.

Bone is an example of a solid in humans as it demonstrates many of the properties of solids: properties of strength, stiffness and toughness. It is important, however, not to neglect the dynamic nature of bone as a living tissue. Habitual physical activity subjects bones to stresses and strains which promote bone growth and remodelling. In some diseases, such as osteoporosis, the mechanical property of toughness is severely compromised. One strategy that can therefore be used to reduce the number of osteoporosis cases is to promote physical activity throughout life, with a particular emphasis on adolescent and menopausal women.

- Most solids have the appearance of rigidity and do not take the shape of containers in which they are placed.
- Since the particles within the solids are held in approximately fixed positions, there is less empty space in which atoms can move.
- The atoms of a solid vibrate to and fro around a fixed point; this vibration and the potential energy of the bonds of the atoms is known as internal energy.
- At room temperature, the average kinetic energy as indicated by the speed of the molecules of a solid are equal to several hundred miles per hour.
- Heating is the transfer of energy from a body of higher temperature to one of lower temperature by radiation, convection or conduction.
- The specific heat capacity of a solid involves the quantity of heat required to increase one unit of mass by one unit of temperature.
- Heating a solid increases the vibration of the molecules and the solid expands.
- The greater the number of collisions of atoms, and therefore the amount of energy transferred by a solid, the higher the thermal conductivity.
- Conduction requires contact to be made between the molecules of two surfaces in order for heat to be transferred.
- Factors such as the mass and thermal resistance of the contacting surfaces, the thickness of the conductor, the temperature gradient between the two surfaces, and the area of connecting surfaces must also be considered when discussing conduction.
- Silver and copper are the best conductors, whilst polythene is considered to be the worst.
- Radiation is not influenced by the medium that it is travelling through.
- At rest, radiation is an important mechanism for heat loss in the human body.
- There are three kinds of solids: crystalline (face centred cubic, hexagonal close packing, body centred cubic and tetrahedral), amorphous and polymers.
- The transference of heat for humans is an important process for thermo-regulation; at rest, radiation can account for a large percentage of the heat loss by the body.
- The human body can be described as a homeotherm and must maintain a thermal balance; if thermal balance is not maintained, and body heat content begins to increase, death can occur.
- The use of different solids in the form of sports equipment has had a major impact on the development of these sports.

BIBLIOGRAPHY

American College of Sports Medicine (1995) Position stand on osteoporosis and exercise. *Medicine and Science in Sport and Exercise*, 27 (4): i–vii.

Drinkwater, B.L. et al. (1995) C.H. McCloy Research Lecture: Does physical activity play a role in preventing osteoporosis? *Research Quarterly in Exercise and Sport*, 65: 197–206.

Duncan, T. (1997) *Advanced Physics*, 4th edition. London: John Murray Publishers.

Pascoe, D.D., Shanley, L.A. and Smith, E.W. (1994) Clothing and Exercise. I: Biophysics of heat transfer between the individual, clothing and environment. *Sports Medicine*, 18 (1): 38–54.

Taaffe, D.R., Snow-Harter, C., Connolly, D.A., Robinson, T.L., Brown, M.D. and Marcus, R. (1995) Differential effects of swim versus weight bearing activity on bone mineral status of eumenorrheic athletes. *Journal of Bone Mineral Research*, 10: 586–593.

Uvarov, E.B. and Isaacs, A. (1986) *The Penguin Dictionary of Science*, 6th edition. London: Penguin Group.

FURTHER READING

Eston, R. and Reilly, T. (2001) *Kinanthropmetry and Exercise Physiology Laboratory Manual. Tests, Procedures and Data*, 2nd edition. London, Routledge.

Martyn-St James, M. and Carroll, S. (2006) Progressive high-intensity resistance training and bone mineral density changes among premenopausal women: Evidence of discordant site-specific skeletal effects. *Sports Medicine*, 36(8): 683–705.

PART 2

FORCE, PRESSURE, ENERGY AND ELECTRICITY

CHAPTER FIVE

FORCE AND PRESSURE

AIMS OF THE CHAPTER

This chapter aims to provide an understanding of the scientific principles of force and pressure as applied to exercise and sport. After reading this chapter, you should be able to:

■ Define the units of force and pressure.
■ Explain the importance of force and pressure in exercise and sport.
■ Apply the principles of force and pressure to exercise and sport.

INTRODUCTION

In the study of exercise and sport, it is the effect of force application on the human body which is of interest. In engineering, the usual safety factor built into materials, and associated physical structures, is over two times the force that is applied on a regular basis. This level of caution is known to result in a low probability of a failure because of mechanical stress. Similar safety factors are built into materials and structures that have to withstand pressure (i.e. force per unit area), such as gas cylinders. An extreme engineering example is a lift, where it is important that failure does not occur! A cable supporting the lift can usually withstand eleven times the maximum load specified by the manufacturers (Diamond, 1993). Interestingly, the human body also seems to have been designed (evolved) with a safety factor in many of its structural and physiological systems. Examples in the human body include the lungs and kidneys, of which we have two when one is enough. In relation to forces, bones and tendons do not normally break until forces of two to five times peak natural force has been applied (Diamond, 1993).

Throughout this chapter the emphasis will be placed on the effect of the application of force and pressure on the human body. Once the concepts of force and pressure have been defined, the various units used in measurement of force and pressure will be examined. The application of force and pressure produces a **mechanical stress**, and the consequences of such stress will be addressed. Since forces can only be applied to solid objects, whereas pressure can be applied to all physical states, the information in this chapter is closely related to that in Chapters 2–4.

SCIENTIFIC PRINCIPLES OF FORCE AND PRESSURE

Movement of an object (i.e. motion) depends on the application of **force**. Force is the effect that causes an object to start or stop moving as well as increasing or decreasing the rate of motion of a moving object. The application of a force can cause a body to accelerate either positively or negatively. Sir Isaac Newton (1642–1727) defined the **laws of motion**, and hence the laws that govern the effect of forces. These laws are important in the study of exercise and sport, and relate to some of the information in this chapter. These laws can be summarised as:

force, pressure, energy and electricity

- Newton's first law: *Law of inertia* – an object will continue in its state of rest or motion unless acted upon by an external force.
- Newton's second law: *Law of acceleration* – the rate of change of momentum of a body is directly proportional to the force causing it, and the change takes place in the direction in which the force acts.

$$F = m \times a \qquad .. \qquad .. \qquad .. \qquad .. \qquad .. \qquad .. \qquad .. \qquad .. \qquad (5.1)$$

- Newton's third law: *Law of action–reaction* – to every action created by a force, there is an equal and opposite reaction.

When applying these laws, it should be remembered that the laws are only true for **rigid bodies**. Since the human body is not a rigid object, the laws should therefore be applied cautiously.

UNITS OF FORCE AND PRESSURE

A quantity with a magnitude (i.e. size) only is known as a **scalar quantity**. Force is a **vector quantity**, which means it has a directional component in addition to a magnitude (see Chapter 9). A force is visualised through the action it has on an object. Specifically, **acceleration** is the **kinematic** (i.e. movement) effect associated with the action of a force. The magnitude of a force is equal to the product of mass (kg) and acceleration ($m.s^{-2}$) (see Equation 5.2). The unit of measurement of force is the **newton** (N). One newton is the force which when applied to a mass of 1 kg causes it to accelerate at $1 \ ms^{-2}$.

$$\text{Force (N)} \quad = \quad \text{Mass (kg)} \quad \times \quad \text{Acceleration } (m.s^{-2}) \qquad .. \qquad (5.2)$$

Whilst forces are important in exercise and sport, it is often a combination of the magnitude of the force and the time over which it acts which is related to performance. The product of force (N) and time (s) is **impulse** (N.s) (see Equation 5.3).

$$\text{Impulse (N.s)} \quad = \quad \text{Force (N)} \quad \times \quad \text{Time (s)} \qquad .. \qquad .. \qquad (5.3)$$

Pressure is the force applied per unit area, and is calculated by dividing force (N) by area (m^2) (see Equation 5.4). The unit of measurement of pressure is the **pascal** (Pa), where 1 Pa is equal to $1 \ N.m^{-2}$.

$$\text{Pressure (Pa)} \quad = \quad \frac{\text{Force (N)}}{\text{Area } (m^2)} \qquad .. \qquad .. \qquad .. \qquad .. \qquad .. \qquad (5.4)$$

Although the pascal is the unit of pressure that is recognised by the international system of units, other units of pressure are widely used. For example, pressure is often measured with a column of liquid, where the height of the liquid in the column reflects the pressure exerted upon it. Since mercury is a very heavy liquid, it is often the liquid of choice. This is because a smaller column is required to demonstrate graduations of pressure with a heavy liquid. Consequently, pressure is often recorded in millimetres (mm) of mercury (Hg) (i.e. mmHg). Since atmospheric pressure is often determined with a column of mercury, the usual units reported are mmHg. It is known that atmospheric pressure varies around 760 mmHg at sea level. There are 760 mmHg to 100 000 Pa (or 100 kPa) (see Equation 5.5). The unit Barometric pressure (Bar) is also related to the unit mmHg, with 1.01325 Bar being equal to 760 mmHg (see Equation 5.6). The Bar is used frequently when measuring ambient pressure in various environments, especially high-pressure environments such as diving for example.

$$100\ 000\ \text{Pa} \quad = \quad 760\ \text{mmHg} \qquad .. \qquad .. \qquad .. \qquad .. \qquad .. \qquad (5.5)$$

$$1.01325\ \text{Bar} \quad = \quad 760\ \text{mmHg} \qquad .. \qquad .. \qquad .. \qquad .. \qquad .. \qquad (5.6)$$

For further information about units, particularly units of pressure, consult appendices in the back of standard physiology textbooks such as Astrand and Rodahl (2003), McArdle et al. (2007), Powers and Howley (2004) and Wilmore and Costill (2004).

TYPES OF FORCE

The forces studied in exercise and sport can be divided into two categories: internal forces and external forces. Internal forces act within a body to produce and control movement, and external forces act between the human body and the environment. A typical example of an internal force is a muscular force, and a typical example of an external force is a **ground reaction force**. Internal forces are more difficult to measure directly than external forces.

When studying the human body during exercise and sport, it is often more appropriate to consider **torque** (or turning moment) rather than force. Torque is the product of force (N) acting on an object and the perpendicular distance (m) between the point of application of the force and the centre of rotation of the object (see Equation 5.7). Torque is often a more appropriate measure since the human body consists of many joints or **levers**. Force produced by the muscles is transferred to external objects through these lever systems.

$$\text{Torque (N.m)} \quad = \quad \text{Force (N)} \quad \times \quad \text{Perpendicular distance (m)} \qquad (5.7)$$

Various other types of force are known to act on the body during exercise and sport. **Drag** is the force opposing the motion of a body travelling through a liquid or gas. When an individual is moving through air, during running for example, a drag force due to the still air is experienced. This drag force is sometimes increased because of a head wind, the velocity of which should be added to the velocity of the runner in drag force calculations. Depending on the type of fluid (i.e. liquid or gas), various components of a drag force are important. Pressure drag is the opposing force caused by the negative pressure created behind a moving object. Wave drag is the force opposing motion caused by the creation

70

of a wave on the surface of a liquid. Surface drag is the force opposing motion caused by the tension on the surface of a liquid.

STOP AND THINK

How does a competitive swimmer attempt to reduce the drag experienced when travelling through the water?

Frictional forces are an important consideration during exercise. For example, the only way in which an individual can translate the force produced by muscle contraction to effective locomotion is with the aid of frictional and **gravitational forces**. Frictional forces arise whenever one body or object attempts to move across the surface of another. Frictional forces always oppose the intended motion. The frictional force increases in response to the applied force (tending to cause the motion) and whilst no movement is occurring the friction is equal to the applied force (they cancel each other out). Eventually the applied force is increased to such an extent that the object starts to slide, at this point the friction has reached its upper limit in magnitude known as **limiting friction**. As sliding takes place, the frictional force is reduced, but still presents an opposition to motion. The frictional force during sliding is known as sliding friction and is equal to the reaction force (R) (the force perpendicular to the force causing the object to move) multiplied by the coefficient of friction (μ) (see equation 5.8).

$$\text{Frictional force (N)} = \text{Coefficient of friction} \times \text{Reaction force (N)} \qquad (5.8)$$

RESOLVING FORCES

When attempting to quantify the magnitude and direction of a force (i.e. a force vector), two approaches can be taken. The forces can either be added together to give an overall force vector, known as **composition of forces**, or resolved in defined directions, known as **resolution of forces**. A graphical technique can be used to quantify a force vector, which is known as a **force parallelogram**. The parallelogram law states:

> If two forces acting at a point are represented in magnitude and direction by the sides of a parallelogram drawn from the point, their resultant is represented by the diagonal of the parallelogram drawn from the point.

Using this technique, forces are drawn from a point, where the magnitude of each force is proportional to the length of a line, and the direction of each force is indicated by the direction of the line. By then creating a completed parallelogram, the diagonal line from the point of origin to the far corner represents the composed force vector (see Figure 5.1).

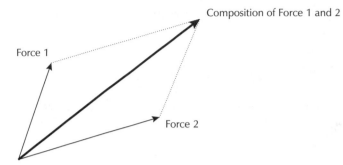

Composition of Force 1 and 2

Force 1

Force 2

Figure 5.1
Composing forces
with the parallelogram
technique

Forces can also be composed and resolved using mathematical techniques. By knowing the magnitude of the force and the angle between the direction of resolution and the direction of the force, the magnitude of a force acting in a particular direction can be quantified. The mathematics used to perform this transformation is known as **trigonometry** (see Chapter 9).

MEASUREMENT OF FORCE

Strain gauges are commonly used to measure the magnitude of a force. In an exercise and sport setting, however, it is normally torque rather than force which is measured. Various types of strain gauges are available. Force may be determined through electrical resistance, mechanical or optical principles. It is common to find an electrical resistance strain gauge in an exercise and sport laboratory. The basic principle of operation is that by applying a force to a length of wire, the wire changes length and cross-sectional area changes accordingly. Since resistance is dependent upon length and cross-sectional area, these mechanical changes have an impact on the electrical resistance of the wire, which in turn affects the voltage output. A process of **calibration** is then used to relate particular voltages with known forces.

Force platforms (or plates) are typically used to measure forces applied in exercise and sport. The platform is installed in the ground and measures the resultant external force acting at the platform's surface. The platform senses the deformation produced by the applied force. There are two main types of force platform: those which utilise strain gauges and those which utilise piezo electric crystals. With strain gauges, the electrical resistance of the plate changes with strain. With the piezo electric-based plates, the deformation produced by an applied force causes the electrical charge in the plate to change. A force platform utilises Newton's third law of motion: for every action force (applied by human body), an equal but opposite ground reaction force is measured by the platform. A force platform measures three ground reaction force components: a vertical force, a horizontal force in a forwards/backwards direction (anterior–posterior force) and a horizontal force in a side to side direction (medio-lateral force). The vertical force is usually labelled (Fz), the horizontal force in the direction parallel (anterior–posterior force) to the motion is

72

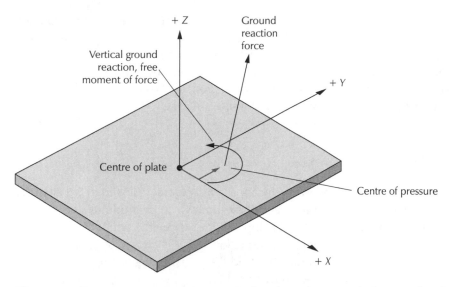

Figure 5.2 Force measurement in a vertical and two horizontal planes with a force plate

labelled (Fy) and the horizontal force perpendicular (medio-lateral force) to the motion is labelled (Fx) (see Figure 5.2).

MEASUREMENT OF PRESSURE

As mentioned earlier in the chapter, pressure is often measured with a column of liquid. Although mercury is often used because of its high density, other substances are also used. For example, when examining the pressure that can be produced on inspiration or expiration, a column of water known as a manometer is often used (see Figure 5.3).

The water naturally tends to find the point of least potential energy, and therefore levels out in the U-shaped tube, so that two columns of water of the same height reside either

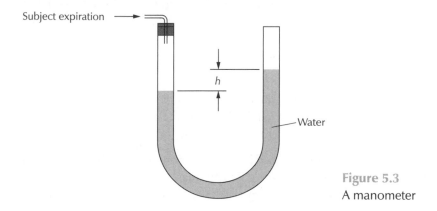

Figure 5.3
A manometer

side of the U-bend. If an individual then inspires or expires into one end of the tube, the inspiratory/expiratory pressure can be determined from the change in height of the water (h) (i.e. mmH_2O). Pressure in pascals is calculated by dividing the force (i.e. the mass of the water moved against the acceleration as a result of gravity) by the cross-sectional area of the tube. The mass of water moved is equal to the product of volume (i.e. height change × cross-sectional area) and density of the water (i.e. ∼ 1.0 $kg \cdot L^{-1}$).

STRESS AND STRAIN

The way in which an object responds to the application of force is linked to the elasticity of the structural material. The degree of **elasticity** is known as the **modulus of elasticity**. It is given the symbol E, and is equal to the applied stress (given the symbol σ) divided by the resulting strain (given the symbol ε) (see Equation 5.9). The applied stress is measured in units of pressure (Pa) (see Equation 5.10) and the resulting strain is measured as the percentage change in length (%) (see Equation 5.11).

$$\text{Elasticity (E)} = \frac{\text{Stress } (\sigma)}{\text{Strain } (\varepsilon)} \quad .. \quad .. \quad .. \quad .. \quad .. \quad (5.9)$$

Where:

$$\text{Stress (Pa)} = \frac{\text{Force (N)}}{\text{Area (m}^2)} \quad .. \quad .. \quad .. \quad .. \quad .. \quad (5.10)$$

$$\text{Strain (\%)} = \frac{\text{Change in length (m)}}{\text{Original length (m)}} \quad .. \quad .. \quad .. \quad (5.11)$$

In the case of tension forces, a solid object usually has a limit of tolerance, known as the **tensile limit**, where the material fractures. Prior to this point, the material will pass from an elastic region of deformation to a plastic region of deformation. The point of transition from elastic to plastic deformation is known as the **yield point**. In the elastic region, the structure of the material is deformed by the tension force and then returns to its original structure with the removal of the force. In the plastic region of deformation, the structure of the material is deformed irreversibly resulting in a permanent length change of the object.

Some solid materials can be placed under tension, but not compressed. Elastic is a good example of such a material. Within the human body, tendons, ligaments and muscle can all be placed under tension, but not compressed.

The human body has many properties of a solid in that the various parts can be compressed *and* placed under tension. However, as is the case with many solids, the human body is not rigid. Mechanical stress placed on the human body cannot, therefore, be treated as

74

though forces are being applied to a rigid body. The consequence, as mentioned earlier, is that Newton's laws of motion cannot always be applied.

In the case of the human body, as with other solid objects, it is functionally useful to consider whether any forces applied are repetitive or isolated events. The technical phrase is **chronic** application of mechanical stress for repetitive force application, and **acute** mechanical stress for isolated force application. When a single impact is considered, such as an unintentional collision, this would be referred to as an acute stress. When repeated impacts are considered, such as those experienced during running, these would be referred to as a chronic stress. Although the process of application of the force may differ, the end result is usually similar if the tolerance of a material is exceeded. In the human body, the consequence of exceeding the tolerance of a material is an injury. An injury which develops over the short term, such as that during a collision, is known as an acute injury. Conversely, an injury which develops over a longer period is known as a chronic injury.

APPLICATION OF SCIENCE TO EXERCISE AND SPORT

THE RELATIONSHIP BETWEEN JOINT TORQUE AND JOINT ANGLE

The measurement of force production by the knee extensor muscles is a regular laboratory practical in the study of exercise and sport. Since it is the measurement of force about a fixed point (i.e. the knee joint) which is considered in such a practical, the correct term is 'torque'. In order to determine torque produced by joints in the body, an isokinetic dynamometer is often used (see Figure 5.4). The dynamometer measures the torque produced by a joint as an individual performs muscle contraction at a pre-determined and constant joint angular velocity.

The maximal torque produced by the knee extensor muscles is determined when the participant performs a maximal voluntary contraction (MVC). Maximal torque is often determined at a range of knee angles, and consequently a range of muscle lengths. In this situation, the torque is determined with the muscles working isometrically. '**Isometric** muscle activity' is the term used when the muscles are attempting to shorten, but fail to do so because of a high external load (i.e with an angular velocity of 0 m.s^{-1}). Figure 5.5 shows typical results from a participant performing a series of maximal voluntary isometric contractions ranging from a flexed (30°) to an extended (150°) knee joint. The results show that the highest torque is produced when the knee is about half way between flexion and extension (i.e. 90°). As the joint moves towards the extremes, the maximal isometric force is reduced. Therefore, when maximal torque is discussed it is essential to make reference to the joint angle.

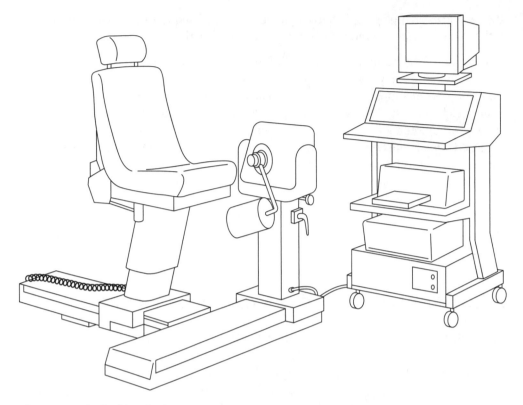

Figure 5.4 An isokinetic dynamometer

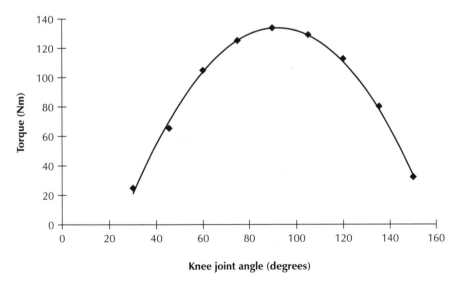

Figure 5.5 The torque–angle relationship during maximal voluntary isometric contractions of the knee extensor muscles

force, pressure, energy and electricity

THE RELATIONSHIP BETWEEN JOINT TORQUE AND JOINT ANGULAR VELOCITY

When considering the torque produced by a joint, it is necessary to consider the velocity of shortening of the muscles in addition to the muscle length. Since torque about a joint is being considered, it is more appropriate to consider the angular velocity of shortening rather than linear muscle shortening velocity. In the first application, an angular velocity of $0°\cdot s^{-1}$ was considered because the contraction was isometric (i.e. no shortening of the muscles or movement of the limb). The result of a series of trials at differing velocities is a torque–velocity relationship. In Figure 5.6 a typical torque–velocity relationship is shown. Torque is normally highest at the lowest velocity, and decreases in a curvilinear fashion as velocity is increased. In fact, when a muscle is lengthened, but resisting the lengthening, the highest torque is produced. A muscle contraction at a pre-determined velocity is known as an **isokinetic** contraction. Normal muscle activity when the velocity of contraction is constantly changing is known as **isotonic** contraction.

THE INTERPRETATION OF GROUND REACTION FORCE DATA

In the study of exercise and sport, the force plate is often used to examine the ground reaction force caused by a participant walking, running or performing jumping movements.

For a participant running over a force plate, a typical trace is provided in Figure 5.7. Graph (a) in Figure 5.7 shows Fz during a single stance phase during running. The first peak

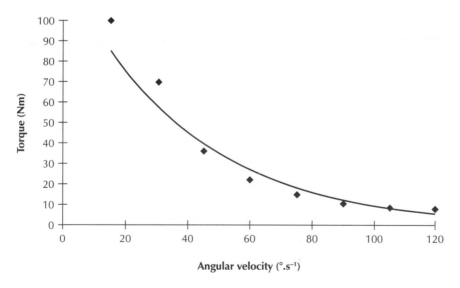

Figure 5.6 The torque–angular velocity relationship during maximal voluntary knee extension exercise

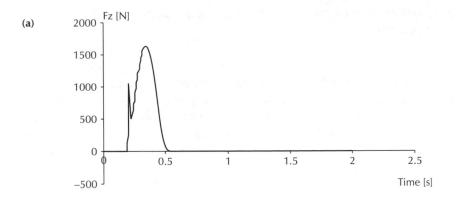

(a)

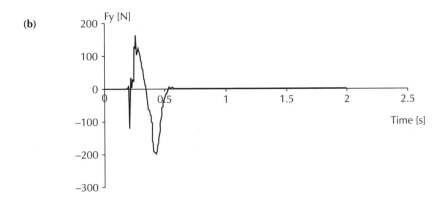

(b)

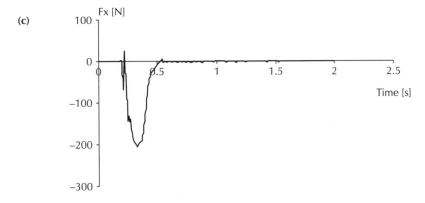

(c)

Figure 5.7 Typical force traces recorded for a running trial in vertical (a) and horizontal (b and c) directions with a force plate

(known as the **impact** or **passive peak**) is usually observed as the foot strikes the ground, followed by the second peak (known as the **active peak**) as the muscles in the leg work against the acceleration caused by gravity which is pulling the runner towards the ground. In graph (b) (i.e. Fy), the negative peak is the result of the initial deceleration (i.e. braking force) following foot contact, and the positive peak is the result of final acceleration (i.e. propulsive force) prior to take off. In graph (c) (i.e. Fx), the positive portion of the curve is the result of movement of the centre of gravity of the body over the foot in contact with the ground. Force traces, such as those in Figure 5.7, have many clinical uses in addition to those in exercise and sport.

THE IMPULSE–MOMENTUM RELATIONSHIP

Collisions exist in many sports. A collision occurs when two or more objects make contact with each other. These objects can either be inanimate objects (such as a ball or the ground) (Figure 5.8) or the human body. The forces produced between objects in a collision occur for a short duration and these collisions can be classified as elastic (such as when two snooker balls collide) or inelastic (such as when a shot putt embeds itself into the ground).

During these collisions an impulse is experienced by each of the objects involved in the collision. The impulse is dependent on the magnitude and duration of the force applied during the collision (see Equation 5.3).

Momentum is the resistance to stopping and therefore has implications for collisions. Momentum (ρ) is defined as the product of the mass (m) and velocity (v) of an object (see Equation 5.12).

$$\text{Momentum (kg·m·s}^{-1}) = \text{Mass (kg)} \times \text{Velocity (m.s}^{-1}) \qquad .. \qquad .. \qquad (5.12)$$

Elastic collision

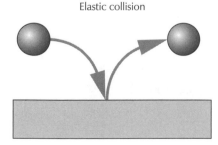

Figure 5.8 An elastic collision between a ball and the ground

Impulse causes a change in momentum of an object. Impulse (I) is equal to the change in momentum produced and is therefore related to momentum by:

Impulse (N) = Mass (kg) × Change in velocity (m.s^{-1})   ..   ..   (5.13)

Knowledge of this impulse–momentum relationship is vital to an understanding of many sports techniques. The relationship is a cause and effect one, whereby a correction of momentum can be achieved by modifying the impulse being applied. Impulse, and hence the change in momentum, can be determined from force data using graphical integration (see Chapter 9).

STOP AND THINK

Is it possible for an approach in the long jump to be too fast? Why?

(Note: both horizontal and vertical impulse is generated during a takeoff.)

SELF-TEST

1. What are the three laws of motion?

2. What visible signs show that a force is acting on an object?

3. What is the unit of measurement of force?

4. Which physical state can force act upon?

5. What variable is derived from force multiplied by time?

6. What are the two main types of force platform?

7. Give an example of when limiting friction is reached?

8. What is the modulus of elasticity?

9. How is the change in length related to strain energy?

10. Under what conditions can pressure act upon a fluid?

11. Give three units for the measurement of pressure?

12. What is the relationship between force and pressure?

13. Draw and label a manometer and give one use.

14. Draw a graph of the relationship between force and muscle length.

15. What is the relationship between impulse and momentum?

force, pressure, energy and electricity

CONCLUSION

The effect of force is observed through changes in motion, and hence Newton's laws of motion are important in understanding the effect of force. However, Newton's laws are only valid for rigid bodies, so application of these laws to the human body should be performed cautiously. Force is the product of mass and acceleration of an object. When forces are generated by muscle contraction in the human body, it is normally torque about a joint that is measured. Functionally torque is important since it is the product of the force applied and the perpendicular distance between the joint and the point of application of the force. Whilst force can be applied to solid objects only, pressure (i.e. force per unit area) can be applied to both solids and fluids (i.e. liquids or gases). With regard to exercise and sport, the time over which force is applied is important, and is known as impulse. Knowledge of the impulse–momentum relationship is vital in understanding sports technique. In an exercise and sport laboratory, force may be measured between an object and the ground through the use of a force plate. Additionally, torque about a joint can be measured when the muscle is working isometrically, isokinetically or isotonically through the use of an isokinetic dynamometer.

KEY POINTS

- The effect of force is observed through the change in motion of an object.
- Force is equal to the product of the mass and acceleration of an object.
- Newton's first law of motion is the law of inertia: a force is required to stop, start or alter motion of an object.
- Newton's second law of motion is the law of acceleration: the acceleration of an object is proportional to the force acting on it, and takes place in the direction of the force.
- Newton's third law of motion is the law of action–reaction: to every action created by a force, there is an equal and opposite reaction.
- The duration over which a force acts is functionally important, and is known as impulse.
- Pressure is force per unit cross-sectional area.
- Pressure can act on all states of matter, but only on liquids and gases if they are contained.
- Force can be measured using a force plate.
- Torque is the force operating about a point of rotation, and is calculated as the product of the force and the perpendicular distance between the point of rotation and the point of force application.
- Torque is functionally important in exercise and sport since force is applied in the human body through a series of levers.

- Joint torque–velocity relationships give a functional insight into muscle force-shortening velocity relationships.
- The impulse–momentum relationship is a cause and effect one, whereby a correction of momentum can be achieved by modifying the impulse being applied.

BIBLIOGRAPHY

Astrand, P-O. and Rodahl, K. (2003) *Textbook of Work Physiology: Physiological Bases of Exercise*, 4th edition. Singapore: McGraw-Hill.

Diamond, J. (1993) Evolutionary physiology. In Boyd, C.A.R., Noble, D. (eds), *The Logic of Life: The Challenge of Integrative Physiology*. Oxford: Oxford University Press.

McArdle, W.D., Katch, F.I. and Katch, V.L. (2007) *Exercise Physiology: Energy, Nutrition and Human Performance,* 6th edition. Baltimore: Williams and Wilkins.

Powers, S.K. and Howley, E.T. (2004) *Exercise Physiology: Theory and Application to Fitness and Performance*, 5th edition. Boston: McGraw-Hill.

Wilmore, J.H. and Costill, D.L. (2004) *Physiology of Sport and Exercise*, 3rd edition. Champaign, IL: Human Kinetics.

FURTHER READING

Bartlett, R. (1997) *Introduction to Sports Biomechanics*. London: E & F N Spon.

Dyson, G. (1985) *Dyson's Mechanics of Athletics*, 8th edition. London: Hodder and Stoughton, Chapters 3 and 4.

Enoka, R.M. (2002) *Neuromuscular Basis of Kinesiology*, 3rd edition. Leeds: Human Kinetics.

Hay, J.G. (1993) *The Biomechanics of Sports Techniques*, 4th edition. Englewood Cliffs, NJ: Prentice-Hall.

Hopper, B.J. (1973) *The Mechanics of Human Movement*. London: Granada Publishing, Chapters 3 and 4.

Kreighbaum, E. and Barthels, K.M. (1996) *Biomechanics: A Qualitative Approach for Studying Human Movement*, 4th edition. London: Allyn and Bacon, Chapter 2.

CHAPTER SIX

ENERGY

AIMS OF THE CHAPTER

This chapter aims to provide an understanding of the scientific principles of energy, work and power as applied to the theory which underpins exercise and sport. After reading this chapter, you should be able to:

- Appreciate the units of energy, work and power and manipulate them.
- Understand the different forms of energy.
- Conceptualise work, power and efficiency.
- Apply energetic concepts to exercise and sport.

INTRODUCTION

Energy is a very important consideration, not only in exercise and sport, but also in daily activities. The human body relies upon a supply of energy to continue to move and to perform essential daily functions. Energy is used for growth, repair, digestion and storage of food, and of course physical activity. The continual supply of energy to the human body is through the diet, and hence the importance of nutrition for prolonged physical performance, where energy expenditure is substantial. Unlike plants, the human body cannot obtain energy directly from the sun (i.e. photosynthesis), and therefore relies upon plants, and the animals that eat those plants, for energy. When considering energy, it is important to understand the implications of the first law of **thermodynamics**, which states:

> Energy can neither be created nor destroyed, just changed from one form to another.

Throughout this chapter many examples will be provided whereby energy is converted from one form to another. When this process takes place in the human body, a significant amount of energy is usually converted to heat in addition to other forms of useful energy. The continual production of heat is one way in which the human body maintains a temperature of about 37°C, despite a cooler surrounding environment.

In this chapter the emphasis will not be placed upon how the body obtains its energy. This important area in the study of exercise and sport is covered elsewhere in detail (e.g. McArdle et al., 2007; Maughan et al., 1997). Instead, emphasis will be placed on the different classifications of energy, and their potential in explaining physical performance.

KEY APPLICATIONS TO EXERCISE AND SPORT

The energy store size, and the rate at which the energy stores can be mobilised and used, are essential for human performance of physical activities. For example, the performance of the marathon runner is normally limited by the size of the store of carbohydrate in the

84

body, particularly the stores in the muscles of the legs. The performance of a 400 m runner is less dependent on the overall carbohydrate store size and more dependent on the rate at which the energy can be made available for muscle contraction and relaxation. The rate at which work is done during physical activities is known as power output, and this is often a key determinant of exercise and sport performance. A further key determinant of exercise and sport performance is how efficiently the body is able to convert energy into useful work; a more efficient performer will use less energy to achieve the same amount of work, which is a particular advantage when fuel stores are limited.

UNITS OF ENERGY

The common language that describes a quantity of energy is referred to as a unit, and further information on the subject of units for different measurements is given in Chapter 1. In the study of exercise and sport, it is important to be able to establish how much, or the quantity of energy. Comparisons may then be made between how much energy exists in different forms or how much energy is used by the body to do a certain amount of work.

The international system for classifying units expresses energy as a **joule** (J). One joule is the amount of energy required to displace the point of application of a force of 1 newton (N) through a distance of 1 metre (m) in the direction of the force (see Equation 6.1).

$$\text{Energy (J)} = \text{Force (N)} \times \text{Displacement (m)} \qquad .. \qquad .. \qquad .. \qquad .. \qquad (6.1)$$

However, the international system of units have not yet been fully adopted by every country in the world, so some countries (and individuals) still use the old unit of energy: the **kilogram calorie** (kilocalorie; kcal). A kilogram calorie is the amount of energy required to heat 1 kg (i.e. 1 litre) of water by 1°C under standard conditions (i.e. from 14.5 to 15.5°C) (see Equation 6.2).

$$\text{Energy (kcal)} = \text{One litre water temperature change (°C)} \qquad .. \qquad .. \qquad (6.2)$$

Although it is not an ideal situation to have people using different units for expressing energy, the conversion between the two units is quite easy. There are ~4186 J (or 4.186 kJ) to a kcal, so a figure in kcal should be multiplied by 4186 to convert into Joules (see Equation 6.3).

$$1 \text{ kcal} = 4186 \text{ J} \qquad .. \qquad .. \qquad .. \qquad .. \qquad .. \qquad .. \qquad .. \qquad (6.3)$$

So, for example, if an energy drink contained 420 kcal per litre, it could be calculated that 1758 120 J (i.e. 420 × 4186) or 1758 kJ of energy was contained per litre of the drink.

Whilst the continued use of two different units for the measurement of energy is undesirable, this situation may unwittingly serve a useful purpose. This purpose relates to the definition of energy. The definition of energy that is often used is related to the unit of the international system of units, the joule. The definition of energy being, 'the capacity to do **work**'. However, when applied to physical activity, this definition has limitations, since energy may be expended when no external work is performed (Winter, 1990). Consider the situation when an individual is trying to lift an object that is too heavy. Although energy is expended, no work is done, since the object is not moved. So for the physical activity situation, a more appropriate definition of energy may be, 'the capability to perform exercise' (Winter, 1990). The fact that a unit of measurement of energy is still used (i.e. the kcal) that does not involve displacement in the line of action of a force in its definition is potentially useful in this regard.

CHEMICAL ENERGY

All **chemical energy** has been previously derived from the energy of the sun. Common forms of chemical energy used to supply energy to the home include coal, gas, and oil, which are either used to generate electricity by first being converted to mechanical energy, or used to directly supply heat.

The idea that chemical energy is stored in food, and that the energy stored within the human body is in the form of chemical energy, is often less well understood. Energy in the form of food may be digested by the body until it is in a form that the body can either use immediately, or transport to storage sites. Since the body does not have a continual supply of energy from outside, unlike the energy supply to a home (e.g. natural gas supply for heat and cooking), the body must store energy for use at a later point. Once this energy arrives at the storage sites (e.g. glucose in the blood is delivered to the muscles), it is further transformed into the required form for storage (e.g. muscle glycogen). The stored energy within the body can then be released as and when required to allow the body to perform mechanical work and to go about other processes. Such other processes include the digestion of food, maintenance of a stable internal environment, repair and growth.

The human body can only directly utilise one form of chemical energy. This is the energy contained within the bonds between phosphate and a substance known as adenosine (adenine and D-ribose). Adenine is usually bound to three phosphates via ribose and three high-energy bonds. This substance is known as a nucleotide, and is called **adenosine triphosphate** (ATP) (see Figure 6.1). As each of the high-energy bonds are broken, the released energy can be used by the body in a useful way. The fuel stores within the body are then used to reform the broken high-energy bonds.

Since the human body only has a small supply of ATP, it must continually re-synthesise this useful form of chemical energy. In fact, the body can only continue to exercise strenuously for about 2 seconds before the ATP stores would be completely used up if no re-synthesis were to take place. Fortunately, the body is very adept at using the fuel stores to continually re-synthesise the ATP store. To compare the amount of energy stored as ATP within a normal 70 kg body with other types of fuel, it is necessary to convert the size of

86

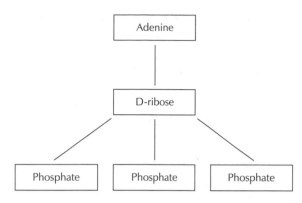

Figure 6.1
Adenosine triphosphate (ATP) which provides the human body with energy in a form that can be directly used

all the energy stores within the body to the common unit of energy, the joule. Table 6.1 shows the amount of energy which may be contained within each fuel store.

Clearly, the size of each store of energy within the body varies enormously between individuals. However, it is interesting to note that usually the body contains a far greater storage of energy as **fat** than it does as other forms. Although the store of energy as protein is large, **protein** is not normally used as an energy source. **Carbohydrate** energy is very important to the body, especially during exercise; however, the store of energy in this form is far smaller than the store of energy as fat. Even compared with the store of energy as carbohydrate, the ATP energy store is extremely small.

MECHANICAL ENERGY

Only a relatively small amount of chemical energy is converted to useful energy in the human body at rest; the remainder being converted to heat. This is why the human body is referred to as being inefficient; something we will be discussing later in the efficiency section (see p. 94). Depending upon the type of activity, about 70 per cent of the chemical energy may be converted to heat during physical activity.

However, once the chemical energy is converted to mechanical energy through the conversion of chemical energy in the muscles, the body is able to perform various physical

Table 6.1 Typical amount of energy stored within a 70 kg human body (~15 % body fat) in different forms

Fuel store	Energy (kJ)	Percentage of total
Carbohydrate (muscle, liver, blood)	5000	0.8
Fat (adipose, muscle, blood)	500 000	83
Protein	100 000	16
Adenosine triphosphate, ATP	10	0.002

tasks. Such physical tasks might range from **involuntary** tasks such as contraction of the heart muscle or the respiratory muscles to **voluntary** tasks such as writing or sprinting for the bus. The ability of the body to convert chemical energy into mechanical energy is why the body is sometimes referred to as a machine, although not a particularly efficient one! Most of the mechanical energy generated by the body can be quantified (i.e. put in a numerical form) by examining the amount of useful work done. However, because the body is not always designed optimally to perform mechanical tasks, some chemical energy is wasted.

In the study of exercise and sport, it is possible to determine the amount of energy expended by an individual to perform a given task. The energy expended will be the sum of the useful work done plus energy lost as heat and energy lost in other forms (e.g. sound). The total **energy expenditure** is usually measured in an indirect way through the examination of gas exchange at the mouth (see Chapter 2 for further details). If, for example, an individual expends 1000 kJ in order to run 5 km, it is interesting to examine what this amount of energy relates to in terms of an amount of chemical energy in the form of food (see Table 6.2). The ability to quantify energy expenditure is very useful in exercise and sport, especially when relating physical activity to nutritional requirements.

KINETIC AND POTENTIAL ENERGY

It is important to be able to distinguish between different forms of mechanical energy. An example often used to explain two energy types is a water-driven electricity generator. The water is stored behind a dam until it is required, and in this position it has all its energy stored as **potential energy**. When the water is required to turn the water wheel, the dam is opened and the potential energy caused by the water's position under the influence of gravity is converted to **kinetic energy**.

Potential energy is calculated by multiplying the mass (in kg) of an object by the acceleration caused by gravity (in m·s^{-2}) acting on the object and the vertical displacement (i.e. height) of the object (in m) (see Equation 6.4). Kinetic energy is calculated by dividing the mass

Table 6.2 Amount of various foods that provide 1000 kJ

100 g of white bread
61 g of cornflakes (Kelloggs)
62 g of rice crispies
59 g of cheddar cheese
225 g of cod fish
260 g of banana
150 g of chicken meat
400 g of whole milk
270 g of potato

(in kg) of an object by two, and then multiplying by the square of the velocity (in m·s^{-1}) (see Equation 6.5).

Potential energy = mass (kg) $\times$ gravity (m·s^{-2}) $\times$ height (m)   ..   (6.4)

Kinetic energy = ½ mass (kg) $\times$ velocity^2 (m·s^{-1})   ..   ..   ..   (6.5)

The transformation of energy between potential and kinetic energy can also be observed when elastic is stretched and then released. As the elastic is stretched, it gains potential energy, which is known as strain energy. The maximal gain in strain energy is reached just before the elastic attains its elastic limit, otherwise known as the yield point (beyond this point energy is lost and the elastic takes on plastic properties). If the elastic is then released, potential energy is converted to kinetic energy. The change in length of elastic (m) is proportional to the force applied (N), which is known as Hooke's law (see Equation 6.6).

Change in length (m) $\propto$ Force (N)   ..   ..   (6.6)

The gain in strain energy is related to the ability of the elastic to store energy on lengthening (k) and the change in length of the elastic (x) (see Equation 6.7).

Strain energy = ½ k x   ..   ..   (6.7)

The mechanical properties of muscle and connective tissue are very much like those of elastic, except for a damping effect (i.e. a shock absorber). Kangaroos make extremely good use of the elastic properties of the tendons in their legs. Interestingly, kangaroos also become slightly more efficient as their hopping speed increases.

STOP AND THINK

Try to investigate the contribution of the elastic properties of the muscle and connective tissue in your own legs by comparing the height jumped with two jumping techniques. First, try a vertical jump starting from a crouched position (i.e. with your legs bent). Second, try a vertical jump starting from a standing position and using a counter-movement. You will observe that the height jumped using the second technique is greater because of the elastic contribution of the muscle and connective tissue in the legs.

We can find examples of the transformation of energy during exercise and sport. A simple example is the pole-vault. As the pole-vaulter approaches the take-off, the pole-vaulter has generated much kinetic energy in a horizontal direction. As the pole is deformed, most of the pole-vaulter's kinetic energy is converted to potential energy in the pole. As the pole-vaulter is propelled upwards, the potential energy stored within the pole is converted to kinetic energy of the pole-vaulter once again, but in a vertical direction. When passing over the bar, the pole-vaulter has maximum potential energy, since all the kinetic energy has been converted to potential energy.

WORK

Essentially, in terms of physical activity, work is the useful end product of the chemical energy used. The useful work done by the body can be accurately measured in some types of activity. It is when the useful work done by the body is compared with the chemical energy used, that a measure of the body's work efficiency is obtained (see efficiency section, p. 94).

Work is measured in joules (J) (the same unit of measurement as used for energy), and is calculated by multiplying the distance an object is displaced (in metres, m) by the force opposing the displacement (in newtons, N) (see Equation 6.8 and Figure 6.2). Notice the similarity with equation 6.1.

Work done (J) = Force (N) × Displacement (m)   ..   ..   ..   (6.8)

At this point it is clear to see that 1 newton metre is the same as 1 joule (i.e. 1 N.m = 1 J).

In many exercise and sport situations, it is difficult to assess the amount of useful work done. It was for this reason that a standardised situation was set up in exercise and sport laboratories where the useful work done by an individual could be determined. The situation is described in detail in application three (see p. 96).

It is very difficult to directly determine the useful work done by a runner, but since running is a very common mode of exercise, such a measure would be useful. Various attempts have been made to crudely estimate the work done by a runner, one of which is described below, and another is given in application two (see p. 96).

The potential energy equation (6.4) may be used for determining work done when running up a gradient. The work done (or useful energy output) is equal to the mass of the runner

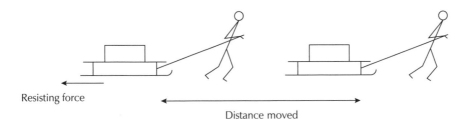

Resisting force

Distance moved

Figure 6.2 Work done in dragging a sledge between two points

multiplied by the acceleration caused by gravity acting on the runner and the vertical displacement (or gain in height). If the runner has a body mass of 70 kg and the gain in height was 100 m, the work done would be:

$$\text{Useful work done or gain in potential energy} = \text{mass} \times \text{gravity} \times \text{height}$$

$$= 70\,\text{kg} \times 9.81\,\text{m·s}^{-2} \times 100\,\text{m}$$

$$= 68670\,\text{J or } 68.7\,\text{kJ}$$

As was mentioned earlier, the above estimate is very crude; the reason being that in addition to the overall gain in height, the runner gains and loses height with each stride which is not accounted for in the present example. It is partly for this reason that running along a perfectly horizontal road or track at a constant velocity still requires significant work to be done in addition to that to overcome air resistance.

POWER

Often in the study of exercise and sport, it is useful to know the amount of work being done per unit time, or put simply, how quickly work is being done. The rate at which work is being done is often the factor that determines success in exercise and sport tasks, and is termed **power**.

The definition of power is work (in joules, J) per unit time (in seconds, s). The internationally accepted unit of power is the **watt** (W) (see Equation 6.9).

$$\text{Power (W)} = \frac{\text{Work (J)}}{\text{Time (s)}} \qquad \cdots \quad \cdots \quad \cdots \quad \cdots \quad \cdots \quad \cdots \qquad (6.9)$$

Since work has the same unit as energy, the joule, power is also energy per unit time. This is why the rating of a light bulb is also presented in watts.

Since the power generated during exercise is often the main determinant of **performance**, the power that an athlete can achieve is often used as a proxy measure for performance. In studies of exercise and sport, the maximum power generated during an exercise test, or the power sustained over a set period of time, is often referred to. Sometimes individuals are required to exercise at a set power for as long as possible to examine the **capacity** for exercise. Again, this measure is often used as an indicator of performance capability. Figure 6.3 shows some examples of power maintained during a range of physical activities in comparison with other familiar power consumers.

It is often useful to compare power produced by individuals during physical activities to get a measure of the differences between individuals or the demands of their specialist sports events. For example, it is interesting to consider that most normal individuals could

91

Power (watts)

4000 A single jump

3000

2500 A 5 second sprint

2000

1500

1000 A 30 second sprint or a one bar electric fire

750 A modern microwave oven

500 A cyclist breaking the world hour cycling record

250 A runner travelling at 16.0 km/h

100 A light bulb

only maintain a power output on a bicycle of about 100 watts for an hour, whereas a cyclist breaking the hour record would maintain a power of ~450 watts for the hour.

The ability of an athlete to produce instantaneous power, or power over a very short period of time, is important for many athletic events. This ability would be useful for events involving jumping, throwing, or accelerating very quickly (e.g. a sprint start). It is possible to estimate power production by asking an athlete to perform a vertical jump. The vertical jump test is often referred to as a Sargeant jump, after a medic Dr Dudley Sargeant who was practising at Harvard University in the 1870s (Sargeant, 1906). Providing the body mass of the athlete is known, the height achieved by the athlete allows determination of the gain in potential energy, and therefore the energy produced. So using Equation 6.4, if the athlete's body mass is 70 kg, and the height jumped is 0.80 m, the gain in potential energy is:

92

force, pressure, energy and electricity

$$\text{Potential energy} \quad = \quad \text{mass} \times \text{gravity} \times \text{height}$$

$$= \quad 70 \text{ kg} \times 9.81 \text{ m·s}^{-2} \times 0.80 \text{ m}$$

$$= \quad 549.36 \text{ J}$$

As long as the time is known over which the energy is converted, the power can be calculated using Equation 6.9. If the time from the start of muscular force production to take off is 0.4 s, the power produced is:

$$\text{Power} \quad \frac{\text{Energy or work (J)}}{\text{time (s)}} \quad = \quad \frac{549.36 \text{ J}}{0.4 \text{ s}} \quad = \quad 1373.4 \text{ W}$$

For determination of power produced over a short duration, power may be calculated through the gain in potential energy when sprinting up steps, and then dividing the value by the time taken to climb the steps. This step test is referred to as the Margaria step test, after Rudolf Margaria (Margaria, 1966). Such short duration power production is required for a short sprint in a team game for example. If an athlete has a body mass of 80 kg and the height of the steps is 2.0 m, and the athlete took 1.1 s to climb the steps, power would be calculated as follows:

$$\text{Gain in potential energy (J)} \quad = \quad \text{mass} \times \text{gravity} \times \text{height}$$

$$= \quad 80 \text{ kg} \times 9.81 \text{ m·s}^{-2} \times 2.0 \text{ m}$$

$$= \quad 1569.6 \text{ J}$$

The power is therefore:

$$\text{Power (W)} \quad = \quad \frac{\text{Gain in potential energy (J)}}{\text{Time (s)}}$$

$$= \quad \frac{1569.6 \text{ J}}{1.1 \text{ s}}$$

$$= \quad 1426.9 \text{ W}$$

A test has also been developed in which it is possible to measure the power produced over longer periods of time on a **cycle ergometer** (see Figure 6.5). This test is known as a Wingate test, and is named after the Wingate Institute in Israel where it was developed in the 1970s. The Wingate test is described later in this chapter (see p. 98), and a typical power curve from a Wingate test is given in Figure 6.6.

EFFICIENCY

It is very useful to compare the rate at which the body is using energy (energy input, usually referred to as energy expenditure) with the rate at which useful work is being done (energy output). Since energy input and useful energy output are being considered, this comparison is known as **efficiency**. Efficiency (%) is energy output (J) divided by energy input (J) multiplied by 100 (see Equation 6.10).

$$\text{Efficiency (\%)} = \frac{\text{Energy output (J)}}{\text{Energy input (J)}} \times 100 \qquad .. \qquad .. \qquad .. \qquad (6.10)$$

An example of the determination of efficiency during physical activity is now provided. On a cycle ergometer in the laboratory, it is possible to measure the amount of energy being utilised, or the energy used for the exercise, and the amount of useful energy produced, or work done during exercise. If a duration of a minute is considered, it may take 20 000 J of energy to exercise steadily on a cycle ergometer whilst producing 3600 J of energy as useful work. The efficiency of the human body in this situation is therefore:

Using Equation 6.10:

$$\text{Efficiency (\%)} = \frac{\text{Energy output (J)}}{\text{Energy input (J)}} \times 100$$

$$\text{Efficiency (\%)} = \frac{3600}{20\ 000} \times 100$$

$$\text{Efficiency} = 18\ \%$$

At this point, care must be taken about how efficiency is defined. Notice that, until now, efficiency has been referred to as the relationship between the energy expenditure of the body (energy input) and the useful work done (or energy output) during the exercise. However, it is important to be more specific about the energy expenditure by the body during exercise.

Gross efficiency refers to the energy expenditure during exercise as being the energy for the activity plus the energy for other needs of the body at that time, whereas net efficiency refers to the energy expenditure for the exercise alone, without the energy for other needs of the body. The question then arises, how it is possible to separate what energy is used for the exercise and what is used for other requirements of the body? The answer is that the energy utilisation at rest must be measured to establish the energy used for requirements other than the exercise. If in the above example it is assumed that of the 20 000 J used during exercise, 5000 J are used to support resting energy expenditure, the net efficiency is:

94

$$\text{Efficiency (\%)} \quad = \frac{3600}{15\ 000} \times 100$$

$$\text{Efficiency} \qquad = \quad 24\ \%$$

Some researchers even suggest that the energy cost of cycling without a load should be subtracted from the overall energy expenditure during exercise, which provides a measure of work efficiency (Whipp and Wasserman, 1969). During cycling work efficiency is reported to be about 30 per cent.

Interestingly, during running exercise humans are more efficient than when cycling because of the energy stored with each stride within the muscles and connective tissues in the form of potential energy. Although a range of values are given in the literature for running efficiency, it is likely that a value in the region of 50 per cent is realistic.

APPLICATION OF SCIENCE TO EXERCISE AND SPORT

ENERGY CONVERSION DURING RUNNING

An example of the storage of potential energy occurs during running (see Figure 6.4). As the foot of a runner strikes the ground, large impact forces (sometimes over three times body weight) are absorbed by the muscle and connective tissue in the leg. Fortunately, some of the kinetic energy is converted into potential energy and stored within the muscles and connective tissue. As the hip, knee and ankle joint extend, the potential energy is converted to kinetic energy once again. This ability of the muscles and connective tissue to convert kinetic energy to potential energy for later use results in the use of less chemical energy. Consequently, physical activities which make use of this phenomenon are known to be more efficient, something that was discussed previously in the efficiency section (see p. 94).

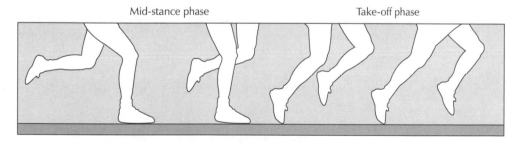

Mid-stance phase Take-off phase

Figure 6.4 Storage of potential energy during the running action whilst the foot is in contact with the floor

ESTIMATING WORK DURING RUNNING IN THE LABORATORY

When running on a non-motorised treadmill in a laboratory, it is possible to estimate the work done by a runner when running on a level gradient. The work done is determined by attaching a harness round the waist of a runner and then adding a known mass over a pulley at the back of the treadmill. The work of the runner is calculated by determining the product of the force the runner is moving against and the displacement in relation to a fixed point on the treadmill belt (i.e. distance). If we know that the mass added is 5 kg and the distance travelled is 1 km, using Equation 6.8:

Work done $\quad$ = $\quad$ Force $\times$ displacement

and since force $\quad$ = $\quad$ mass $\times$ gravity

Work done $\quad$ = $\quad$ mass $\times$ gravity $\times$ distance

$\quad$ = $\quad$ 5 kg $\times$ 9.81 m·s^{-2} $\times$ 1000 m

$\quad$ = $\quad$ 49 050 J or 49 kJ

As mentioned earlier, this is a crude method of estimating the work done by a runner. This is because it is assumed in this calculation that the runner does not do work to move in a vertical plane against the acceleration caused by gravity. Simply by observing a runner, it can be seen that motion does not just occur in a horizontal direction.

MEASURING WORK IN THE LABORATORY WITH A CYCLE ERGOMETER

The cycle ergometer (see Figure 6.5) is a very useful piece of equipment, in that the work done by an individual can be easily quantified. Just as in the definition of work presented earlier in the chapter (i.e. force $\times$ distance), the assessment of useful work is made by knowing how far the individual is moving the ergometer (i.e. distance) and multiplying this by the opposing force. The question is, how is the distance and the opposing force calculated on the cycle ergometer?

Distance = Number of pedal revolutions $\times$ Distance flywheel moves each revolution (m)

Force = Mass on weight pan (kg) $\times$ Acceleration due to gravity (m·s^{-2})

In the case of typical friction-loaded cycle ergometers that are used in the laboratory, the distance the fly-wheel moves for each revolution of the pedals is set at 6 m. Also, the acceleration caused by gravity is constant at 9.81 m·s^{-2}. So the only factors that change

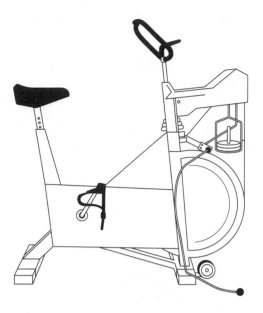

Figure 6.5 A cycle ergometer used for measuring work done in exercise tests

(i.e. variables) are the number of pedal revolutions and the mass on the weight pan. Let's assume for the following example that the pedals will be turned at a rate of 60 revolutions per minute (rev·min⁻¹). Also, the mass on the weight pan will be 1.0 kg.

Work (J) =	Force (N)			×	Distance (m)		
Work (J) =	Mass (kg)	×	Acceleration (m·s⁻²)	×	Revs	×	Distance per rev (m)
Work (J) =	1.0	×	9.81	×	60	×	6
Work (J) =	9.81			×	360		
Work	= 3531.6 J (in a period of one minute, or 3.5 kJ·min⁻¹)						

Since the number of pedal revolutions in a minute was considered in the example calculation, you will notice that the answer was the work done in a minute, rather than the work done over any other time period. Whilst we usually quantify pedal revolutions over a minute period (i.e. revolutions per minute), the amount of work done is usually calculated over the period that the work takes place. So it would be more useful in terms of calculating work done to consider the total number of pedal revolutions during the work period. However, there are some situations when the work performed over a period of time is the desired figure, as you have seen in the section on power (see p. 91), and can see in the next application.

Since the cycle ergometer represents a real exercise situation very effectively, it will not be surprising to learn that much of the research in the area of exercise physiology has traditionally been performed using this type of activity. During other modes of activity which individuals would normally choose to use for exercise, it is far more difficult to assess the useful work done. For example, although attempts have been made to estimate work done during running, most attempts make several questionable assumptions.

DETERMINING POWER OUTPUT DURING CYCLING

Since work done can be measured during cycling, it is a relatively simple further calculation to determine power during cycling. Power is the work done per unit time, where time is in seconds. If the calculated work done in the previous example is used (i.e. 3531.6 J), which was over a minute period (i.e. 60 s), using Equation 6.9:

$$\text{Power (W)} = \frac{\text{Work (J)}}{\text{Time (s)}}$$

$$\text{Power (W)} = \frac{3531.6 \text{J}}{60 \text{ s}}$$

$$\text{Power} = 58.9 \text{ W}$$

Work done each second (i.e. power) can be determined relatively easily using friction-loaded cycle ergometers. This concept has been put to good use in what is known as the Wingate test mentioned earlier. As seen in the following application, four variables influence the work done, and therefore the power output:

1. The mass placed on the weight pan of the ergometer.
2. The acceleration caused by gravity acting on the mass.
3. The distance travelled by the fly-wheel for each revolution of the pedals.
4. The number of revolutions of the pedals per second.

The Wingate test is based upon keeping three of the four possible variables mentioned above constant: the mass placed on the weight pan of the ergometer, the acceleration caused by gravity acting on the mass, and the distance travelled by the fly-wheel for each revolution of the pedals. The only variable during the test, and hence the one that will determine the power, is the rate at which the pedals are turned (revolutions per second). Since it is relatively simple to measure the revolutions per second, the power produced at intervals throughout a test can be quickly calculated following a test.

For a Wingate test, a participant is asked to pedal as fast as possible for 30 seconds. Prior to the test, the mass placed on the ergometer must be determined. The mass must be such that the participant is not trying to pedal faster than possible at the start of the test when fresh, but also not having to stop pedalling at the end of the test when fatigued.

The following data were collected from a participant during a Wingate test in which the mass placed on the ergometer was 5.0 kg. It is also known that the acceleration caused by gravity is 9.81 m·s^{-2} and the distance travelled by the fly-wheel for each revolution of the pedals is 6.0 m.

Time (s)	1	2	3	4	5	6	7	8	9	10
Revs per second	2.40	3.40	3.70	3.60	3.40	3.20	3.10	2.90	2.60	2.40

Time (s)	11	12	13	14	15	16	17	18	19	20
Revs per second	2.40	2.30	2.20	2.15	2.10	2.07	2.04	2.02	2.01	2.00

Time (s)	21	22	23	24	25	26	27	28	29	30
Revs per second	2.00	1.98	1.96	1.93	1.92	1.91	1.92	1.88	1.89	1.88

For the first time point, power is calculated as follows:

Power   =   mass   ×   acceleration   ×   dist per rev   ×   RPS

where RPS = revolutions per second

Power   =   5.0 kg ×   9.81 m·s^{-2} ×   6.0 m   ×   RPS

Power   =   294.3   ×   2.40

So for the first second:

Power   =   706 W

Figure 6.6 is the graph of power against time for the data given previously, and is a typical power trace for a Wingate test. It can be seen that power increases quickly in the first two seconds, and then reaches a peak prior to a steady decline at 6 seconds. Such a trace provides useful information when studying the energy system contribution during short-term exercise.

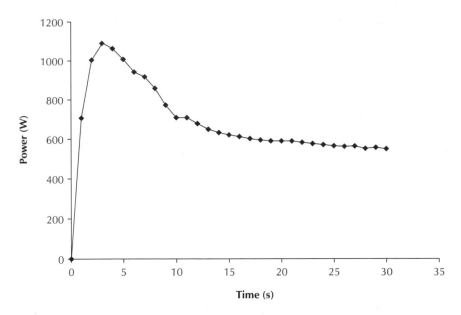

Figure 6.6 A power curve over time recorded during cycle ergometry

SELF-TEST

1. How many joules is 20 kcal?

2. If a runner expends 12 000 J in a race, has the runner used more energy than the 30 kcal energy bar consumed following the race?

3. If a sprint up a flight of stairs takes 6 s, and the height of the top step is 8 m, what is the power output of the 80 kg participant?

4. Why might walking be less efficient than running at higher speeds?

CONCLUSION

Energy provision is of critical importance for physical activity. It is useful to be able to quantify energy expenditure and the resulting work done. In the study of exercise and sport, energy expenditure is routinely measured, and related to mechanical work output. The relationship between energy expenditure and work output is known as efficiency. It is also useful to quantify the rate at which work is being done. Work rate is referred to as power, and is of great importance in many sporting events. Power output is often closely related to exercise performance.

Figure 6.7 illustrates the relationship between energy, work, power and efficiency.

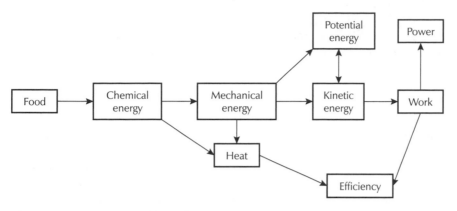

Figure 6.7 Schematic of the relationship between energy, work, power and efficiency

- The human body obtains all energy through diet.
- The SI unit for energy is a joule (J), which is the amount of energy required to move the point of application of a force of 1 N through a distance of 1 m.
- An additional unit of energy is the kilogram calorie (kcal). A kilogram calorie is the amount of energy required to heat 1 kg of water by 1°C under standard conditions.
- There are 4200 J (or 4.2 kJ) to a kcal.
- The body consumes and stores energy in a chemical form.
- Adenosine triphosphate, ATP, is the only form of energy which the body can directly use.
- ATP stores will only allow strenuous exercise to continue for about 2 s, unless they are replenished.
- About 70 per cent of chemical energy stored in the body is converted to heat during physical activity, and less than 30 per cent is converted to useful work.
- The elastic properties of the muscles and connective tissue allow the body to convert kinetic energy into potential energy.
- In terms of physical activity, work is the useful end product of the chemical energy used.
- Work (in joules) is calculated by multiplying the distance an object is moved (in metres, m) by the opposing force in the direction of movement (in newtons, N).
- The rate at which work is being done is important in many sporting events.
- Power (in watts) is calculated by dividing work (in joules) by the time (in seconds, s).
- Efficiency (%) is calculated by dividing work done (in joules) by energy expenditure (in joules), and then multiplying the answer by 100.

■ Running is more efficient than cycling exercise because of the relatively large storage of potential energy within the muscles and connective tissue during each stride.

BIBLIOGRAPHY

Bar-Or, O., Dotan, R. and Inbar, O. (1977) A 30-second all-out ergometric test – its reliability and validity for anaerobic capacity. *Israel Journal of Medical Sciences*, 13: 329.

Margaria, R. (1966) Measurement of muscular power in man. *Journal of Applied Physiology*, 21: 1662.

Maughan, R.J., Gleeson, M. and Greenhaff, P.L. (1997) *Biochemistry of Exercise and Training*. Oxford: Oxford University Press.

McArdle, W.D., Katch, F.I. and Katch, V.L. (2007) *Exercise Physiology: Energy, Nutrition and Human Performance*, 6th edition. Baltimore: Williams and Wilkins.

Sargeant, D.A. (1906) *Physical Education*. Boston: Ginn and Co.

Whipp, B.J. and Wasserman, K. (1969) Efficiency of muscular work. *Journal of Applied Physiology*, 26 (5): 644–648.

Winter, E.M. (1990) Assessing exercise performance – the development of terms. *British Journal of Physical Education Research Supplement*, 6: 3–5.

FURTHER READING

Winter, E.M. (1991a) Assessing exercise performance – maximal exercise I. *British Journal of Physical Education Research Supplement*, 9: 12–14.

Winter, E.M. (1991b) Assessing exercise performance – maximal exercise II. *British Journal of Physical Education Research Supplement*, 10: 13–18.

CHAPTER SEVEN

ELECTRICITY

AIMS OF THE CHAPTER

This chapter is designed to provide an understanding of the scientific principles of electricity as applied to the practical issues which underpin exercise and sport. After reading this chapter, you should be able to:

▣ Define electricity.
▣ Understand electrical charge.
▣ Understand the movement of electrons.
▣ State the conservation of electrical energy and Coulomb's law.
▣ State Ohm's law.
▣ Show how the scientific principles of electricity can be applied to exercise and sport.

INTRODUCTION

The topic of electricity is very important not only in exercise and sport but also in our daily lives. The majority of the population are dependent on electricity for their work, social and leisure pursuits. The study and investigation of electricity has a long history which amounts to a classic Who's Who of past scientists. Included in this list are many scientists who have given their names to terms that we use today, such as Count Alessandro Volta who gave us the term 'volt', Georg Simon Ohm who gave us the term 'ohm', and Nikola Tesla who invented the Tesla coil.

KEY APPLICATIONS TO EXERCISE AND SPORT

In exercise and sport many measurements depend upon electricity. The electrical activity of the heart is measured in the form of an electrocardiogram (ECG). This measurement relies on the electrical activity of the myocardium (heart muscle) as it contracts and relaxes. The assessment of body composition is possible because of the electrical conduction properties of the various types of tissue (e.g. fat) in the body. Specifically, the resistance to the flow of a small current is associated with the composition of the body. So, by passing a small electric current through the body, it is possible to determine the composition of the body. This measurement technique is known as bioelectrical impedance analysis (BIA).

SCIENTIFIC PRINCIPLES OF ELECTRICITY

In an atom there are electrons (which possess a negative charge), protons (which possess a positive charge) and neutrons (which possess no charge and are therefore termed neutral). As the electrical charge of one proton and one electron are equal in strength, when the number of electrons and protons are equal, there is no overall charge, and the molecule is said to be neutral. Protons and neutrons in the nucleus are held together tightly, whereas some of the orbiting electrons around the nucleus are held very loosely. Consequently, the electrons can move from one atom to another atom. It was George Johnstone Stoney in 1874 who proposed the model of the charge carrier as a particle.

STATIC ELECTRICITY

As discussed in Chapter 4, solid materials classified as conductors (e.g. most metals) have loosely held electrons, which can move easily. Conversely, materials classified as insulators (e.g. plastic and glass) have tightly arranged electrons so the electrons do not move so freely. However, if two materials are rubbed together there can be movement of electrons from one to the other, even if both are insulators. In fact, the Greeks had observed such facts when amber was rubbed against cloth, wool or fur, some 2000 years ago; it was because of this that George Johnstone Stoney used the Greek word 'electron', meaning amber.

Even now, it is not entirely clear how the movement of electrons occurs. Movement is not thought to be caused by the friction between the two materials per se. At present it is thought the mere contact between the materials may cause the electrons to move. The result of two different materials coming into contact with one another (e.g. rubbing a balloon on a woollen jumper) creates **static electricity** because of an imbalance in the positive and negative charges. The other name often used for static electricity is electrostatics, which is the study of electric charges at rest.

The gold-leaf electroscope (see Figure 7.1) is an instrument used in some high school science work to demonstrate electrostatics and to visually show the effects of a small charge flowing through a thin piece of gold leaf. The electroscope is a square container that holds a metal cap, a perspex plug and a metal rod to which a gold leaf, or pointer, is attached. When a positively charged rod is brought to the surface of a negatively charged metal cap, the potential of the cap is raised. The charge flows onto the leaf and an equal but opposite charge is created inside the case, so that the leaf is deflected. Thus, the deflection of the leaf is approximately proportional to the potential.

The adage that opposites attract is related to charges. A proton (positive charge) and an electron (negative charge) will be attracted to one another, but like charges (e.g. two protons) will repel one another. These attraction forces are clearly demonstrated through the example of a balloon and a woollen jumper. When the balloon is rubbed on the jumper it acquires extra electrons and therefore an increasingly negative charge. If the balloon is then placed on a third object, such as a wall, it will stick to the wall because of an attraction between the positive charges in the wall and the negatively charged balloon. If the object happens to be a good conductor, the negative charges (electrons) in it will move as far away from the balloon as possible. Therefore, the balloon will still stick to the conductor because of the attraction of the positive charges in the latter. Another common example is a spark or small electric shock which is sometimes experienced when you walk

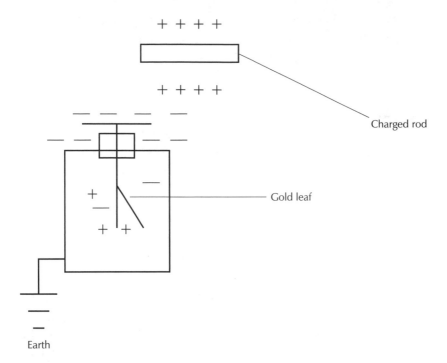

+ + + +

+ + + +

− − − −

− − −

Charged rod

Gold leaf

Earth

Figure 7.1 A gold-leaf electroscope showing the effects of a positive potential

across a rug and then brush another person's hand. When you walk across the rug a large number of electrons are transferred from it to you (i.e. you gain increased negative charge). When you touch the other person, they act as a conductor, and the electrons move rapidly from you to that person. You will recall from Chapter 4 that the human body is a good conductor because it is composed of a large amount of water. However, it should be stressed that water per se is not the prime reason for conduction within the body; it is the dissolved ions, such as sodium and chloride, that assist the flow of the charge.

When two objects are rubbed together one becomes negatively charged and one becomes positively charged. To simplify the decision about which object becomes negative and which positive, scientists have formulated a rank order list (Figure 7.2). Thus whichever object appears higher along the scale gives up electrons and becomes more positively charged; hence the other object (lower along the scale) will become more negatively charged. This list is known as the triboelectric series.

Human hand Glass Human hair Nylon Wool Fur Silk Paper Cotton Hard rubber Polyester Polyvinylchloride plastic

High ◄───► **Low**

Figure 7.2 The triboelectric series

force, pressure, energy and electricity

The imbalance of positive and negative charges, which leads to static electricity, is merely the movement of electrons from one place to another. There is no new creation or destruction of electrons, hence the net electric charge stays the same. This concept is called the **principle of conservation of charge**. This type of principle should seem familiar to you if you have read Chapter 6, since it is similar to the conservation of energy principle.

COULOMB'S LAW

The electric charge of a proton or an electron is measured in coulombs (C). A single positive or negative electrical charge is equal to 1.6×10^{-19} C. Although smaller fractions of charged particles have been found (known as 'quarks'), experimentally it has been difficult to isolate them. Therefore, at present all charged particles (negative or positive) are integer multiples of a 'quantised' charge.

The invisible electrical field created around objects is a product of both the positively and the negatively charged objects. The force of the field around the objects is dependent on the amount of the charge, the distance between the objects and the shape of the objects. Because of the complexity of the situation, electrical charge is often simplified by treating the charged protons and electrons as a 'point source'. The point source applies to charged objects that are much smaller than the distance between them.

Charles Coulomb, in 1785, was the first to describe the strength of electric fields. Coulomb found that the electrical force varied directly with the product of the charges. This means that, the bigger the charge, the stronger the field. He also stated that the field varied inversely with the distance between the charges. In other words, the greater the distance the weaker the field. These experimental relationships are formulated in what is known as Coulomb's law, as shown in Equation 7.1.

$$F = K.q_1.q_2 /d^2 \qquad .. \qquad .. \qquad .. \qquad .. \qquad .. \qquad .. \qquad .. \qquad (7.1)$$

Where F is the electric force (N), $q_1 q_2$ are the two charges (C), d is the distance between the two charges (m) and K is Coulomb's constant, equal to 9×10^9 Nm$^2 \cdot$C^{-2}.

Therefore, from Equation 7.1, if the distance between two charged particles is doubled, the force is reduced by three-quarters. If the charge is doubled, the force is increased by a factor of four.

The discussion so far has dealt only with electric charges at rest (static electricity or electrostatics). Although static electricity and current electricity are the same phenomena, and result in very similar effects, the former deals with very small charges. In current electricity the charge is much greater, and this is the type of electricity which we rely upon every day.

CURRENT ELECTRICITY

When electricity passes through a material such as a wire, electric current can be described as flowing through the material. However, the electric current is more accurately described as an organised 'drift' of electrons. The size of the current is the rate at which the electrons flow. Hence, electrons will be attracted to the positive charge within a wire (or any other material in which the current is travelling) whilst being repelled at the opposite end of the wire because of the negative charge (remember like charges repel). Even though electrons within a wire are travelling at many thousand metres per second, the potential difference between two points imposes an average overall velocity of a few centimetres per second upon the high speed of the electrons. It is incorrect to think that a particular electron has to travel from one end of a wire to the other. It is perhaps easier to relate to the concept of 'drift' for electrons within materials. The important effect is more of a 'falling domino' scene, whereby one electron will invade the space of the nearest electron and repel it leading to that electron then moving into the space of the next electron and so on. This domino effect results in the electrical energy travelling at the speed of light $(3 \times 10^9 \text{ m·s}^{-1})$. Therefore, electricity should be considered to be a form of kinetic energy when it is flowing in a wire.

Electrical current is measured in amperes. One ampere is equal to 1 coulomb per second:

$$1 \text{ A} = 1 \text{ C·s}^{-1}$$

A more detailed and technical definition often found in physics textbooks is:

> The electric current which, when flowing through two straight parallel conductors of infinite length and negligible circular section and one metre apart, causes a force between the wires of 2×10^{-7} newtons per metre.
>
> (Duncan, 1994: 272)

An understanding of electricity in the context of atoms and matter should aid in your understanding of energy and forces. Electricity, by virtue of the position of the protons and electrons, can be described as possessing potential energy in much the same way that a battery can store electricity. This potential is associated with another known unit of electricity, the volt. The volt is a measure of the difference in potential energy between two points, known as the potential difference. Potential difference is very similar in concept to the potential gradient of liquids discussed in Chapter 3. A potential gradient allows a liquid to flow from one point to another providing there is a difference in the pressure at the entrance and exit points. Electrons tend to flow to the point of least potential energy. Electricity can be thought of as a method of transferring energy from one location to another. Another way to look upon the voltage, or potential difference, is in terms of the driving force. The volt can be defined as:

the potential difference such that one ampere of current will be driven through a resistance of one ohm.

(Duncan, 1994)

In the above definition of the volt, the term 'resistance' was used. Resistance is measured in ohms, after Georg Ohm. An ohm is signified by the Greek capital letter omega (Ω). The resistance of matter is a function of the type of material, and the length and thickness of the material. The resistance to electricity will therefore impede the flow of electrons. The ohm's law (Equation 7.2) describes how current, voltage and resistance relate to one another:

$$I = V/R \qquad .. \qquad .. \qquad .. \qquad .. \qquad .. \qquad .. \qquad .. \qquad (7.2)$$

where I is the electrical current, V is the potential difference, and R is the resistance of the conductor. The formula can be rearranged to give the resistance of a conductor:

$$R = V/I \qquad .. \qquad .. \qquad .. \qquad .. \qquad .. \qquad .. \qquad .. \qquad (7.3)$$

The three main factors in electricity mentioned so far – potential difference (voltage), current and resistance – are illustrated in Figure 7.3. This diagram shows the form of an electric circuit. Notice the direction of the arrows: they are deliberately pointing from the positive terminal of the battery towards the negative terminal. However, from the information given, we have understood that direction of the electric current is from negative to positive. This apparent contradiction can be explained as follows. Historically, the direction of electrical current was thought to go from positive to negative, as if the

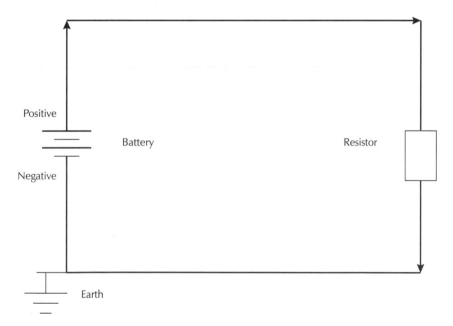

Figure 7.3 An electric current circuit

positive charge was responsible for the flow of charge. Therefore, in all schematics of electrical current, the direction of the arrow for flow was from positive to negative. However, it is now known that the flow is from negative to positive and that electrons are responsible for this flow of charge. Since the effect of the negative charge moving to the positive is exactly the same as the positive charge moving to the negative, this apparent contradiction should not cause a problem.

STOP AND THINK

Would a thicker and shorter wire have a lower or higher resistance than a thinner and longer wire of the same material?

Since electricity is a force that transfers potential energy to kinetic energy, it is possible to express electricity in units of energy (such as joules) or units of power (such as watts). As stated in Chapter 6, the joule is the SI unit of energy or work, and 1 joule of work is done when a force of 1 newton acts through a distance of 1 metre. The watt is the SI unit of power, and 1 watt is 1 joule of work done per second. In electrical terms it is common to come across the term kilowatt-hour (kW.h). This is a non-SI unit of energy, and is defined as the energy consumed in 1 hour by an electrical appliance working at a power of 1 kilowatt (1000 watts), such that 1 kW.h equals 3.6×10^6 joules. If the energy change, or work done, is represented by W (take care not to confuse this symbol with the abbreviation W for watts) and measured in joules (recall that 1 volt = 1 J per coulomb) then:

$$W = Q \times V \qquad\qquad\qquad\qquad\qquad\qquad (7.4)$$

where Q is coulombs and V is potential difference in volts.

Since $Q = I \times t$

$$W = V \times I \times t \qquad\qquad\qquad\qquad\qquad (7.5)$$

where I is current (in amperes) and t is time (in seconds).

To be translated into power (P), the formula for work (W) must now incorporate the factor of time because by definition power is the rate of work per unit time. Therefore, the formula now becomes:

$$P = (V \times I \times t) / t \qquad\qquad\qquad\qquad (7.6)$$

or

$$P = V \times I$$

110

Electric current can be either what is known as direct current (d.c.) or alternating current (a.c.). A torch or a car battery are examples of a direct current, whilst mains electricity is an example of an alternating current. The mains electricity which is delivered to our homes has a potential of approximately 240 V. If the equation $P = V \times I$ is rearranged to $I = P/V$, then we can calculate that a typical 120 W lamp running off 200 V would draw a current of 0.66 A.

APPLICATION OF SCIENCE TO EXERCISE AND SPORT

Any technology that requires computerisation or motorisation will require electricity. For example, navigational equipment in sports such as sailing is often battery powered.

In electricity there are four main areas to relate to physiology and these include:

1. Law of conservation of electrical charge.
2. Opposite charges attract.
3. Energy is needed to separate protons and electrons.
4. Conductors and insulators.

STOP AND THINK

Why would dissolved ions such as sodium and chloride assist the flow of charge within the human body?

A DEFIBRILLATOR

A defibrillator is basically a large capacitor which delivers an electric shock to the heart. A capacitor is designed for storing electric charge, so a defibrillator therefore has an electric potential or potential voltage. A conducting pathway must be made available for a capacitor to discharge, thereby releasing the stored electrical energy. By placing what are known as the paddles of the defibrillator on the chest of the patient, the pathway is completed. A switch in the circuit is then closed, thus allowing the capacitor to discharge the current in a few milliseconds. The switch is then opened, breaking the pathway for the electricity, and the defibrillator recharges in preparation for the next occasion. A defibrillator has a potential of about 7500 volts and the charged capacitor has a stored energy of 400 J.

A defibrillator is used to deliver an electric shock by discharging a high voltage through the heart. The electric shock is used to overcome the heart's irregular rhythm, and if successful allows the heart to then beat in a normal rhythm again. A discharge of 200–360 J will usually result in depolarisation of the heart muscle (the myocardium). After an electric shock the heart should be capable of providing its own electrical stimulus, thereby returning to a normal ECG wave formation.

The rhythm of a patient's heart is disturbed (arrhythmia) when the normal electrical conduction circuit of the heart is bypassed. Normally, the electrical circuit involves a passage from the sinoatrial node, through the atria to the atrioventricular node, through the Purkinje fibres and through the ventricles. Sometimes when this circuit is not followed (e.g. ventricular fibrillation), the irregular electrical pattern must be disrupted by the action of the defibrillator, and the normal electrical activity restored. There are many reasons why an arrhythmia might occur, but commonly a myocardial infarction (heart attack) is the reason. The quicker the normal rhythm is restored, the better the chances of survival of the patient.

THE ELECTROCARDIOGRAM (ECG)

The electrocardiogram (ECG) is one of the most widely used instruments in both hospitals and exercise physiology laboratories. The ECG is a graphic representation of the electrical forces produced by the heart. An ECG relies on the body's water and salt content to allow the heart's voltage of approximately 1 mV to be detected at the surface of the skin. The heart has a natural rhythm originating from the sinoatrial node, which is known as the heart's natural pace maker. The electrode leads of a three-lead ECG which are often labelled I, II and III, are used to detect both the magnitude and the direction of the heart's electrical impulse. Prior to an ECG waveform being determined, the skin has to be prepared to allow for optimal conductance of the electrical signal. This procedure often includes shaving off any excess body hair and the removal of dead skin cells by vigorous rubbing with an alcohol wipe. Electrodes are then placed onto the prepared skin. The standard placement of the electrodes is for lead I to be placed just below the left collar bone (clavicle); lead II to be placed on the sixth rib on the left-hand side in a vertical line with lead I, and lead III to be placed on the eighth rib on the right-hand side. Leads I, II and III are positive, negative and earth leads respectively. The ECG is able to convert the electrical signal into what we see as the heart's electrical waveform (see Figure 7.4). The original ECG lead system was devised by a scientist called Einthoven. The system uses what is known as Einthoven's triangle to determine the sum of all the electrical activity within the heart. By assessing the magnitude and direction of the electrical signal to lead I, to lead II and from leads I to II, and by using Pythagoras' theorem and simple geometry, the signal is converted into a waveform of electrical activity of the heart which can then be interpreted. Heart rate monitors use a similar principle to determine heart rate with the use of two electrodes that form part of the chest strap.

BIOELECTRICAL IMPEDANCE

Bioelectrical impedance analysis (BIA) is a common technique used in body composition assessment. It is based on the fact that electrical current is passed more easily through fat-free tissues and extracellular water than through fat tissue. The reason for this is the greater

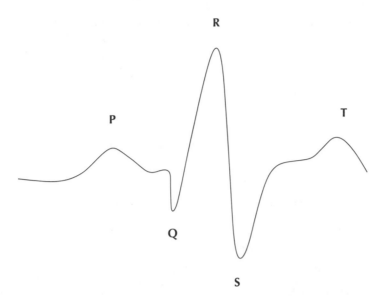

Figure 7.4
An electrocardiogram
(ECG) trace showing
the PQRST complex
of electrical activity

content of electrolyte in fat-free tissue. Thus BIA will record a lower resistance for lean tissue than for fat tissue, and hence the impedance of the electricity is directly associated with fat tissue.

The protocol used in measuring body fat by the BIA method typically involves requesting a participant not to eat for 4 hours nor to exercise 12 hours prior to the measurement being taken. Similarly, abstinence from alcohol for 24 hours prior to the test is also requested. The instrument requires the participant to be in the supine position and as relaxed and still as possible. One electrode is placed on the phalangeal-metacarpal joint on the dorsal surface of the right hand and the second electrode is placed on the medial side of the right wrist. A third electrode is placed just below the metatarsal arch of the superior side of the right foot and another on the medial side of the right ankle. A small, undetectable electrical signal (50 kHz, 800 µA) is passed through the body and a resistance to the current is recorded. The impedance figure plus details of gender, stature, body mass and age are then used to predict body density. This figure is then converted to percentage body fat using an equation formulated by Siri (1961).

Although the technique is quick, easy to use and non-invasive, there are a number of confounding factors which can easily distort the true value. The first factor is the participant's hydration level. Numerous studies have shown that the hydration level of the participant alters the recorded value. For example, a deficit of body water will decrease the impedance value and the participant will record a lower percentage body fat. Conversely, a hyperhydrated state will result in an artificially high body fat percentage. The temperature of the skin also affects the predicted body fat score: measurements taken in warmer climates typically result in lower impedance values than measurements taken in colder climates.

The BIA technique is thought not to be as accurate as other body composition techniques, such as skinfolds and hydrodensitometry. In fact, because the BIA method has been validated against skinfold testing it can never be more accurate than skinfold testing itself. However, although it should be used with caution, it does provide another non-invasive technique for predicting percentage body fat (Williams and Bale 1998).

SELF-TEST

1. How does an insulator differ from a conductor?

2. How strong are magnetism and gravity compared with electrical force?

3. Construct a flow diagram to show how coulombs, amperes, volts and ohms all relate to one another.

4. Describe how electrical behaviour is similar to that of liquids.

5. Find examples of direct and alternating current.

6. Review Figure 6.3 in Chapter 6, noting the power outputs of human performances and power consumption of common electrical appliances.

7. What is the electrical output of the heart and suggest why an ECG signal can be distorted during an exercise test?

8. Electromyograms (EMG) measure skeletal muscle electrical activity. Explain why the concept is similar to that of an ECG instrument.

CONCLUSION

Electricity is a force which relates to the atomic model. The study of electricity involves looking at the interactions of electrons. In electrostatics (or static electricity), the attraction of positively and negatively charged protons and electrons is central to the effects shown by the electrical force. The imbalance of the positive and negative charges responsible for static electricity is caused by the movement of the protons and electrons on an object, which results in a net electrical force. Therefore, energy is neither created nor destroyed, conforming to the principle of conservation of charge.

As an object carries both negative and positive charges, it creates an electrical field. The force of this field is dependent on the amount of the charge, the distance between objects and the shape of the objects. As a result of research by Charles Coulomb, the strength of electrical fields was found to vary directly with the product of the charges. This finding led to the law known as Coulomb's law.

Electricity can flow through conducting materials such as metal, and this current is measured in amperes. One ampere is equal to 1 coulomb per second. The driving force or potential difference contributing to this electric current is known as the voltage. To establish the relationship between the electric current and the voltage, the resistance of the material must be known. Resistance is a function of the type of material and its thickness. The work of Georg Ohm led to a law known as Ohm's law, which describes the relationship between current, voltage and resistance of a conductor. As electricity is a force, it is possible to express it using units of work or power. The properties of electricity are used in several instruments in the study of exercise and sport.

BIBLIOGRAPHY

Duncan, T. (1994) *Advanced Physics*, 4th edition. London: John Murray.
Siri, W.E. (1961) Body composition from fluid spaces and density: analysis of methods. In J. Brozek and A. Henschell (eds), *Techniques in Measuring Body Composition*. Washington, DC: National Academy of Sciences/National Research Council, pp. 223–244.
Williams, C.A. and Bale, P. (1998). Bias and limits of agreement between hydro-densitometry, bioelectrical impedance and skinfold calliper measures of percentage body fat. *European Journal of Applied Physiology*, 77: 271–277.

FURTHER READING

Isaacs, A. (1963) *Introducing Science*. Middlesex: Penguin, pp. 139–142.
James, D.V.B., Barnes, A.J., Lopes, P. and Wood, D.M. (2002) Heart rate variability: response following a single bout of interval training. *International Journal of Sports Medicine*, 23: 247–251.

PART 3

SCIENTIFIC TRANSFERABLE SKILLS

CHAPTER EIGHT

DATA ANALYSIS

AIMS OF THE CHAPTER

This chapter aims to provide an understanding of the principles of data analysis which underpin exercise and sport investigations. After reading this chapter, you should be able to:

■ Understand the importance of data analysis in exercise and sport investigations.
■ Link hypothesis testing and data analysis principles.
■ Link study design with appropriate data analysis techniques.
■ Identify the fundamental principles of scientific data analysis.
■ Interpret data analysis outcomes in an exercise and sport context.

INTRODUCTION

Considerable thought and planning usually precedes any scientific investigation, from the stage of isolating the problem and identifying the question, through to designing the study. In this chapter some of the important principles upon which scientific investigations are based will be considered. Without a basic understanding of the principles of the scientific method, hypothesis testing and study design, it is difficult to consider data analysis. Consideration of the construction of a scientific investigation, from the identification of the problem to the analysis of the data, should help to improve understanding of why certain types of data analysis are utilised. The remainder of the chapter will consider the different types of data that may be collected when conducting experimental type investigations in exercise and sport, and the possibilities for appropriate analysis. Covering all of these areas in one chapter is a challenge, so we would refer interested readers to Williams and Wragg (2004) for further detail.

In the study of exercise and sport, it is often necessary to collect information either through measurement or questionnaires and surveys. Sometimes information is also gathered through interviews, focus groups and observation of individuals and their behaviour. When an experimental type of scientific investigation takes place, the information is usually collected through **direct measurement**, and this is the type of quantitative information that will be considered in this chapter. For further information regarding the analysis of quantitative data from observational type studies, see Kuzma and Bohnenblust (2001). For an overview regarding the analysis of quantitative or qualitative data from questionnaires, surveys and interviews, see Gratton and Jones (2004). For further information regarding the analysis of qualitative data, which may be collected through questionnaires, interviews, focus groups, or observation, see Patton (1980), Silverman (1993), and Derzin and Lincoln (1994, 1998).

The advantage of making a direct measurement is that little ambiguity surrounds the influence of the investigator on the resulting quantitative data. The data may, therefore, be collected by different investigators, who should all obtain similar results. Direct

120

measurement ensures a degree of reliability between investigators (inter-investigator reliability) since the data is collected objectively. However, the findings of an experimental investigation of this type are not without some subjective influence. First, the design of the study will be influenced by the investigator, which may in turn influence the findings. Additionally, interpretation has to take place by the investigator once the data has been collected in order to place the findings in context and draw conclusions. Finally, publication bias may influence whether the findings are made available to the wider academic community.

This chapter will not cover particular statistical tests in detail, but if you want to access such information Hinton (1995) is a good place to start. Data analysis is normally performed by students in higher education using widely available computer software, and familiarity with such software is increasingly important in the workplace. See Field (2005) for further information on the application of statistical software commonly used in exercise and sport.

KEY APPLICATIONS TO EXERCISE AND SPORT

Most students undertaking a course in the broad exercise and sport area are required to conduct a research investigation at some point during their studies. In exercise and sport sciences courses, students are often required to undertake an experimental investigation, and for some students an experimental investigation is conducted as part of a final year dissertation. The design and conduct of an experimental investigation is challenging, and this chapter should provide an interesting overview. Whatever the particular area of specialism of the student, all students working in the broad exercise and sport area will need to critically understand and interpret the findings of experimental research which is normally published in peer-reviewed academic journals. This chapter will help students to understand why studies have been conducted in a particular way, and how the outcomes of the data analysis should be interpreted.

SCIENTIFIC APPROACH

Scientists in the area of exercise and sport, like scientists in other subjects, work within an established **scientific paradigm**. The underlying principle in science is that understanding is advanced as theories are tested. Scientific theories are proposed, which are then rigorously tested. If the tests establish that the theories are inadequate, the theories should either be adapted to account for the new findings, or discarded. This scientific approach was advocated by Sir Karl Popper (1902–1994), and remains the dominant approach in experimental research.

Experimental investigations are designed in order to test particular aspects of our under-standing. The design of the investigation must be such that our understanding can be challenged with a degree of confidence. It is important to recognise that much data analysis is performed in order that a theory can be challenged with a degree of confidence. In this regard, confidence is usually expressed as a probability or percentage. For example, an investigator might accept a probability of 95 times out of 100, or 95 per cent. However, the area of research often dictates acceptable probability levels. For example, in medical research where lives are at stake, 95 per cent probability may not be acceptable.

The first step in designing an experimental investigation is the formation of testable hypotheses, based upon the identified problem or **research question**. The design of the investigation will then test the hypotheses, and allow focused conclusions to be drawn (see Figure 8.1).

HYPOTHESIS TESTING

The *Collins English Dictionary* definition for a **hypothesis** is a suggested explanation for a group of facts or phenomena which are accepted as a basis for further verification, or an assumption used in an argument. A hypothesis is normally broken down into two components: a null hypothesis (abbreviated as H_0), and an alternative hypothesis (abbreviated as H_1). If we consider the example of an experimental investigation that is

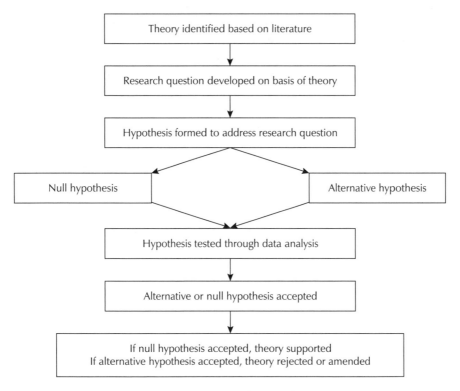

Figure 8.1 Flow diagram of the process of scientific investigation

scientific transferable skills

attempting to determine whether a particular intervention has an effect, the null hypothesis usually states that there is no effect caused by the intervention, while the alternative hypothesis states that there is an effect caused by the intervention. If the investigators are confident of the direction of effect, they will normally make that explicit in the alternative hypothesis. For example:

Null hypothesis (H_0): Ingestion of water does not decrease race times
Alternative hypothesis (H_1): Ingestion of water does decrease race times

Whether or not the investigators accept or reject the hypotheses is based upon the data analysis. The employed data analysis techniques are selected based upon their ability to determine whether the hypotheses should be accepted or rejected. At this point a word of caution is required. It must be understood that the hypotheses are only ever rejected or accepted with a degree of confidence. For example, it is never possible to say that on every occasion the null hypothesis is true. Although at first thought, that fact may not seem adequate for scientific investigations, the concept of a degree of confidence serves a very useful purpose. In every experiment, **random errors** will occur for one reason or another. If a hypothesis is only accepted if every observed result agreed with the hypothesis, the findings of a study would always be influenced by the random errors. Random errors are the deviation in a measurement for reasons relating to errors of the investigator or factors related to control of confounding variables. The degree of confidence is determined by the investigator, and implemented through the chosen statistical test. The degree of confidence (or confidence limit) is often selected based on several factors (for further information, see statistical power section, p. 141). Further detail on how to include hypotheses in a scientific report can be found in Chapter 10.

STUDY DESIGN

When considering the most appropriate study design for experimental investigations, two key questions should be considered:

1. What is the best design that tests the hypotheses?
2. Does the design lend itself to a conventional form of data analysis?

Both of the above considerations are, however, inextricably linked. The design must allow the hypotheses to be tested, which is only possible if appropriate data analysis can be performed. It is the **inferential data analysis** (see section 'inferences from findings', p. 135) that allows an investigator to claim with confidence that the results within the examined sample may be generalised to the whole population.

Since it is rare in the study of exercise and sport to be able to examine a whole population, it is normal to select a **sample** from the population for examination. However, the way in which the sample is chosen from the population may influence the findings dramatically.

It is usually necessary to select a representative sample from the population, and failure to do this will result in what is known as a biased sample. A representative sample shares the same characteristics as the population. The key question is then, how is a representative sample selected? Various approaches are implemented to achieve a representative sample, including random sampling and purposeful sampling. Random sampling ensures that each member of the population has an equal chance of being selected for the sample. Purposeful sampling ensures that the characteristics of the group are representative of the characteristics of the sample.

For the remainder of the experimental design part of the chapter, a sample will be referred to as a group. It is normal to refer to a group when discussing the participants in relation to the experimental investigation, but to a sample when discussing the participants in relation to data analysis principles.

In experimental investigations, the following study designs are often employed in exercise and sport:

- A group that represents a cross-section of the population of interest.
- A single group which is tested prior to and following an intervention.
- A control group and an experimental group which are tested prior to and following an intervention.
- A case study performed on a small number of participants who are exposed to an intervention at various time points.

The reason for having a **control group** that is monitored, despite the lack of an intervention, is to determine whether the results in the **experimental group** are caused by the intervention alone. If a similar change is observed in the control group, it cannot be claimed with confidence that the results are caused by the intervention. In some situations it is possible to have a control and experimental group that swap over. The control group becomes the experimental group, and the experimental group becomes the control group. This is known as a **cross-over** type design (e.g. Kreider et al., 1990). Sometimes it is not possible to implement such a design if the experimental intervention is not retractable. For example, if it is known that the administration of a drug to the experimental group will have lasting results, it is not possible for that group to become the control group. A cross-over type design is generally considered to be stronger than the simpler control and experimental group design.

A single group is often used to examine the effect of an intervention. This particular approach is weaker than a control and experimental group. However, such an approach is sometimes unavoidable. For example, if an investigator wishes to test the effect of a drug which is strongly suspected to only have beneficial effects on patients health, and no negative side-effects, it may be considered unethical to allow one group of patients access to the drug, but not another group. Under this condition, a single group experiment is unavoidable. There are, however, various ways to strengthen the design considerably, even with just one single group. A design that is considered to be relatively strong is a

124

repeated measures design, where the participants all act as their own controls. Usually the participants will be observed prior to an intervention, during the intervention, and following the intervention. If the observed responses return to pre-intervention values when the intervention is removed, it is possible to state with a degree of confidence that the observed change is caused by the intervention. If a single group design must be used because of ethical considerations, as discussed earlier, it is possible to further strengthen the design. Rather than simply have all participants exposed to the intervention at the same time, the application of the intervention could be staggered. With this approach, all participants receive the intervention that is perceived to be beneficial. The benefit of the staggered approach is the opportunity to observe whether any change in the response of the participants who have the intervention administered early is a result of the intervention or something else. If a change is also observed in the response of the participants who have not been administered the intervention, the observed change is likely to be caused by another factor. The other factor may simply be a 'placebo effect' (or Hawthorne effect), which is the term used to describe a change for no apparent reason apart from the fact that the participants think they had been given the intervention.

A similar approach of staggering the application of an intervention is adopted in investigations that use a small group of participants. A **case study** approach often relies on the application of innovative strategies to determine whether any observed change is caused by the intervention or not. Inferential analysis of findings is the usual method of determining with a degree of confidence whether any observed effect is caused by an intervention. However, inferential data analyses are normally dependent upon relatively large group (sample) sizes. With a case study approach, the number of participants may be anything from one to five or more. To account for the small number of participants, but still allow a statistical approach to the analysis, a multiple baseline is used. The multiple baseline is simply an extension of the repeated measures design referred to above, where participants act as their own control. However, the intervention is applied and taken away several times with a multiple baseline design. By adopting this approach, enough information is collected to allow analysis of the findings via inferential statistical tests. Again, such an approach is not possible when an intervention is not retractable. However, it is possible to modify the design to stagger the application of the intervention between participants if more than one participant is used. Once the intervention has been applied, it cannot then be removed without a residual effect. This latter approach is similar to the staggered repeated measures design with larger groups. Table 8.1 summarises some of the various experimental designs used in the study of exercise and sport and their relative merits.

Through the previous discussion it is clear that, in experimental investigations, the design of a study cannot be separated from the method of data analysis. The inferential data analysis simply allows the appropriate hypothesis to be accepted with a degree of confidence. The type of analysis will be heavily dependent upon the study design. Often, the more complicated the experimental design, the more complicated the analysis – a trap many a student has fallen into! However, by understanding the principles of data analysis, this knowledge will partly inform the choice of experimental design.

Table 8.1 Experimental designs used in the study of exercise and sport

Study design	Differences [a]	Relationships [b]	Own control [c]
Cross-sectional		✓	
Experimental group	✓	✓	✓
Control and exp. group	✓	✓	
Cross-over	✓	✓	✓
Repeated measures	✓	✓	✓
Multiple baseline	✓	✓	✓
Case study			✓

(a) Differences – The ability to determine differences in outcomes between conditions.
(b) Relationships – The ability to determine relationships between variables.
(c) Own control – The participants act as their own control.

ANALYSIS PRINCIPLES

Whilst it is not the aim of this chapter to cover particular statistical tests which may be of use to a student of exercise and sport, the intention is to provide enough information to enable the reader to understand the principles underlying all relevant data analysis techniques. In addition, it is intended that the information provided will enable the reader to choose an appropriate statistical test. Several texts provide useful information on the details of specific statistical tests. For a basic level text see Williams and Wragg (2004) or Hinton (1995), for an intermediate level see Vincent (1995), and for an advanced level see Howell (1997).

Data analysis is usually divided into two categories: **descriptive** and inferential analysis. Once data has been collected in its raw form, it is usually necessary to undertake some analysis prior to presentation of the data. As the term suggests, descriptive analysis of data enables an observer to obtain important information in order to appreciate the data. Often data presented in its raw form is not the best representation to allow an observer to examine the data. The descriptive analysis of the data, however, does not allow an observer to make a judgement about how the findings from the sample under investigation might be generalisable to the population; an inferential analysis of the data is required for this purpose. Prior to either form of analysis, it is necessary to establish what type of data is under investigation.

TYPE OF DATA

In order to choose the most appropriate analysis technique for either describing data or drawing inferences from the data, it is essential to first consider the type of data being handled. The type of data is categorised according to the scale of measurement used. The four categories are outlined below:

- Nominal
- Ordinal
- Interval
- Ratio.

Nominal data are those which are categorised. However, no relationship exists between the categories, and the categories cannot be ordered in any way. For example, human participants may be categorised according to their hair colour. For example, category one could be black hair, two could be brown hair, etc. There is no way of ordering these categories in any meaningful way. We cannot state that category two is better or higher than category one. Perhaps a more meaningful example for exercise and sport would be the sport played by participants. If a study recruited individuals who engaged in running (category 1), football (2), swimming (3), cricket (4), cycling (5) and rowing (6), there would be no way to order such categories. The sport categories could, however, be further categorised into team or individual, or water or land-based sports.

Ordinal data are those which are categorised, and may also be ordered in some way. However, it is not possible to say that the difference between two categories is the same as the difference between other different categories. For example, human participants may be categorised according to their perception of how strenuous an exercise task appeared. The degree to which the task was strenuous could be rated between one and five, with one being very easy and five being very hard. From this information it is possible to claim that the participants in category 2 found the task less strenuous in contrast to participants in category 4. However, it is not possible to claim that participants in category 4 found the task twice as strenuous compared with participants in category 2. So although the categories can be ranked, the numbers ascribed to each category cannot be treated mathematically.

Both nominal and ordinal data are classified as being **categorical data**. Such data are analysed in a standard way, and statistical tests known as non-parametric tests are normally used to draw inferences from categorical data.

Interval data are measured from a continuous scale of measurement, where the differences between successive increments are uniform. However, such data has no fixed zero reference point. The point that takes the value 0 is arbitrary. Interval data can be treated mathematically, however, certain rules do not apply. It is not possible to apply ratio manipulations to such data. An example of interval data is the measurement of temperature. Different temperature scales have different fixed zero reference values. For example, the Celsius scale has the freezing point of water as its zero. The boiling point of water is a further fixed reference point of 100. Each increment between 0 and 100 is known as a degree (°) on the Celsius scale. The kelvin scale has the same magnitude degree increments, but a zero value corresponding to −273° on the Celsius scale. So 0° on the Celsius scale corresponds to 273° on the kelvin scale. Therefore, doubling a figure on the Celsius scale has a different effect from doubling a figure on a kelvin scale.

Ratio data are exactly the same as interval data, except that they are appropriate to perform ratio manipulations of the data. In other words, it is possible to state that a score of 40 is twice as high as a score of 20. Most data that is collected on a continuous scale of measurement is ratio data. An example of ratio data would be the height (stature) of participants in a study. The zero value is absolute (i.e. no height), and the increments are uniform. For example, someone who is 150 cm tall is only three-quarters of the height of someone who is 200 cm tall.

Both interval and ratio data are classified as being continuous data. Inferences are drawn from continuous data using parametric statistical tests (see choosing a statistical test section, p. 139). For a summary of the four types of data see Table 8.2.

STOP AND THINK

For each category of data, can you think of one variable commonly measured in exercise and sport?

Throughout the remainder of this chapter, the emphasis will be on interval and ratio data, since these continuous data types are normally derived from the direct measurement techniques employed in experimental investigations in exercise and sport. Fortunately, a large range of analysis procedures are possible with continuous data.

DESCRIPTION OF FINDINGS

Descriptive analysis is the transformation of data into a 'user-friendly' form. In order to describe the data, it is necessary to present the data in a way that allows the observer to quickly obtain the most important information. Normally such information is related to the central point (central tendency) of the data, and the degree of spread (variation) about this centrality. This information can be expressed in a variety of forms as shown in Table 8.3.

The data in the second column of Table 8.3 is the resting heart rate (HR) of 30 individuals immediately after waking up in the morning. The participants in the study were all female

Table 8.2 Characteristics of the different types of data

Scale	Categorised	Ranked	Addition/Subtraction	Multiplication/Division
Nominal	✓			
Ordinal	✓	✓		
Interval	✓	✓	✓	
Ratio	✓	✓	✓	✓

scientific transferable skills

athletes, between the ages of 18 and 29 years. In order to standardise the measurement, all HR values were determined in a supine position after each participant had been awake for five minutes.

By examining column 2 in Table 8.3, it is difficult to arrive at any conclusions from the data. Importantly, it is also difficult to determine whether any erroneous values have been entered into the column by mistake. For example, to find the middle value would be a difficult task because of the organisation of the data in column 2. Likewise, the minimum and maximum values could not be obtained at a glance. However, when the data are organised through a ranking system, which in the case of column 4 is in ascending order, it becomes easier to locate the middle, minimum and maximum value at a glance. From column 4 it is clear that the middle value is between the 15th and 16th ranked value, since

Table 8.3 Calculation of descriptive statistics based upon resting heart rate (HR, beats·min^{-1}) from 30 female participants

Participant	HR	Rank	Ranked HR	Descriptive statistics	
1	59	1	43		
2	68	2	46		
3	55	3	47	**Median**	59
4	57	4	49	**Minimum**	43
5	51	5	50	**Maximum**	73
6	59	6	51	**Range**	30
7	55	7	52	**Lower Q**	54
8	71	8	55	**Upper Q**	64
9	61	9	55	**Mode**	58
10	58	10	55	**Mean**	58
11	46	11	56	**St deviation**	8
12	59	12	57		
13	49	13	58		
14	62	14	58		
15	73	15	58		
16	64	16	59		
17	58	17	59		
18	43	18	59		
19	55	19	59		
20	59	20	61		
21	67	21	61		
22	61	22	62		
23	64	23	64		
24	52	24	64		
25	50	25	64		
26	47	26	67		
27	58	27	68		
28	72	28	71		
29	64	29	72		
30	56	30	73		

the column contains 30 observations. The middle value is therefore 58.5 beats per minute (b·min^{-1}). Since heart rate is measured in whole beats per minute, this value would normally be rounded up to 59 b·min^{-1}. The minimum and maximum values are located easily from the top and bottom values, respectively, in column 5, that is, 43 and 73 b·min^{-1}. The middle value is known as the **median**, and provides a measure of the central tendency of the data. By taking the minimum from the maximum value (i.e. 73 – 43 = 30 b·min^{-1}), a measure of the variation of the data is provided, which is known as the **range**.

By continuing to think about the number of observations, questions also arise about the location of proportions of the data about the median value. For example, it might be useful to know how far from the median the highest and lowest quarter (or quartile, Q) of the data reside. This value, known as the quartile range, is useful in further examining the spread of the data. So for the data in Table 8.3, the lower quartile (or 25 per cent of the observations) are determined as the observations ranked 1 – 7.5 in column 4. To determine the value corresponding to the 7.5 observation, the 7th and 8th observations are added, and then divided by 2, that is, (52 + 55)/2 = 53.5 b·min^{-1}. Again, the figure must be rounded up to the nearest whole heart rate (i.e. 54 b·min^{-1}). Since the median value is 59 b·min^{-1}, a quarter of the data reside 5 b·min^{-1} below the median. Likewise, the upper quarter of the data can also be determined easily from column 4, residing 5 b·min^{-1} above the median. This is because the 22.5 observation (i.e. highest 25 per cent of observations) are above 64 b·min^{-1}. The inter quartile range, which provides an insight into the spread of the data, is calculated by subtracting the lowest quartile cut-off value from the upper quartile cut-off value, that is, 64 – 54 = 10 b·min^{-1}. Another way of looking at this situation is that 50 per cent of the closest observations to the median range by 10 b·min^{-1}.

From column 4, it is also possible to determine the most frequently observed heart rate. This value is known as the **mode**, and provides a further measure of the central tendency of the data. From column 5, it is apparent that 59 b·min^{-1} was recorded on four occasions, which was more frequent than any other value. It is often easier to find the mode if a **histogram** of the data is produced. A histogram of the data is shown in Figure 8.2.

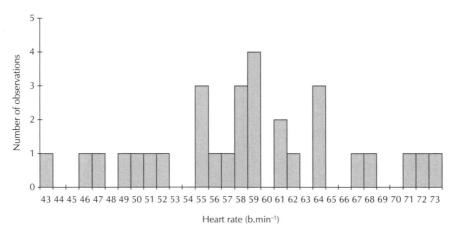

Figure 8.2 Histogram showing the frequency of observation of the range of heart rates

A histogram also provides us with a graphical representation of the distribution of the data (frequency distribution). The histogram reinforces the information presented above in a tabular form. For example, it is clearly shown that that a large proportion (i.e. at least 50 per cent) of the observations are between 54 and 64 b·min⁻¹.

All the measures of spread and central tendency of the data presented so far are suitable for description of ratio, interval and ordinal data. The mode is also suitable for a description of nominal data. With interval and ratio data, further tools are available to describe the centrality and spread of the data.

If all the data is added together and then divided by the number of observations, the **mean average** is determined (see Equation 8.1).

$$\text{Mean average } (\overline{x}) = \frac{\sum (x_1 + x_2 + ...)}{n} \qquad .. \qquad .. \qquad .. \qquad .. \qquad .. \qquad (8.1)$$

Where: $\overline{x}$ is the mean average;

$\sum$ is the sum of observations

x is an individual observation, where x_1 is observation 1, etc.

n is the number of observations

The mean provides a further measure of the centrality of the data, providing interval or ratio data is being described. For the data presented, the mean is determined by adding the heart rate values for all participants, and then dividing by the number of participants, giving a value of 58 b·min⁻¹. The advantage of the mean as a measure of central tendency is that all the observed values are taken into account in its determination, unlike the other measures of central tendency. The mean therefore provides a better average of the data in general, and is the preferred measure of central tendency.

At this point, it is worth comparing the three measures of central tendency determined for the heart rate data. From Table 8.3 it is clear that the median, mode and mean provide similar values of 59, 58 and 58 b·min⁻¹ respectively. Comparisons of these measures of central tendency provide a simple check of the pattern of distribution of the data, which is important prior to applying an inferential data analysis technique. Inferential data analysis assumes that the data are **normally distributed** (see Figure 8.4). A distribution is considered to be 'normal' when the data are distributed evenly about a central point. A visual inspection of the histogram can usually confirm that the data are normally distributed. A further check is to ascertain whether the central points agree, as determined by the three methods of determining central tendency. If the mean, median and mode all produce similar values, then the data are regarded as being normally distributed.

With interval and ratio data, it is also possible to develop further information regarding the spread of the data about the central value, in addition to the range and the quartile range. The **mean absolute deviation** (MAD) is one such measure of the spread of the data. To determine the MAD, the difference between each individual observation and the mean is determined, and then these differences are expressed as positive values (see Table 8.4). The sum of the differences is then determined. If the differences were expressed as positive and negative values, rather than just positive values, the differences would cancel each other out when summed together. Finally, the sum of the positive difference values is divided by the number of observations (see Equation 8.2).

$$\text{Mean absolute deviation (MAD)} = \frac{\sum (|\bar{x} - x_i|)}{n} \qquad .. \qquad .. \qquad .. \qquad (8.2)$$

Where: x_i is each individual observation

Table 8.4 shows that the mean absolute deviation is 6 b·min^{-1} for the chosen example. The higher the MAD, the greater the spread of the data.

The **variance** is another measure of the spread of the data, and is determined by finding the difference between the mean and each individual observation. Each difference value is then squared. The average of all the squared difference values is then determined by adding together all the squared differences and dividing by the number of observations (see Equation 8.3).

$$\text{Variance} = \frac{\sum (\bar{x} - x_i)^2}{n} \qquad .. \qquad .. \qquad .. \qquad .. \qquad .. \qquad .. \qquad (8.3)$$

The process for determining the variance is shown in Table 8.4, and results in a value for the variance of 56. A value known as the **standard deviation** (SD) may then be determined by taking the square root of the variance value, which results in a value of 7 b·min^{-1} (see Equation 8.4). Both the variance and the SD value are used to describe the degree of spread of the data.

$$\text{Standard deviation (SD)} = \sqrt{\frac{\sum (\bar{x} - x_i)^2}{n}} \qquad .. \qquad .. \qquad .. \qquad .. \qquad (8.4)$$

In order to understand more fully the significance of the SD, it is sometimes useful to graphically represent the tabulated information. Figure 8.3 shows lines representing one SD from the mean and two SDs from the mean in relation to the mean average of the individual observations, and the individual observations themselves. The lines on the graph illustrating one SD from the mean provide markers between which 67 per cent of observations from the sample lie. The lines on the graph representing two SDs from the mean provide markers between which 95 per cent of observations from the sample lie. The lines on the graph representing one and two SDs, are referred to as the 67 per cent

132

Table 8.4 Calculation of variance, standard deviation and mean absolute deviation based upon resting heart rate (HR, beats·min⁻¹) from 30 female participants

HR	$\bar{X}$	$\bar{X} - X_i$	$(\bar{X} - X_i)^2$	$\sqrt{(\bar{X} - X_i)^2}$	Descriptive statistics
59	58	−1	1	1	Absolute deviation: 173
68	58	−10	100	10	Mean absolute deviation: 6
55	58	3	9	3	Variance: 56
57	58	1	1	1	Standard deviation: 7
51	58	7	49	7	
59	58	−1	1	1	
55	58	3	9	3	
71	58	−13	169	13	
61	58	−3	9	3	
58	58	0	0	0	
46	58	12	144	12	
59	58	−1	1	1	
49	58	9	81	9	
62	58	−4	16	4	
73	58	−15	225	15	
64	58	−6	36	6	
58	58	0	0	0	
43	58	15	225	15	
55	58	3	9	3	
59	58	−1	1	1	
67	58	−9	81	9	
61	58	−3	9	3	
64	58	−6	36	6	
52	58	6	36	6	
50	58	8	64	8	
47	58	11	121	11	
58	58	0	0	0	
72	58	−14	196	14	
64	58	−6	36	6	
56	58	2	4	2	

and 95 per cent confidence intervals respectively. The SD values are normally written in text by initially stating the mean average (i.e. 56 b·min⁻¹ in this example) plus or minus the SD (i.e. $\bar{X} \pm$ SD is 56 ± 7 b·min⁻¹).

The SD is sometimes expressed in relation to the mean, resulting in a value known as the **coefficient of variation** (CV). To calculate the CV, the SD is divided by the mean, and then the answer is multiplied by 100. By multiplying by 100, the answer is expressed in the form of a percentage (%) (see Equation 8.5).

$$\text{Coefficient of variation (CV) (\%)} = \left(\frac{\sqrt{(\bar{x} - x_i)} / n}{\bar{x}} \right) \times 100 \qquad .. \qquad .. \qquad (8.5)$$

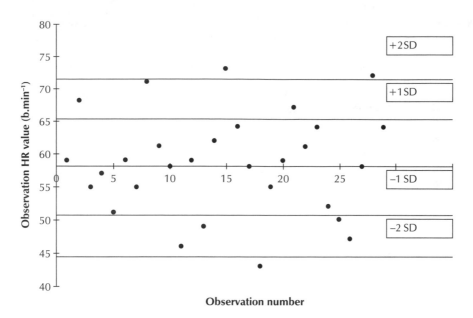

Figure 8.3 Graphical representation of standard deviation in relation to individual heart rate observations

The CV is a standardised measure of the variation, and is therefore very useful when comparing the variation between two sets of data. From the heart rate data considered in the earlier examples, the coefficient of variation is 12.5 per cent (i.e. (7/56) $\times$ 100). For example, if the core temperature of the female subjects in our sample was also measured, in addition to heart rate, it would be possible to compare the amount of standardised variation in both measures by using the CV.

At this point it should be clarified that although the SD and MAD both provide a measure of spread for the sample under consideration, the SD is known as a more reliable representation of the spread of the population data from which the sample was taken. It is for this reason that the SD is more widely used to illustrate the spread of data within an investigation.

The importance of the relationship between a sample, and the population from which the sample was taken, becomes more apparent as we move on to drawing inferences from findings. When we need to infer something from the data, the population characteristics are always used as the reference point. Although a sample of only 30 participants were selected from the population in the earlier example, it is known that with that many participants the descriptive characteristics of the sample will be similar to those of the population providing representative sampling has taken place.

scientific transferable skills

INFERENCES FROM FINDINGS

When inferences are drawn from data sets, relationships or differences are usually determined. However, the **population** from which the sample was derived is always taken as the reference point, and findings from the sample are applied to the population. It is now interesting to see how particular questions are addressed.

To check whether a single observation belongs to a population, information is required about the mean and SD of the population. It is then necessary to examine the difference between the population mean and the observation, in relation to the population SD. It is already known that if an observation is less than the value of one SD from the mean of the population, it can be stated with confidence that the observation is not from another population. If the observation is less than two SD from the population mean, it can still be stated with confidence that the observation is not from another population. However, if the observation falls outside the value of the second SD away from the population mean, it is likely that the observed value is not from the population. In fact, it can be stated with 95 per cent confidence that the observed value is from another population. If the observation falls outside the value of the third SD away from the population mean, it can be stated with 99 per cent confidence that the observed value is not from the population. It is sometimes easier to understand the concept of **confidence intervals** if a graphical representation of the population under consideration is provided (Figure 8.4).

Figure 8.4 represents what is known as a standard normal curve, which is the curve produced when, for standardised data, the standard deviation number is plotted on the x-axis in relation to the position of the mean. Earlier, it was mentioned that to ascertain whether an observation is from a population, the difference between the value of the observation and the population mean should be determined in relation to the population SD. For example, if the observation falls outside the second standard deviation ($\pm$ 2 SD in Figure 8.4), it is with 95 per cent confidence that it can be stated that the observed value is not from the population.

In the area constrained below the curve, 67 per cent of observations reside between $\pm$ 1 SD, 95 per cent of the observations reside between $\pm$ 2 SD, and 99 per cent of the observations reside between $\pm$ 3 SD. Although 67 per cent, 95 per cent, and 99 per cent confidence intervals have only been mentioned so far, it is possible to find a specific confidence level for any observation. Such confidence levels are determined by relating the standardised observed value to the standardised normal curve (Figure 8.4). Tables of values have been produced for this purpose. The value obtained from such tables simply relates to the proportion of the curve below or above the standardised value respectively.

It is sometimes possible to specify that if the observed value is not from the population, it is from a population with a greater mean average, or from a population with a lesser mean average. If this is the case, only half of the curve is relevant for comparative purposes. For example, if it was to be stated with confidence that the observed value was either from the population under consideration, or a population with a greater mean average, only

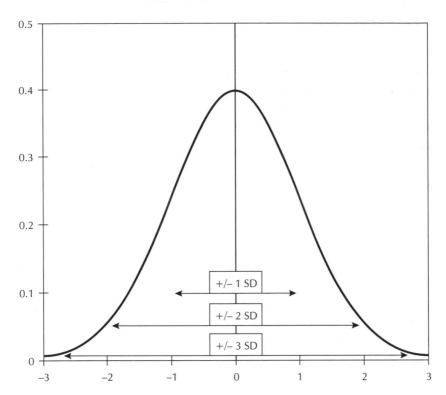

Figure 8.4 Graphical representation of a standard normal curve

the right-hand side of the curve would be of relevance. In that case, 5 per cent of the populations observations are to the right of the 95 per cent confidence interval on the right-hand side of the curve. In contrast, when the whole curve was considered, because a directional effect could not be specified, only 2.5 per cent of the populations observed values would be contained in the same area. Tests to evaluate whether an observed value is from a different population are known as one tailed if the direction of the alternative population can be specified, and two tailed if the direction of the alternative population cannot be specified.

Although the value of a single observation in relation to a known population has been considered, a sample in relation to a population could also be considered, to establish whether the sample is from the population. Consideration could also be given to whether two samples come from the same population. The only difference when a sample is considered, rather than an individual observation, is that a population made up of several samples is discussed, rather than several individual observations. Each sample is assumed to have a similar SD, but a different mean value. Instead of considering the population SD, the equivalent value is known as the **standard error of the mean** (SEM). So rather than a SD of observed values within a population, a standard error of sample means is considered. In the same way that the difference between an individual observed value was compared to the population mean relative to the SD, the sample mean is compared to the population mean in relation to the SEM.

As well as looking for differences between data sets, the relationships between data sets often require consideration. For example, is there a relationship between the number of years spent in training and the performance in a particular athletic event? Questions regarding performance and the relationship between another variable (i.e. training years in this example) are frequently asked in the study of exercise and sport. Although a non-linear relationship sometimes exists between two variables in the study of exercise and sport, only linear relationships will be considered here. Linear models are used to describe linear relationships. Often, the first step in establishing whether a relationship exists between two variables is to produce a **scatter plot** as shown in Figure 8.5, which was produced from the data presented in columns 1 and 5 in Table 8.5. Such visual presentation of data is often required in order to observe a relationship between two variables.

From the scatter plot (Figure 8.5) it is clear that a relationship does exist between the number of years spent training and the athletes' 100 m sprint time. In fact, the relationship is what is referred to as being negative, where one variable gets smaller as another gets larger. To see whether a relationship is negative or positive, imagine a line through the middle of the data: a line of best fit. The slope of that line illustrates whether the data is negatively or positively related. In the case of the data presented in Figure 8.5, performance time is getting smaller as the number of years spent training gets larger. A negative relationship is always viewed as a negative slope on a scatter plot.

Although the scatter plot in Figure 8.5 seems to show a relationship, it is often necessary to test the strength of the relationship. The strength of the relationship is viewed graphically by how close the data points are to the line of best fit. The strength of the relationship can also be quantified, by what is referred to as the **correlation coefficient** (r). In Table 8.5, the variety of columns, in addition to the columns for the training duration (in years) and the 100 m sprint time (in seconds), are used in the calculation of r. The columns in the table provide the observed values (column 1 and 5 respectively), the mean average of the observed values (2 and 6 respectively), the differences between the mean average and the observed values (3 and 7 respectively), the square of the differences (4 and 8 respectively), and the product of the observed values (column 9). The r– value is calculated by first determining the sum of the products of the observed values, and then dividing this value by the square root of the product of the sum of squares for both variables (see Equation 8.6).

$$\text{Correlation coefficient (r)} = \frac{SP}{\sqrt{SS_x SS_y}} \quad .. \quad .. \quad .. \quad .. \tag{8.6}$$

Where: $SP = \sum XY - \dfrac{(\sum X)(\sum Y)}{n}$

$$SS_x = \Sigma\, X^2 - \frac{(\Sigma\, X)^2}{n}$$

$$SS_y = \Sigma\, Y^2 - \frac{(\Sigma\, Y)^2}{n}$$

where: SP =   Sum of products

      SS_x =   Sum of squares for x-variable

      Ss_y =   Sum of squares for y-variable

The r– value for the data in the present example is –0.76, indicating a negative relationship between number of years training and performance in the 100 m sprint.

In addition to drawing inferences about differences between variables, inferences can also be drawn about the strength of a relationship between variables. The confidence in such inferences can also be determined. The correlation coefficient (r) from a sample can be compared with a population normal distribution of r– values to establish whether the r– value is derived from the population or not. Again, the confidence level with which the claim is made can take on a range of values. So it is possible to ascertain both the strength of a relationship and whether the relationship was from a particular population. It is vitally important to note at this point that the strength of a relationship and the significance of the relationship provide no insight into whether the relationship between the variables is causal. A causal relationship is one in which the change in one variable explains the change in the other variable.

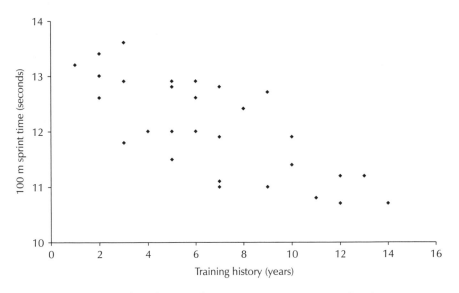

Figure 8.5 Scatter plot of years of training against 100 m sprint time

scientific transferable skills

Table 8.5 Calculation of derived values based upon training duration (years) and performance times (seconds) of male 100 m sprinters

Years training	$\bar{X}$	$\bar{X} - X_i$	$(\bar{X} - X_i)^2$	Performance time (s)	$\bar{Y}$	$\bar{Y} - Y_i$	$(\bar{Y} - Y_i)^2$	$X_i \cdot Y_i$
2	7	5	25	13.4	12.1	−1.3	1.7	−6.5
10	7	−3	9	11.9	12.1	0.2	0.0	−0.6
12	7	−5	25	10.7	12.1	1.4	2.0	−7
6	7	1	1	12.9	12.1	−0.8	0.6	−0.8
4	7	3	9	12	12.1	0.1	0.0	0.3
1	7	6	36	13.2	12.1	−1.1	1.2	−6.6
8	7	−1	1	12.4	12.1	−0.3	0.1	0.3
9	7	−2	4	12.7	12.1	−0.6	0.4	1.2
5	7	2	4	12	12.1	0.1	0.0	0.2
7	7	0	0	12.8	12.1	−0.7	0.5	0
3	7	4	16	13.6	12.1	−1.5	2.3	−6
2	7	5	25	13	12.1	−0.9	0.8	−4.5
1	7	6	36	13.2	12.1	−1.1	1.2	−6.6
14	7	−7	49	10.7	12.1	1.4	2.0	−9.8
12	7	−5	25	11.2	12.1	0.9	0.8	−4.5
3	7	4	16	11.8	12.1	0.3	0.1	1.2
7	7	0	0	11.9	12.1	0.2	0.0	0
5	7	2	4	11.5	12.1	0.6	0.4	1.2
7	7	0	0	11.1	12.1	1	1.0	0
9	7	−2	4	11	12.1	1.1	1.2	−2.2
6	7	1	1	12.6	12.1	−0.5	0.3	−0.5
5	7	2	4	12.9	12.1	−0.8	0.6	−1.6
11	7	−4	16	10.8	12.1	1.3	1.7	−5.2
13	7	−6	36	11.2	12.1	0.9	0.8	−5.4
10	7	−3	9	11.4	12.1	0.7	0.5	−2.1
5	7	2	4	12.8	12.1	−0.7	0.5	−1.4
3	7	4	16	12.9	12.1	−0.8	0.6	−3.2
6	7	1	1	12	12.1	0.1	0.0	0.1
7	7	0	0	11	12.1	1.1	1.2	0
2	7	5	25	12.6	12.1	−0.5	0.3	−2.5

Mean			Sum	Mean			Sum	Sum
7			401	12.1			22.7	−72.5

CHOOSING AN APPROPRIATE STATISTICAL TEST

In addition to information on the basic concepts underlying interval and ratio data analysis, it is also necessary to provide information on the range of appropriate data analysis tools available. With knowledge of the concepts underlying statistical treatment of data, an informed decision can be made about the most appropriate test for a particular purpose. However, it is not essential to understand how to perform each statistical test by hand, particularly as such tests are normally performed with the help of purpose-designed statistical packages.

A range of tests are available for determination of differences between samples. The following tests are suitable for a variety of situations when the data are measured on an interval or ratio scale.

The independent t-test is used to determine differences between two samples when the samples do not include the same participants. It is therefore not possible to pair the data for analysis, so the descriptive characteristics of the complete samples are used in the analysis. Whether a one-tailed or two-tailed test is used, will depend on the hypothesis being tested. Earlier in the chapter it was mentioned that if the direction of change is stated in the hypothesis, a one-tailed test should be used. At the same level of significance, the choice of a one-tailed test will increase the chance of finding a difference if one exists. A one-tailed test is, therefore, considered a more powerful test (see section on statistical power, p. 141).

The related t-test is used to determine differences between two samples when the samples include the same participants. Such an experimental design is referred to as being repeated measures. For analysis, the data are treated as paired data, since the same participants appear in both samples. The related t-test is sometimes referred to as a paired t-test. A related t-test is considered to be more powerful than an independent t-test. Again, with this type of test, a one or two-tailed test should be chosen, depending upon the wording of the hypotheses.

The independent measures analysis of variance is used to determine differences between two or more samples, when the samples include different participants. Again, it is not possible to pair the data in this situation, so whole sample characteristics are used in the analysis. Since two or more samples are compared with this type of test, a further test is necessary to determine the location of any significant differences, if any should arise. Such tests are known as **post-hoc** tests, and are named after their inventor, for example, Tukey, Scheffé, Newman-Keuls.

The repeated measures analysis of variance is used to determine differences between two or more samples, when the samples include the same participants, that is, paired data. As with a related t-test, a repeated measures analysis of variance is more powerful than an independent measures analysis of variance. Again, a post-hoc test must be used to locate any differences demonstrated with the analysis of variance.

It is important to note that the tests mentioned above should only be used when the data conform to certain standards. These prerequisites include interval or ratio data, which are normally distributed. If the data are not normally distributed, inferences may still be drawn by employing other tests which are normally used with ordinal data. In this situation, the independent t-test can be replaced by the Mann-Whitney test, the related t-test by the Wilcoxon test, the independent measures analysis of variance by the Kruskal-Wallis test, and the repeated measures analysis of variance by the Friedman test.

STATISTICAL ERRORS AND POWER

Statistical errors occur when the incorrect hypothesis is accepted/rejected based on the available data (see Figure 8.6). For example, if the alternative hypothesis is accepted, but the null hypothesis should have been accepted, this is known as a type I statistical error. In other words, if a difference is claimed between two sets of data when there is no difference, a type I statistical error has been made. Alternatively, if the null hypothesis is accepted, but the alternative hypothesis should have been accepted, this is known as a type II statistical error. In other words, if it is claimed that no difference exists between data sets when a difference does exist, a type II statistical error has been made.

So what factors lead to these inappropriate conclusions? The answer to this question is best viewed graphically. From Figure 8.7 it is observed that the chosen confidence level (alpha level) defines the alpha (α) area under the left curve. The beta (β) area is then the area to the left of the α level constrained by the right curve. The β area is the proportion of the right curve that passes the predefined α level.

By relating the α and β areas to hypothesis testing, it is possible to see how statistical errors are made, and more importantly how statistical errors may be prevented. If the chosen α level is too relaxed, thereby resulting in a large α area, the chances are increased of concluding that there is a difference, when no difference is actually present. So a relaxed α level may result in a type I statistical error. Likewise, if the β area is too large, there is an increased chance of concluding that there is no difference, when a difference is actually present. A β level is never set prior to performing a statistical test however, so this situation must be examined in a slightly different way.

Rather than specify that the β area must be as small as possible, the area to the right of the α level which is constrained under the right curve can be maintained as large as possible. This area is quantified as being the area under one whole curve minus β (i.e. $1 - \beta$), and is also referred to as the statistical power of the test of differences. So the statistical power of a test is defined as the area $1 - \beta$. Therefore, rather than talk about the β level, the statistical power can be considered. The statistical power of the test is what influences the chance of making a type II statistical error; the larger the statistical power, the smaller the chance of making a type II statistical error.

	Null hypothesis is true (e.g. no difference)	Null hypothesis is false (e.g. difference)
Null hypothesis accepted	Correct decision	Incorrect decision (Type II error)
Null hypothesis rejected	Incorrect decision (Type I error)	Correct decision

Figure 8.6 Evaluation of statistical errors

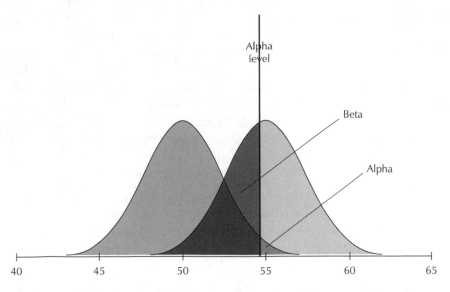

Figure 8.7 Area of normal distributions defined as alpha (α) and beta (β)

Whilst the size of the alpha level may be specified prior to performing a statistical test, it is not so simple to change the power (1 – β). Three factors influence the power:

1. The number of participants (n).
2. The effect size (γ) of the treatment.
3. The alpha (α) level.

The more participants in a study, the greater the power. This is the case because as the participant number is increased, the shape of the normal distribution curve changes, effectively becoming narrower. A narrower curve results from less variation about the mean, so less overlap is likely between curves when comparing samples.

The effect size (usually denoted by Greek symbol gamma: γ) is the difference between the means in relation to the variation in the data (Equation 8.7).

$$\text{Effect size } (\gamma) = \frac{\overline{X}_1 - \overline{X}_2}{\text{SD}} \qquad .. \qquad .. \qquad .. \qquad .. \qquad .. \qquad .. \qquad (8.7)$$

If the difference between the means is large in relation to the variation in the data, the effect size (γ) will be large, which will increase the power. Similarly, if the variation in the data is reduced, the effect size (γ) will be increased, thereby increasing the power. Both an increase in the difference between means and a decrease in the variation about the means lead to less overlap between the normal distribution curves when comparing samples.

The more relaxed the α level, the greater the power. However, by increasing power through relaxation of the α level, the chance of making a type I error is increased. By relaxing the α level, the overlap between the curves is not reduced. This would, therefore, be the least desirable way to increase the power of the test. The most desirable methods involve an increase in participant numbers (n) and/or effect size (γ), without decreasing the α level. In this way, the chances of making both a type II and a type I error are minimised.

Although it is not necessary to know the intricacies of the calculation of statistical power, it is useful to have an idea of the factors which influence statistical power. With this knowledge, it is possible to appropriately interpret outcomes from published studies. For example, a study that found no statistical difference between two groups, but only had five subjects in each group, might usefully be investigated further in terms of the power to detect a difference. In this example, the power may be found to be low, in which case the alternative hypothesis cannot be rejected with confidence. Knowledge of statistical errors is also required when designing experiments. Often investigators will perform prospective power analysis to establish the required subject numbers.

ASSESSING RELIABILITY AND VALIDITY

An investigator should ensure that measurements in exercise and sport are both reliable and valid. Since measurements are usually objective in experimental investigations in exercise and sport, inter-investigator reliability is usually good. Inter-investigator reliability will usually be good if direct measurements are taken from equipment with no requirement for interpretation, providing equipment is properly calibrated. Inter-investigator reliability may be investigated by asking two or more investigators to make the same measurement under identical conditions. If the measurement or data collection technique is complicated, or requires skills developed through training, inter-investigator reliability may be poorer.

With a stable response from a participant, and using identical equipment and data collection techniques for repeat measurements, it is possible to investigate the reliability of the measurement. A number of repeat measurements should be made and then the data are assessed to determine the mean average and standard deviation; based on these values the coefficient of variation may be determined (i.e. (mean/SD) $\times$ 100). The acceptable reliability will be based on the effect size in a study. For example, if it is expected that a 9 per cent effect will be observed, a coefficient of variation of 5 per cent may be acceptable; however, if a 2 per cent effect is expected, a coefficient of variation of as little as 0.5 per cent may be required. Alternative approaches to determine reliability are available that require repeat measurements on several participants (see Norton et al., 2000).

Data cannot be valid if they are not reliable; the reason being that it is impossible to make a valid measurement if the measurement cannot be shown to produce the same results time and time again under the same conditions. Normally, tests of validity compare the outcome of one measurement approach with another measurement approach to determine if the outcomes from the two approaches agree. Normally one measurement approach is considered to be the criterion (or gold standard) approach. The extent to which the outcomes of the alternative approach agree with the outcomes of the criterion approach determines the degree of validity of the alternative measurement approach.

Although difference tests have traditionally been used to test for validity, it is now well acknowledged that such an approach is rather crude. More commonly, the relationship between outcomes from two measurement approaches is used to determine validity. If the correlation between the two measurements is strong, and it is shown that the two samples are significantly similar, the alternative measurement is said to be valid in relation to the criterion measurement. A range of limitations have been identified with this method of assessment of validity, and further information is provided by Bland and Altman (1986).

SELF-TEST

1. Describe the scientific approach to experimental investigations.
2. Present an example of a null hypothesis and an alternative hypothesis.
3. How are hypotheses and data analysis related?
4. What are the two key points to consider when designing experiments?
5. Outline the four types of data and their defining characteristics.
6. Which of the four types of data are categorical and which are continuous?
7. What are the two types of inferential data analysis?
8. List three measures of central tendency.
9. List five measures of spread.
10. Which measure of central tendency takes account of all the observed values?
11. Which measure of central tendency is suitable for use with categorical data?
12. Which measures of spread are suitable for use with continuous data only?
13. What is the difference between the standard deviation and the standard error of the mean?
14. Which measure of central tendency and spread is used to determine the coefficient of variation?
15. How is a distribution of data simply tested for normality?
16. What statistic is used to compare values relative to their respective populations?
17. What is the difference between a one- and two-tailed test?
18. How are hypotheses related to one- and two-tailed tests?

19. What is a confidence interval?

20. How are confidence intervals used in statistical tests?

21. How are confidence intervals related to the chance of making a type I error?

22. Show graphically how the power of a test is determined.

23. Which method is commonly used to determine the validity of a measurement?

24. Explain why a measurement cannot be valid if it is not reliable.

25. Describe inter-investigator reliability, and explain how it may be improved.

CONCLUSION

In experimental investigations, data analysis cannot be discussed in isolation from study design and hypothesis testing. Studies should not be designed without giving considerable thought to the required data analysis. Additionally, hypotheses are tested through appropriate data analysis, and conclusions may be misleading if inappropriate data analysis is performed. Particular attention must be given to the type of data to be analysed; specifically whether the data is nominal, ordinal, interval or ratio level. Often data analysis is broadly divided into descriptive and inferential analysis. Descriptive analysis allows information to be derived from a set of data quickly. Inferential analysis allows claims to be made about the sample of data in relation to a population or another sample. Inferences are possible about either the differences between samples, or the relationship between samples. Such claims are then used in order to accept or reject hypotheses with a degree of confidence. The confidence interval is set by the investigator prior to the study, and often a 95 per cent confidence interval is selected. The chance of making a type I statistical error is then small (i.e. 5 per cent). The chance of making a type II statistical error is assessed through the power of the statistical test, and it is normally advised to increase this figure to 80 per cent (i.e. 20 per cent chance of making a type II error). The reliability and validity of measurement approaches may also be determined using inferential data analysis. The importance of knowledge of data analysis cannot be over emphasised for a student of exercise and sport.

KEY POINTS

- Experimental investigation is based upon the formation of testable hypotheses.
- Hypotheses are tested through inferential data analysis.
- Data can be categorised as being **one** of four types: nominal, ordinal, interval **or** ratio.

- Descriptive data analysis should present required information to an observer in an easily accessible form.
- Measures of central tendency and spread are fundamental to descriptive data analysis.
- Many inferential statistical tests are dependent upon normally distributed data.
- When a direction of change is hypothesised, a one-tailed test should be used.
- A type I statistical error is when a difference is accepted, although no difference actually exists.
- A type II statistical error is when no difference is accepted, although a difference actually exists.
- Measurements implemented in scientific investigations should be both reliable and valid.

BIBLIOGRAPHY

Bland, J.M. and Altman, D.G. (1986) Statistical methods for assessing agreement between two methods of clinical measurement. *Lancet*, 1: 307–310.

Derzin, N.K. and Lincoln, Y.S. (1994) *Handbook of Qualitative Research*. London: Sage.

Derzin, N.K. and Lincoln, Y.S. (1998) *Collecting and Interpreting Qualitative Materials*. London: Sage.

Field, A. (2005) *Discovering Statistics Using SPSS*. London: Sage.

Gratton, C. and Jones, I. (2004) *Research Methods for Sport Studies*. London: Routledge.

Hinton, P.R. (1995) *Statistics Explained: A Guide for Social Science Students*. London: Routledge.

Howell, D.C. (1997) *Statistical Methods for Psychology*. Belmont: Wadsworth.

Kreider, R.B., Miller, G.W., Williams, M.H., Somma, C.T. and Nasser, T.A. (1990) Effects of phosphate loading on oxygen uptake, ventilatory anaerobic threshold, and run performance. *Medicine and Science in Sport and Exercise*, 22 (2): 250–256.

Kuzma, J.W. and Bohnenblust, S.E. (2001) *Basic Statistics for the Health Sciences*, 4th edition. London: McGraw-Hill.

Norton, K., Marfell-Jones, M., Whittingham, N., Kerr, D., Carter, L., Saddington, K. and Gore, C. (2000) Anthropometric assessment protocols. In C.J. Gore (ed.), *Physiological Tests for Elite Athletes*. Leeds: Human Kinetics, pp. 83–85.

Patton, M.Q. (1980) *Qualitative Evaluation Methods*. Beverly Hills, CA: Sage.

Silverman, D. (1993) *Interpreting Qualitative Research*. London: Sage.

Vincent, W.J. (1995) *Statistics in Kinesiology*. Champaign, IL: Human Kinetics.

Williams, C. and Wragg, C. (2004) *Data Analysis and Research for Sport and Exercise Science*. London: Routledge.

FURTHER READING

Atkinson, G. and Nevill, A.M. (1998) Statistical methods for assessing measurement error (reliability) in variables relevant to sports medicine. *Sports Medicine*, 26 (4): 217–238.

Hopkins, W.G. (2000) Measures of reliability in sports medicine and science. *Sports Medicine*, 30 (1): 1–15.

Hyllegard, R., Mood, D.P. and Morrow, J.R. (1996) *Interpreting Research in Sport and Exercise Science*. St Louis, MI: Mosby-Year Book.

Jackson, A.S. (1989). Application of regression analysis to exercise science. In M.J. Safrit and T.M. Wood (eds), *Measurement Concepts in Physical Education and Exercise Science*. Leeds: Human Kinetics, pp. 181–205.

Oliver, J., Armstrong, N. and Williams, C.A. (2007) Reliability and validity of a soccer-specific test of prolonged repeated-sprint ability. *International Journal of Sports Physiology and Performance*, 2: 137–149.

CHAPTER NINE

NUMERICAL CALCULATIONS

AIMS OF THE CHAPTER

This chapter aims to provide an understanding of the numerical calculations which are fundamental to the theories underpinning exercise and sport. After reading this chapter, you should be able to:

■ Understand calculation methods used in exercise and sport.
■ Utilise the calculation methods to determine variables of interest in exercise and sport.
■ Provide examples of when the methods are required within the study of exercise and sport.

INTRODUCTION

When studying exercise and sport, it is important to have a good knowledge of the numerical methods which are critical for understanding key theories. The ability to do this not only provides a better understanding but also allows you to calculate variables of interest. The majority of the methods discussed in this chapter are those used in the areas of biomechanics and physiology.

The use of numerical calculations in the study of exercise and sport is made clear through examples in which they are utilised to determine variables of interest, such as force and acceleration.

TRIGONOMETRY

When applying mathematics to mechanical systems such as the human body, you will often use variables such as mass, distance and time. These variables are known as **scalars** and they are described by their quantity or magnitude, given by a number, and the appropriate unit. Some variables, however, cannot simply be characterised by a number. These variables also require a direction. A **vector** is defined as any variable which is completely specified by a scalar magnitude and a direction. How the direction of any vector is defined needs to be specified (e.g. by an angle taken from the horizontal). Examples of vectors are displacement, velocity, acceleration and force. Displacement can be defined as a distance with a direction and similarly velocity can be defined as speed with a direction.

If a vector, such as displacement, is defined by its horizontal and vertical components both the magnitude and the direction of the displacement vector can be determined by resolving the two components. In Figure 9.1, a and b are the horizontal and vertical components respectively, c is the resultant displacement vector and θ (theta) defines the direction of vector c which is the angle between the horizontal a and the resultant displacement vector c.

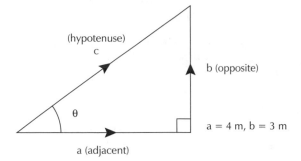

Figure 9.1 A right-angled triangle

(hypotenuse)
c

b (opposite)

θ

a = 4 m, b = 3 m

a (adjacent)

Magnitude

In Figure 9.1 you can find the magnitude of the resultant displacement vector c using Pythagoras' Theorem:

$$a^2 + b^2 = c^2 \qquad .. \qquad .. \qquad .. \qquad .. \qquad .. \qquad .. \qquad .. \qquad .. \qquad (9.1)$$

Therefore;

$$c = \sqrt{a^2 + b^2}$$

$$c = \sqrt{4^2 + 3^2}$$

$$c = \sqrt{16 + 9}$$

$$c = \sqrt{25}$$

$$c = 5 \text{ m}$$

Note: the magnitude of the resultant vector is always larger than both its horizontal and vertical components.

Direction

The three basic trigonometric functions of a right-angled triangle (see Figure 9.1 for definition of sides and angles) are:

$$\sin \theta = \frac{b}{c} = \frac{\text{opposite}}{\text{hypotenuse}} \qquad .. \qquad .. \qquad .. \qquad .. \qquad .. \qquad .. \qquad (9.2.1)$$

$$\cos \theta = \frac{a}{c} = \frac{\text{adjacent}}{\text{hypotenuse}} \qquad .. \qquad .. \qquad .. \qquad .. \qquad .. \qquad .. \qquad (9.2.2)$$

$$\tan \theta = \frac{b}{a} = \frac{\text{opposite}}{\text{adjacent}} \qquad \qquad \qquad \qquad \qquad \qquad (9.2.3)$$

Opposite is the length of the side of the triangle opposite the angle θ, adjacent is the length of the side of the triangle between the angle θ and the right angle and hypotenuse is the length of the side of the triangle opposite the right angle. It might be helpful to use the acronym SOHCAHTOA (Sine=Opposite/Hypotenuse, Cosine=Adjacent/Hypotenuse, Tan=Opposite/Adjacent) to remember the functions 9.2.1–9.2.3.

To calculate the direction of the displacement vector, θ (defined as the angle from the horizontal), any of the three equations from above can be used since a, b and c (the lengths of all sides of the triangle) are all known.

Using equation (9.2.3):

$$\tan \theta = \frac{b}{a} = \frac{3}{4} = 0.75$$

$$\theta = \tan^{-1}(0.75)$$

$$\theta = 36.9°$$

This means that the tangent of the angle 36.9° is equal to 0.75. In this example, θ was calculated using the **inverse (inv)** and **tangent (tan)** functions on a calculator.

Force vectors

It is often useful to resolve a force vector into components in order to calculate the magnitude of a force acting in a particular direction. It is sometimes necessary to find components horizontally or vertically (e.g. when determining projectile motion), while at other times it is more useful to find the components parallel to and at right angles to a given plane (e.g. when a object is travelling on an inclined surface). The component of a force in any direction is the product of the magnitude of the force and the cosine of the angle between the force and the required direction. The component of a force in a direction perpendicular to that force is zero.

Example
If a skier of mass 75 kg is skiing down a mountain at an incline of 30° to the horizontal, what is the magnitude of the force acting in the direction of travel (assuming no friction)?

The force, R which is acting at 90° (perpendicular) to the direction of travel is known as the **reaction force**. The component of the reaction force in the direction of travel is therefore zero. The only force which will produce a force in the direction of travel is the body weight (W). The mass of any object/body is measured in kilograms (kg). People often refer to this quantity as the weight of the object/body. However, body weight is measured in newtons (N), as it is a **force**, and is equal to the mass of the object/body multiplied by the acceleration caused by gravity (9.81 m·s^{-2}) (Hay, 1993). As force is a vector, all forces have a direction in which they act. Body weight is an unusual force in that it always acts in the same direction, which is downwards towards the centre of the Earth.

STOP AND THINK

How do an astronaut's mass and weight vary as they get closer to the moon?

When an athlete is standing in a stationary vertical position, which force opposes the body weight in order to keep the athlete on the surface on which they are standing?

The sum of the angles in a right-angled triangle is always equal to 180°. Therefore, in Figure 9.2, the angle between the force (W) and the direction of travel (the direction of F) is equal to 60°.

Calculation of the magnitude of force, F, acting in the direction of travel:

$F = W \times \cos (60)$

$F = (\text{mass} \times \text{acceleration due to gravity}) \times \cos (60)$

$F = (75 \text{ kg} \times 9.81 \text{ m·s}^{-2}) \times \cos (60)$

$F = 368 \text{ N}$

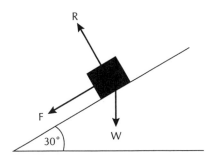

Figure 9.2 Resolving force components

KINEMATICS OF A BODY

Kinematics is the study of the motion of a body (defined as an object with a mass). This includes the displacement, velocity and acceleration of the body as well as the path it follows. The kinematics of a body contain no reference to either force or mass.

If a body travels with a constant acceleration (a) for a given time interval (t), then its velocity will change from its initial velocity (u) to its final velocity (v) whilst it travels a displacement (s). If you know any three of these five variables, you can calculate the remaining two using a set of equations known as the equations of constant acceleration. For the acceleration to be constant, and therefore for the equations of constant acceleration to be used, the body must either be in a vacuum or in flight. Gravity acts on a body when in flight by vertically accelerating it at a rate of 9.81 m·s^{-2} towards the centre of the Earth (Hay, 1993). There is no acceleration in the horizontal direction.

Equations of constant acceleration

If a body's velocity changes from u to v in t seconds, its acceleration over t is:

$$\text{acceleration} = \frac{\text{change in velocity}}{\text{time taken for change}}$$

$$a = \frac{v - u}{t}$$

By re-arranging this equation, the final velocity of the body at the end of the time period t can be determined:

$$a.t = v - u$$

Therefore:

$$v = u + a{\cdot}t \quad .. \qquad .. \qquad .. \qquad .. \qquad .. \qquad .. \qquad .. \qquad .. \qquad (9.3.1)$$

(For rearranging equations see pp. 163–4.)

From Equation 9.3.1 the other three equations of constant acceleration can be derived and are as follows:

$$s = \frac{1}{2}(u + v){\cdot}t \quad .. \qquad .. \qquad .. \qquad .. \qquad .. \qquad .. \qquad .. \qquad .. \qquad (9.3.2)$$

$$s = u.t + \frac{1}{2}a{\cdot}t^2 \quad .. \quad .. \quad .. \quad .. \quad .. \quad .. \quad .. \quad .. \quad (9.3.3)$$

$$v^2 = u^2 + 2.a.s \quad .. \quad .. \quad .. \quad .. \quad .. \quad .. \quad .. \quad .. \quad (9.3.4)$$

QUADRATIC EQUATIONS

In the study of exercise and sport one variable which is commonly calculated is the time taken for a body/object to travel a certain distance or to a specified point.

Example
If a football is kicked from the ground into the air with a vertical velocity of 5 m·s^{-1}, how long does it take for the ball to get to 1 m above the ground?

In this example the use of equations 9.3.1 to 9.3.4 becomes complex as it is necessary to solve what is known as a quadratic equation. When you have an equation in the form $a{\cdot}x^2 + b{\cdot}x + c = 0$, or can rearrange an equation into this form, then you can determine x using the following equation:

$$x = \frac{-b \pm \sqrt{b^2 - 4{\cdot}a{\cdot}c}}{2{\cdot}a} \quad .. \quad .. \quad .. \quad .. \quad .. \quad .. \quad .. \quad (9.4)$$

For the football example above, we know:

$u = 5$ m·s^{-1}

$a = -9.81$ m·s^{-2} (acting in the opposite direction to the initial velocity)

$s = 1$ m

$t = ?$

Using equation (9.3.3):

$s = u{\cdot}t + \frac{1}{2}{\cdot}a{\cdot}t^2$

Substituting in the known values:

$1 = 5{\cdot}t - 4.905{\cdot}t^2$

Rearranging:

$4.905{\cdot}t^2 - 5{\cdot}t + 1 = 0$

154

Using equation (9.4):

$$t = \frac{-(-5) \pm \sqrt{(-5)^2 - 4 \times 4.905 \times 1}}{2 \times 4.905}$$

$$t = \frac{5 \pm \sqrt{5.38}}{9.81}$$

$t = 0.27$ s and $t = 0.75$ s (see Figure 9.3)

The ball will be at 1m above the ground at two time instants: once on the way up and once on the way down (see Figure 9.3). The time taken for the ball to reach peak height will be half way between 0.27 s and 0.75 s at 0.51 s.

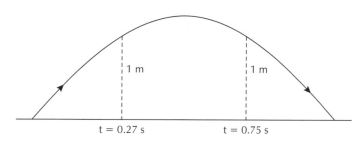

Figure 9.3
Projectile
motion of a ball

DIFFERENTIATION

Gradient of a line

The gradient of a straight line graph is constant and can be calculated using any two points on the line (x_1, y_1) and (x_2, y_2) (see Figure 9.4). The gradient represents the rate of change of variable y with respect to variable x.

$$\text{Gradient} = \frac{\text{change in y}}{\text{change in x}} \quad .. \quad .. \quad .. \quad .. \quad .. \quad .. \quad .. \quad (9.5)$$

$$\text{Gradient} = \frac{y_2 - y_1}{x_2 - x_1}$$

Differentiation is concerned with the rate at which things change. The velocity of an object is the rate at which its displacement changes (i.e. how displacement changes over time). Therefore the gradient of a displacement-time line graph is equal to velocity. The calculation of the gradient of the line, and therefore velocity, is known as graphical differentiation. The change in y is the change in displacement and the change in x is the change in time (see Figure 9.5). Similarly, the gradient of a velocity-time line graph represents the acceleration. Differentiation is the change in variable y with respect to the variable x. In all examples given in this chapter the variable x is time.

Figure 9.5 represents the velocity of a sprinter during a race. The sprinter accelerates for the first 3 seconds then moves with constant speed for 5 seconds before decelerating to rest over 4 seconds. Graphical differentiation can be used to calculate the acceleration and deceleration.

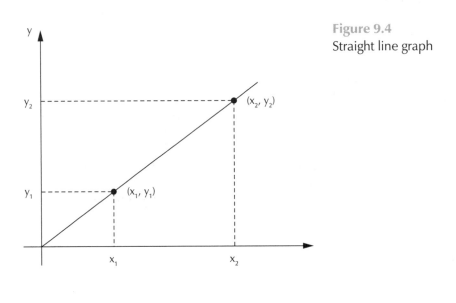

Figure 9.4
Straight line graph

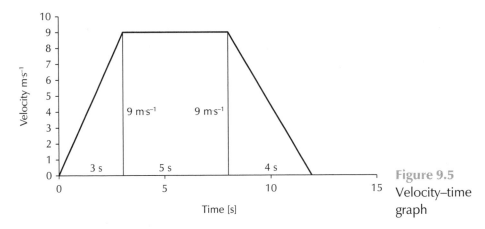

Figure 9.5
Velocity–time graph

Acceleration:

$$\text{gradient of line} = \frac{\Delta \text{ velocity}}{\Delta \text{ time}} = \text{acceleration}$$

$$\text{acceleration} = \frac{9 \text{ m·s}^{-1}}{3 \text{ s}}$$

$$\text{acceleration} = 3 \text{ m·s}^{-2}$$

Deceleration:

$$\text{gradient of line} = \frac{\Delta \text{ velocity}}{\Delta \text{ time}} = \text{deceleration}$$

$$\text{deceleration} = \frac{9 \text{ m·s}^{-1}}{4 \text{ s}}$$

$$\text{deceleration} = 2.25 \text{ m·s}^{-2}$$

Gradient of a curve

In most situations in sport the rate of change of a variable will not be constant and therefore the line of a graph will not be straight (see Figure 9.6). When this is the case, the gradient of the curve is not constant but continuously changing. The gradient at a given point (x, y)

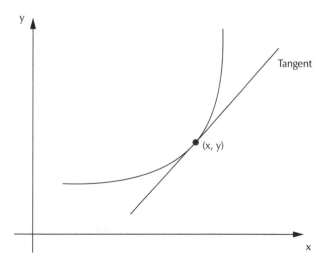

Figure 9.6
Curved graph with tangent

on the curve is defined as the gradient of the tangent to the point on the curve. The tangent at any point on a curve is a straight line which touches the curve at that point (or time) only. The gradient of the tangent will be the rate of change of the variable of interest at that time instant. A tangent to a curve can be drawn onto a graph and its gradient calculated using equation 9.5.

INTEGRATION

Integration is the reverse or inverse process of differentiation. Through the process of integration, you can determine variables such as velocity and displacement from acceleration–time and velocity–time profiles respectively. In addition to these kinematic variables, impulse can be determined from a force–time profile. Integration is effectively the multiplication of a variable by time. Let us first consider the situation when velocity is constant and we have a straight line graph (Figure 9.7). The displacement travelled during the time over which the velocity is exerted can be determined by simply calculating the area under the line on the graph; in other words, multiplying the velocity (y-axis) by the time (x-axis):

$$\text{displacement} = \text{velocity} \times \text{time}$$

$$\text{displacement} = 5 \text{ m·s}^{-1} \times 12 \text{ s}$$

$$\text{displacement} = 60 \text{ m}$$

The displacement travelled by the sprinter represented in Figure 9.5 can also be calculated using graphical integration. The easiest way to calculate the displacement in this example is to break the graph into three parts and calculate the area of each (Figure 9.8).

Note: Area of a triangle = ½ × base of the triangle × height of the triangle.

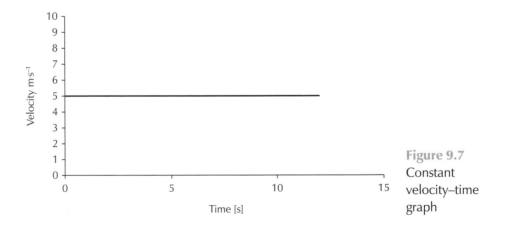

Figure 9.7
Constant velocity–time graph

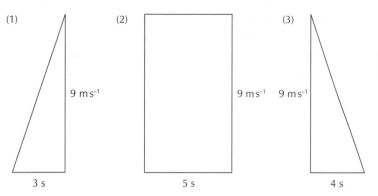

(1) (2) (3)

9 m·s⁻¹ — 9 m·s⁻¹ 9 m·s⁻¹

3 s   5 s   4 s

Figure 9.8
Calculation of
displacement:
graphical integration

area of (1) = ½ × 3 s × 9 m·s⁻¹ = displacement

displacement = 13.5 m

area of (2) = 5 s × 9 m·s⁻¹ = displacement

displacement = 45 m

area of (3) = ½ × 4 s × 9 m·s⁻¹

displacement = 18 m

Total displacement = 13.5 + 45 + 18 = 76.5 m

Impulse

As:

Impulse (Ns) = Force (N) × Time (s)   ..   ..   (9.6)

The integral of force is impulse. If force is constant over a specified time period, calculating impulse over that time period is straightforward and similar to the calculation of displacement in the previous examples. If, however, like in the majority of situations, the force is not constant, the calculation of impulse becomes slightly more complicated. A common method of calculating impulse using graphical integration is the trapezium rule. This method can be used to graphically integrate any variable.

Trapezium rule

The trapezium rule provides a way of estimating the area under a curve through the estimation of integrals (Grimshaw et al., 2007). The trapezium rule works by splitting the area under a curve, within the time interval of interest, into a number of trapeziums (each of width dt). The area of each trapezium is then calculated (see Figure 9.9), and the area of all trapeziums is added together. In Figure 9.9, H_1 and H_2 represent consecutive force data points when determining impulse.

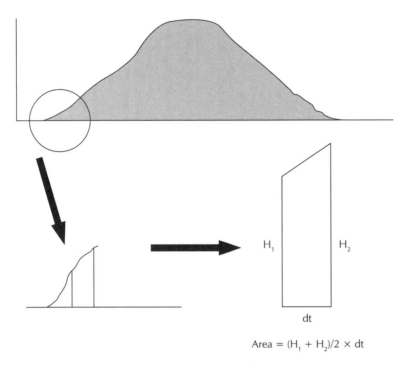

$$\text{Area} = (H_1 + H_2)/2 \times dt$$

Figure 9.9 The trapezium rule

ALGEBRA

Algebra is the area of mathematics that uses symbols to represent numbers, or unknown quantities, in order to solve problems (which may otherwise require the use of trial and error) or investigate relationships between variables. Any equation of the form **y = a·x + b** is linear which means it may be represented as a straight line (linear) graph. The coefficient of x (a), denotes the gradient of the line and b denotes the point at which the line crosses or intercepts the y axis. The greater the value of a the steeper the slope of the line.

If we consider the equations of line graphs representing the velocity of a sprinter (Figure 9.10). Line P represents the velocity of a sprinter during the first 5 s of a 100 m race. The initial velocity is 0 m·s⁻¹. The sprinter accelerates uniformly over the 5 s time period until a velocity of 10 m·s⁻¹ is reached. Because the initial velocity is 0 m·s⁻¹ the value of b is 0 (at y = 0, x = 0). The gradient of the slope of a velocity–time graph represents the acceleration. If the line is straight, the acceleration must be uniform and in the example is equal to 2 m·s⁻²:

$$\text{acceleration} = \frac{\text{change in velocity}}{\text{time taken for change}} = \frac{10 \text{ m·s}^{-1} - 0 \text{ m·s}^{-1}}{5 \text{ s}} = 2 \text{ m·s}^{-2}$$

The gradient of the line and the value of a is therefore 2. Line Q represents the velocity of a sprinter during the first 5 seconds of a rolling 100 m race. The initial velocity (at time = 0 s) is 4 m·s⁻¹. Therefore the value of b in the equation is 4. Again the sprinter accelerates uniformly over the 5 s to reach a velocity of 10 m·s⁻¹. The line will intercept the y axis at 4 and the gradient of the slope, representing the acceleration, will be 1.2 (change in velocity/time taken for the change). Therefore $a = 1.2$ and $b = 4$.

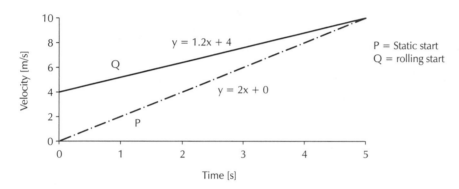

Figure 9.10 Velocity–time traces

SIMULTANEOUS EQUATIONS

There are a number of situations in the study of exercise and sport when the ability to solve simultaneous equations is necessary. This is generally achieved by the method of substitution. One such example, in exercise physiology, is the estimation of energy expenditure using **indirect calorimetry** (see McArdle et al., 2007).

Example
- When 1 g of carbohydrate (CHO) is oxidised, 0.828 O_2 are used and 0.828 of CO_2 are produced releasing 17 kJ of energy.
- When 1 g of fat is oxidised 1.989 O_2 are used and 1.419 CO_2 are produced releasing 39 kJ of energy.

If values for oxygen uptake (VO_2) and carbon dioxide output (VCO_2) are known, the quantities of fat and CHO oxidised per minute can be calculated:

$VO_2 = 1.6\ L \cdot min^{-1}$

$VCO_2 = 1.3\ L \cdot min^{-1}$

Let x g of CHO and y g of fat be oxidised per minute,

Therefore: $VO_2 = 0.828 \cdot x + 1.989 \cdot y$

$VCO_2 = 0.828 \cdot x + 1.419 \cdot y$

Therefore:

$1.6 = 0.828 \cdot x + 1.989 \cdot y\ (1)$

$1.3 = 0.828 \cdot x + 1.419 \cdot y\ (2)$

Subtracting equation (2) from equation (1) gives you;

$0.3 = 0.57 \cdot y$

Therefore:

$y = 0.53\ g\ of\ fat$

The calculated value of y can now be substituted into either equation (1) or equation (2) to calculate x.

$1.6 = 0.828 \cdot x + (1.989 \times 0.53)$

$1.6 = 0.828 \cdot x + 1.054$

$0.546 = 0.828 \cdot x$

$x = 0.66\ g\ of\ CHO$

Energy expenditure $= (0.53\ g\ of\ fat * 39\ kJ) + (0.66\ g\ of\ CHO * 17\ kJ)$

$= 20.7\ kJ \cdot min^{-1} + 11.2\ kJ \cdot min^{-1}$

$= 31.9\ kJ \cdot min^{-1}$

DETERMINATION OF PERCENTAGES

In order that values can be normalised and comparison can take place between participants or trials, values are often expressed as a percentage of some other value. One such example is when whole body centre of mass locations are determined and comparison between members of a group is to be carried out. The height of the centre of mass (CM Ht) is calculated as a percentage of total body height (Ht) in order to allow for comparison between subjects of differing total body height. This is a form of normalisation. To calculate this value, equation 9.7 is used:

$$\text{CM Ht as a percentage of Ht} = \frac{\text{CMHt}}{\text{Ht}} \times 100 \qquad .. \qquad .. \qquad .. \qquad (9.7)$$

A measure which is expressed as a percentage, and used in physiology to indicate reduction in performance caused by fatigue, is the **fatigue index**, which is calculated from repeated sprint times using Equation 9.8:

$$\text{fatigue index} = \frac{\text{fastest sprint time} - \text{slowest sprint time}}{\text{slowest sprint time}} \times 100 \qquad .. \qquad (9.8)$$

REARRANGING EQUATIONS

The rearranging of equations or the transposition of formulae is regularly used in exercise and sport science when attempting to solve problems using the formulae presented in this chapter. The aim of rearranging an equation is to get the variable of interest on one side of the equation on its own. In order to do this, other variables need to be moved from one side of the equation to the other.

General rules of rearranging equations:

- If a quantity is positive (or added) on one side of the equation and you want to move it to the other side of the equation, it will become negative (or subtracted) on the side of the equation you are moving it to (note: a number without a sign in front of it is positive). This is because in order to remove it from the original side of the equation you would need to subtract it from itself (to cancel it out) and whatever you do to one side of the equation you must do to the other. The reverse is true if a quantity is negative.
- Similarly, if a quantity is multiplied on one side of the equation and you want to move it to the other side, it will be divided on the side of the equation you are moving it to. Again, this is because in order to remove it from the original side, you would need to divide it by itself and therefore the same must be done on the other side of the equation. The reverse is true if a quantity is divided.

- When multiplying and dividing, the same action must not only be done to each side of the equation but also to each term within the equation.

Example

If the final velocity (v), initial velocity (u) and acceleration (a) of a kicked football are known, the equation (9.3.4) can be re-arranged in order to calculate the displacement (s) of the ball;

$$v^2 = u^2 + 2 \cdot a \cdot s$$

The first step would be to move u^2 from the right-hand side (RHS) of the equation to the left-hand side (LHS) to leave the term $2 \cdot a \cdot s$ on its own. As u^2 is a positive term on the RHS, it becomes a negative term on the LHS.

$$v^2 - u^2 = 2 \cdot a \cdot s$$

The next step in the rearrangement of the equation is to split the term $2 \cdot a \cdot s$ to get s on its own. In order to remove the $2 \cdot a$ from the RHS (where it is multiplied), it needs to be divided on the LHS:

$$\frac{v^2 - u^2}{2 \cdot a} = s$$

UNITS

As previously discussed in Chapter 1, the standardised units for all variables studied within exercise and sport science are based on the **Système Internationale (SI) units**. There are seven base SI units (Table 1.1) from which all other units can be derived. For ease of understanding and convenience, some SI derived units have been given special names and symbols (such as newtons (N), pascals (Pa) and joules (J)).

Derivation of units for velocity:

$$\text{velocity} = \frac{\text{displacement (m)}}{\text{time (s)}}$$

$$\text{velocity} = \frac{m}{s} \text{ which is usually expressed as } m \cdot s^{-1}$$

Derivation of units for volume:

$$\text{volume} = \text{length (m)} \times \text{width (m)} \times \text{height (m)}$$

$$\text{volume} = m^3$$

scientific transferable skills

Derivation of units for density:

$$\text{density} = \frac{\text{mass (kg)}}{\text{volume (m}^3)}$$

$$\text{density} = \frac{\text{kg}}{\text{m}^3} \text{ which is usually expressed as kg·m}^{-3}$$

SELF-TEST

1. Give an example of a scalar variable and an example of a vector variable.

2. What are the three basic trigonometric functions?

3. State the theorem used to calculate the magnitude of a resultant vector from its horizontal and vertical components.

4. What are the five variables used in the equations of constant acceleration?

5. If a constant velocity of 6 m·s^{-1} is exerted over a time period of 9 s, what is the displacement covered in that time?

6. Give the equation of a line which has a gradient of 3 and intercepts the y-axis at 2.

7. State one purpose for the normalisation of data.

8. What is the fatigue index used to indicate?

CONCLUSION

This chapter has described a number of numerical calculations which are used to solve problems in exercise and sport. These calculations are necessary in order to determine variables of interest in an exercise and sport context which can then be used for further understanding of principles and concepts. Practical examples in this chapter have looked at the determination of both kinetic variables (e.g. forces) and kinematic variables (e.g. displacement, velocity and acceleration) which are studied in exercise and sport.

KEY POINTS

- A scalar is a variable with magnitude only, and a vector is a variable with both magnitude and direction.
- Pythagoras' Theorem is used to calculate the magnitude of a vector when the magnitude of the vector components are known.

- The direction of a vector can be calculated using the basic trigonometric functions (sine, cosine and tangent) when the vector components are known.
- The kinematics of a body during flight can be calculated using the equations of constant acceleration, given three of the five variables (initial velocity, final velocity, acceleration, time and displacement) are known.
- Differentiation is the rate of change of one variable with another (usually time).
- Integration is the reverse process of differentiation.
- A common method of calculating impulse using graphical integration is the trapezium rule.
- The correct units for all variables studied within exercise and sport science are based on the Système Internationale (SI) units.
- Normalisation of data is carried out in order to be able to compare subjects or trials.

BIBLIOGRAPHY

Grimshaw, P., Lees, A., Fowler, N. and Burden, A. (2007) *Sport and Exercise Biomechanics*. Oxon: Taylor and Francis.

Hay, J.G. (1993) *The Biomechanics of Sports Techniques*, 4th edition. Englewood Cliffs, NJ: Prentice-Hall.

McArdle, W.D., Katch, F.I. and Katch, V.L. (2007) *Exercise Physiology: Energy, Nutrition and Human Performance*, 6th edition. Baltimore: Williams and Wilkins.

FURTHER READING

Bartlett, R.M. (1997) *Introduction to Sports Biomechanics*. London: E & FN Spon.

Kamen, G. (2001) *Foundations of Exercise Science*. Baltimore: Lippincott, Williams and Wilkins.

CHAPTER TEN

REPORT WRITING

AIMS OF THE CHAPTER

This chapter aims to provide an understanding of the importance and practicalities of report writing for the study of exercise and sport. After reading this chapter, you should be able to:

■ Adopt a scientific approach to report writing in exercise and sport.
■ Identify the various sections which make up a scientific report.
■ Outline the content of each section of a scientific report.
■ Apply scientific report writing skills to the study of exercise and sport.

INTRODUCTION

When studying exercise and sport, it is important to be able to plan, perform and write up experimental investigations. This chapter will focus on writing scientific reports, and the content of sections that should be included within the report. In addition to a description of how to write a scientific report, a rationale is provided for the approach normally taken. Whether writing up the findings of an investigation in molecular biology or exercise and sport, the process will be similar. The approach to report writing is normally similar irrespective of whether you are an undergraduate student writing up a laboratory report or a professor writing a paper for publication.

Scientific investigation of any subject is based on certain fundamental principles that have been covered in both Chapters 1 and 8. Experimental research normally aims to test whether a theory stands up to rigorous investigation. The main research question is often posed in the form of clear **hypotheses** that can be tested. The findings of the investigation dictate whether or not the hypotheses are accepted or rejected. Normally inferential statistical techniques are used to analyse the results in order to accept or reject the hypotheses with a degree of confidence. This chapter will explain how the fundamental principles of scientific investigations are accounted for in each section of the report. For information about the qualitative research and report writing process, see Graziano and Rawlin (1993) and Silverman (1993).

scientific transferable skills

KEY APPLICATIONS TO EXERCISE AND SPORT

The skills developed through writing up the findings of experimental investigations are transferable to many other report writing tasks. Therefore, a student who has developed an ability to produce a high-quality report on an experimental investigation will be well placed to write other types of report. Given that report writing is such an important part of professional life in many subject areas, skills developed in this area will be extremely valuable to employers of exercise and sport graduates.

Normally, one of the most important written pieces of work to be completed as an undergraduate student in an exercise and sport subject is the **dissertation**. For this piece of work, report writing skills will be critical to success, so these skills should be correctly developed from an early stage in the course. An opportunity to develop these skills will normally be provided through reporting the outcomes of laboratory-based practical sessions. The development of report writing skills is a key part of academic work. The most common medium through which academic work is presented is concise reports, which are published in **peer-reviewed academic journals**. Day (1998) provides extensive guidance on writing and publishing a scientific paper.

WRITING STYLE

An area of scientific report writing, which many students find difficult, is the normal convention of writing in the **third person**. Although it may seem natural to write in the first person, especially in the method section of the report, convention dictates that the third person should be used. The use of the third person should help an author to report details in an objective form. In the following examples, the first paragraph illustrates the use of the first person and the second paragraph shows the preferred use of the third person.

Writing in the first person:

> In **our** last lecture, Prof Harris told **us** that vertical jump height was an indirect way of assessing very short-term power output. He also told **me** at the end of the lecture that **I** would have to be the participant in the following laboratory practical. The practical demonstrated to **us** that power determined from vertical jump height and power directly determined from a force plate differed slightly in the same participant.

Writing in the third person:

> In a previous lecture, Prof Harris explained that vertical jump height was an indirect way of assessing very short-term power output. At the end of the lecture, it was also explained that this author would have to be the participant in the following laboratory practical. The practical demonstrated that power determined

from vertical jump height and power directly determined from a force plate differed slightly in the same participant.

From the above examples of text written in the first and then the third person, it should be possible to observe the differences between the two styles, and see how the writing in the third person appears more objective, and less ambiguous. Reports are also written in the past tense (as is the case in the previous example). Further discussion of this point is included in the method section (see p. 175), since this is an area of report writing which many students have difficulty with.

The importance of concise, clear writing in scientific reports cannot be over-emphasised. For the reader to extract information efficiently, the inclusion of sections and sub-sections within the report must be logical. As you will see in the method section, this can often be a complicated task that requires practice. A report should always be clear and concise, regardless of who the report is intended for. Day (1998) provides extensive guidance of clear and concise scientific writing.

SECTIONS OF A SCIENTIFIC REPORT

A scientific report is normally written with clearly defined sections to lead the reader through all the necessary information. Without such sections, the reader would quickly become confused. Typical sections within a report include the following:

- **Abstract**
- **Introduction**
- **Review of literature**
- **Methods**
- **Results**
- **Discussion**
- **Conclusion**
- **References**.

A reader may also find sections useful if certain information has to be extracted from a report quickly. For example, an abstract will normally provide the reader with detail on the method and main results, and a brief concluding sentence. Sometimes, a quick look at the results section will provide the reader with the main findings of a study. The reader will then have to interpret the results themselves. Often a reader who is very familiar with an area of work will be in a good position to interpret the results, without referring to the author's interpretation.

It is advisable to read some published scientific reports to familiarise yourself with the content of the various sections of a report. A visit to a library that stocks journals in the area of exercise and sport would be useful in order to look at some example reports. Examples of refereed academic journals in exercise and sport are shown in Appendix 4. Many peer-reviewed academic journals are now published on the internet; however, most require a subscription to access the full papers. For some of the journals listed in Appendix 4, type the title into the 'Google' search engine to see if you can access the full papers without a subscription. Google Scholar is a version of the Google search engine that only returns peer-reviewed publications. Some journals allow you to look at a full example paper without a subscription. Looking through papers published in peer-reviewed journals will enable familiarisation with the format of a report in the area of exercise and sport. It is also the case that scientific writing is improved by reading high-quality scientific reports, although it should be acknowledged that the report format will differ slightly according to the journal.

When examining the journal contents, be careful to distinguish between original research papers and review papers. For the purpose of this chapter, original research papers should be consulted. However, to find out how to write a review of literature section, consult some review papers (e.g. Williams, 1997; Gidlow et al., 2006). Some journals make a distinction between two types of original research paper, with a category known as a rapid communication. Such papers are shorter than normal original research papers, to allow the authors to get important findings into print quickly. A rapid communication is usually written in a form consistent with that expected for a laboratory report from an undergraduate student. It is therefore worth examining such reports to observe how the authors manage to include so much information in such a concise manner.

WRITING THE ABSTRACT

Often, to get a flavour for a complete paper, the reader will just look at the abstract. This is why it is important to learn how to incorporate all the necessary information into the abstract to enable the reader to extract a summary of the information found in the full paper. An abstract format is not only included as a section of an original research paper, but is also widely used to inform delegates at a conference about the content of a presentation. Abstracts from most of the exercise and sport journals listed in Appendix 4 are easily accessed through 'PubMed' (sometimes known as 'Medline'). Just type PubMed into the Google search engine to view abstracts from these journals.

Some journals specify the content of the abstract, whilst others allow the reader more freedom. However, in general, an abstract will include an introductory and concluding sentence, along with a description of the method and the main results. The following detail is normally required:

- Single sentence to introduce the investigation
- Primary aim of the investigation
- Method:
    - Participants
    - Study design
    - Protocols

- Measurements
- Equipment
- Data analysis
- Results summary
- Conclusion in relation to primary aim.

A limit of between 150 and 250 words is often applied to an abstract. Normally dissertation abstracts are slightly longer, whilst journal paper abstracts are closer to 150 words. It is normally desirable for the abstract to fit onto a single side of A4.

WRITING THE INTRODUCTION

The primary purpose of an introduction is to allow the reader to understand why the investigation has taken place. The aim of the introduction is to:

1. Enable the reader to place the investigation in context.
2. Provide a rationale for the investigation.
3. Delimit the investigation.
4. State the aim(s) of the investigation.
5. State the hypotheses.

The content of the introduction may differ, depending on the application. Often, an introduction in a journal paper will also review the literature. However, in most cases, a separate introduction and review of literature will be included. If a separate literature review is included, the introduction is the section that leads the reader from a very general context to the specific aims of the study. For example, an undergraduate biomechanics laboratory report included the following extract in its introduction:

> Performance in many sports depends on the ability to generate power over a very short time period. Often short term power production is used to raise the performer in a vertical plane against the force due to gravity . . . In order to assess the difference in power production capability of performers in different sports, vertical jump performance was determined in twelve class members. Six of the participants were basketball players, and six were cyclists.

In the previous extract, the author explained the general context of the study, before explaining to the reader exactly what would be investigated. An introduction helps the reader to contextualise the investigation. Once the study has been placed in context, the hypotheses may be stated. However, in most scientific reports, the hypotheses are stated in the form of open questions. For example:

> The aim of this investigation is to determine whether a prior fatiguing bout of running exercise alters gait during treadmill running.

172

In a dissertation, however, you would normally be required to formally state a null hypothesis and an alternative hypothesis. For example:

Null hypothesis (H_0):   A prior fatiguing bout of running exercise does not alter gait during treadmill running.

Alternative hypothesis (H_1):   A prior fatiguing bout of running exercise alters gait during treadmill running.

Sometimes it is possible to specify the direction of the change in the measured variables within the hypothesis. For example:

H_0:   A prior fatiguing bout of running exercise does not increase the duration of the stance phase during treadmill running.

H_1:   A prior fatiguing bout of running exercise does increase the duration of the stance phase during treadmill running.

For further detail on the formulation of hypotheses, and the association with the choice of statistical test, see Chapter 8. It should be noted that the introduction does not always include the hypotheses. Sometimes the hypotheses are included after the review of literature. The location of hypotheses should be made clear in specific guidelines provided by your department.

It is common to have statements in the introduction supported by **references**, even if the introduction is to be followed by a review of literature. Factual sentences should be accompanied by references which support the statements (see referencing section, p. 185). If, however, the factual information is the author's own thought, then it should be acknowledged that it is a personal comment. For example:

according to this author, it has been observed that many high level athletes take the area of nutrition very seriously.

WRITING THE REVIEW OF LITERATURE

The distinction between the introduction and review of literature is one that many students find unclear. Whereas an introduction contains references, the references are normally for general points of fact and overall findings from published investigations. It is in the review of literature that the author makes reference to the details of studies that have been performed previously in the area and the results of these studies. The author should also attempt to explain why previous studies may have obtained conflicting findings. So, for example, in the introduction the following statement might appear, supported by a reference(s):

Endurance performance is predicted by a range of physiological and biochemical parameters, both at the whole body and cellular level (Jones, 1997).

Alternatively, in the review of literature, a reference may be used in the following way:

In a study that examined eight well-trained cyclists, maximal power produced during an incremental cycling test to exhaustion predicted 60 % of the variation in cycling time trial performance (Smith et al., 1996).

The skill of writing a good review of literature is in linking the findings of previous studies together in a logical order. Even if your study is to be the first in a particular area, it is appropriate to make reference to previous work in related areas. Fortunately, in the study of exercise and sport, most of the techniques available for student work have been widely used before. Normally, there is no shortage of literature to make reference to.

Previous research should be referred to objectively. As the author of a report, it is important to write the review of literature as though the investigation has not been carried out. By taking this approach, the findings of the study should not influence the content of the review of literature. It is important to take this prospective approach, since the review of the literature should play an important part in influencing the approach taken in a scientific investigation. Only when the literature has been reviewed in the area under investigation will the investigator be in an informed position to design the study. In reality, many researchers will read the literature, then plan and execute the study, and finally write the review of literature along with the other sections of the report. By taking a prospective approach to writing the review of literature, the literature will be reported as it was interpreted prior to the study. It is within the discussion that the findings of the investigation are related to those findings reported within the review of literature.

For examples of literature reviews, it is often useful to examine review papers in refereed scientific journals. Such papers are a good place to start a literature search for a project, in addition to finding out about writing a literature review. Have a look at the content of the journal called *Sports Medicine* to see a useful range of literature reviews in exercise and sport. Although referencing techniques are not covered in this section, you will find detailed discussion of this topic in the section on producing the references (see p. 185).

STOP AND THINK

Many students struggle with the literature review, particularly if they have too much literature to report. What ways could you delimit the material you have read to ensure a concise and relevant review of literature? Are there any other ways to present numerous findings succinctly?

WRITING THE METHODS

The description of an investigation is usually referred to as the method section. A frequently asked question is: why is it important to describe the investigation? This question arises, since at first it appears that it is only the results of a study that are important. However, there are two important reasons why the method section of a investigation should be written up:

1. Scientists may wish to repeat the exact investigation to confirm the findings.
2. The method employed may heavily influence the findings.

It is quite often necessary to repeat an investigation, either in an identical way, or by changing part of the method slightly. For example, it may be important to replicate the investigation exactly, as mentioned earlier, in order to add information gained from additional participants. It may also be important to replicate the study exactly, but to use a different group of participants. The findings of the experiment may then become generalisable to a wider population.

There are numerous ways in which a slight change in the methods may influence the findings of an investigation. This point is best illustrated with an example:

> In one study in which the effects of a carbohydrate drink on exercise performance were to be assessed, participants in the experimental group consumed a carbohydrate drink and participants in the control group consumed no drink (study 1). In another study, the experimental group participants consumed a carbohydrate drink, and the control group participants consumed an equivalent amount of water (study 2).

When the studies were examined, it was found that the experimental group performed significantly better than the control group in study 1 but not in study 2. The only difference in the study design was that water was consumed in the control condition in study 2, but not in study 1. This difference in methods is important, since it demonstrates that under the experimental conditions, a carbohydrate drink is better than no drink, but not significantly better than a similar quantity of water. The conclusion from this study may be that the water in the carbohydrate drink is eliciting a large part of the performance improvement, rather than the carbohydrate per se. Hopefully, this example demonstrates the importance of a detailed method section.

When the literature in the area of exercise and sport is examined, what appear to be similar studies often have slightly different methods. A critical and well-read student of exercise and sport will be able to differentiate between methods and to make judgements about the likely effect upon the results of the study.

Because of the complexity of producing a coherent method section, it is essential that the method section of a report is well planned and structured appropriately. It is important to consider the following:

- The usual conventions for describing a study
- The necessary considerations when using human participants
- The correct terminology
- The appropriate style of writing.

The method section of a scientific investigation is usually written in a standardised way. This general format does not differ between a exercise and sport study and a physics study. The methods usually contain detail on the following:

1. Participants recruited to the investigation
2. Study design
3. Protocol(s)
4. Measurement details
5. Data analysis techniques.

In the area of exercise and sport, most of the studies performed will inevitably involve **human participants**. Details on the participants are usually given in the method section in order to describe the population they have been selected from and their physical and physiological characteristics. The process of selection is also normally outlined at this point in the methods. Very strict guidelines exist about the treatment of human participants when they are involved in a scientific investigation (see Chapter 1), and the method section of the investigation report should make reference to the fact that such guidelines have been adhered to. Even in undergraduate laboratory practical work it is good practice to make reference to the treatment of participants in accordance with published guidelines. Normally, it is reassuring to know that undergraduate laboratory practical sessions only include procedures that have been previously cleared with the institution's **ethics committee**. For further discussion of ethical issues and **informed consent**, see Chapter 1.

An example of how the participant section of your method might read is:

Eight well-trained female cyclists (mean $\pm$ s.d.: body mass, 64.1 ± 1.5 kg; height, 1.68 ± 0.11 m; $\dot{V}O_2$ max, 3.81 ± 0.27 L·min^{-1}) agreed to take part in the investigation which was approved by the institutional ethics committee. Following completion of a health screening questionnaire, and reading the details of the investigation, participants gave written consent to take part in the study.

It is usual to give details about groups of participants at the end of the participant description if the study design requires the participants to be split into more than one group. The reader can then immediately see whether the groups are well matched.

The key to a good method section lies in the organisation of the information for the benefit of the reader. A useful way to think about this process is to consider the most general aspects first, then gradually move into the fine detail. Also, describe the investigation in

scientific transferable skills

chronological order (i.e. over time). The importance of an accurate description of the method used to examine a particular issue has already been discussed. In particular, the study design should be clearly outlined. For example:

> A repeated measures design was used, where participants visited the laboratory on three occasions spaced one week apart. On the first occasion, subjects had their mass, height, and maximal oxygen uptake determined. On the second occasion . . .

Further detail on the range of study designs is outlined in Chapter 8. As far as possible, the study design section should be constructed to avoid duplication later in the method section. For example, the study design section should provide details of any intervention used in the study. Once such details are stated at this early point in the methods, they do not need to be repeated later in the methods. For example:

> participants consumed 500 mL of a solution containing 6 % carbohydrate. In the control condition, participants consumed 500 mL of flavoured water.

The protocol(s) should be reported in an accurate and unambiguous way. Accuracy will be achieved if every important part of the protocol is reported in detail. It is also necessary that the general layout of the protocols assists with the understanding and piecing together of information. For example:

> . . . progressive exercise test on a flat motor driven treadmill to determine maximal oxygen uptake and maximum heart rate. During the test, speed increased from 8 km·h^{-1} by 1.2 km·h^{-1}·min^{-1} in increments of 0.1 km·h^{-1} every 5 s. Heart rate and respiratory gas exchange was determined continuously throughout.

Also, notice in the preceding example that the information is presented objectively. This means that the protocol of the study is presented factually, with no attempt by the researcher to interpret what happened. The presentation of information in this way helps to avoid a situation where the information presented might be ambiguous or misleading. Many students find this aspect of the method section particularly difficult. A common mistake is to present a subjective style of writing which incorporates a personal interpretation of what happened, rather than an exact description of what happened. The use of the first person is a further common mistake.

Once the detail of the protocols has been provided, it is then appropriate to describe the way in which measurements took place. Usually in an investigation, several different measurements are taken, and some of the measurements may be repeated during different parts of the protocol. For example, heart rate may be measured in all exercise tests in a study, but the method of measurement only needs to be described once. The level of description required usually includes precise detail, so that exactly the same procedure of measurement may be repeated on a subsequent occasion. For example, if a heart rate monitor is used to measure heart rate throughout a study, the description might be as follows:

> Heart rate was determined via telemetry (Model HR121, name of manufacturer, location of company). Prior to exercise, participants placed electrodes and a transmitter on their chest which were contained in an elasticated strap that was tightened but still allowed unrestricted chest movement. The participants also placed a receiver on their wrist, which stored heart rate on a beat-by-beat basis. On termination of exercise, the stored information was downloaded from the receiver to a computer for subsequent analysis via a . . .

In the previous example, enough information is given about the equipment to enable another scientist interested in making the same measurement to use identical equipment. The method of measurement and the equipment used to record the measurement is usually followed by the necessary information in brackets. In the above example, the model number, and name and location of the manufacturer of the heart rate monitor is provided. A simple example has been given here, however, some of the equipment you may use is more challenging to describe. An example of this type is provided in the second application (see p. 186).

The content of the method section that describes the data analysis should clearly explain how the investigator has treated the raw data. The raw data is simply the information gathered as measurements are undertaken. This information is invariably difficult to interpret in its raw form. Some analysis has to take place before a reader can interpret the information. At a fundamental level of data analysis, some calculations may have to take place to move from raw data to derived variables. In other words, raw data requires manipulation to calculate a derived variable. A simple example of this would be the use of information about the distance covered by a runner and the time taken to cover the distance. With these two pieces of information, speed can be derived (i.e. distance divided by time). The clear description of such a process is very important, since the analysis of data in different ways can lead to different findings.

A further area to be covered in the data analysis section of the methods is the description of the statistical techniques that have been used. Again, the choice of statistical procedure can markedly affect the study findings. The appropriate methods for analysing various types of data are discussed in Chapter 8.

A large amount of variation is present in the format of, and detail provided in, the method section. Part of the reason for such differences lies with the requirements of the particular institution where the investigation has been conducted, or the outlet for publication of the findings. As an undergraduate student, the supervisor of your laboratory practical sessions may provide specific guidelines for the layout of the methods section of required written reports. It is, however, a good idea to look at some examples of method sections in the

scientific transferable skills

published literature. Thomas and Nelson (1996: Chapter 4) provides comprehensive further reading on formulating the method. Hyllegard et al. (1996: Part II) provides a more detailed insight into the formulation of appropriate methods.

WRITING THE RESULTS

In order to present the results appropriately, this section should be read in conjunction with Chapter 8 on data analysis. Whilst Chapter 8 will provide the information necessary to deal with various types of data, this section will enable presentation of the main findings in the most appropriate format.

Normally, a results section of a scientific report will include the following:

- A full description of the participant characteristics
- A written description of the main findings
- Tables and figures of results.

Notice that at no point is any interpretation of the results attempted. Results are only interpreted in the discussion section. It is important to report the results in an objective form, and in the third person. When the results are reported in this way, the reader is able to identify the main findings of the study quickly.

In order for information to be extracted quickly by the reader, the results should also be presented in order of events, if possible. As was the case with the method section, ordering the presented information chronologically, in line with the time course of the experiment, will aid the reader.

The description of the participant characteristics, which is usually the most appropriate starting point, will often be presented in the form of a table. The text, which may accompany such a table, may make reference to the type of participants in the group. Information about the degree of similarity (homogeneity) or difference (heterogeneity) of the group, and the training status of the group may be included. It is often necessary at this point to mention if any participant had to withdraw from the study. If the study required a division of participants into two or more groups, the details of each group would normally be presented. It is important not to repeat information in the text that has been supplied in a table.

The main findings of the study will often be presented in a tabular or graphical form. The old saying, 'a picture [i.e. table or figure] can tell a thousand words' is relevant here, but only if the information is presented in an appropriate form. It is worth spending some time examining good practice when producing tables and figures. For further information see Day (1998).

The term 'figure' may refer to a graph, a schematic, or a picture. A schematic is often used to present information that is difficult to explain in text, due to the inter-relationships between pieces of information. Figure 8.1 is a good example. A picture is used less frequently in scientific reports, however, a picture may be included to illustrate a certain piece of novel equipment. For the purpose of this section on writing the results, only graphs will be considered along with tables, since schematics and pictures are usually included in other sections of a scientific report.

When deciding how to most effectively present the results, often one of the first questions is: what information should be presented as a table and what information should be presented as a graph? Generally, graphs are the presentation form used when data is plotted in relation to a continuous variable; for example, 'time' with a unit of seconds or minutes. Also, graphs are used when comparing two or more groups of data. Tables tend to be used when data relates to a discontinuous variable; for example, subject number. In order to get a feel for the sort information that is normally included in either a graph or a table, look at some scientific reports in exercise and sport journals. In addition, Chapter 8 of this book includes several further examples of different types of tables and graphs.

Tables and figures must be properly titled. The title should be such that the table or figure can be understood without reference to the text. Clearly, therefore, the title has to provide a substantial amount of information in a concise form. In addition, convention dictates that the title for a figure is placed at the side or bottom of the figure, whereas the title for a table is placed at the top of the table (see Table 10.1 and Figures 10.1–10.5 for examples).

The column headings of a table and axes of a graph must be properly labelled. The label should describe what is on the axis or in the column, and provide the unit of measurement in brackets. Failure to include an appropriate unit is a common mistake in student work.

It is preferable to avoid the inclusion of vertical lines in a table (see Table 10.1). It is important that the information in each column is aligned. Sometimes the information is aligned to the left of the column and sometimes to the right. The advantage of aligning numbers to the right of a column is that any decimal points will then line up providing the number of decimal places are consistent within the data in the column.

Horizontal lines are included in tables to isolate the title of a column from the content of a column and to indicate the end of the table. The title of a table usually sits above the first horizontal line and any additional notes or explanations are usually placed below the final horizontal line. If a table contains information about individual participants in addition to group data, a horizontal line is normally included to differentiate the information (see Table 10.1).

Since numerous types of graph are found in scientific reports, a brief explanation will be provided for each type and then examples will be given. Further examples can be found in published articles in peer-reviewed exercise and sport journals.

A **pie chart** is a simple way of presenting data that is categorised (see Figure 10.1). A pie chart expresses the proportion of data that falls within each category as a section of a pie. It is rare to see a pie chart in the exercise and sport literature, since such information is more typically expressed in a percentage form in a table. The reason that such information

Table 10.1 Individual and group training, anthropometric and physiological characteristics for eight well-trained runners (an example of a table)

Participant	Age (Years)	Training history (Years)	Mass (kg)	VO₂ max (L·min⁻¹)
1	40	7	59	4.11
2	31	10	68	5.08
3	35	12	79	4.87
4	47	3	72	3.99
5	29	6	67	3.76
6	36	8	65	4.21
7	35	13	76	4.65
8	32	11	74	4.86
$\bar{X}$	35	9	72	4.49
SD	6	4	5	0.50

Mass, body mass; VO₂ max, maximal oxygen uptake determined during incremental treadmill running. $\bar{X}$, group mean average; SD, group standard deviation.

is tabulated rather than expressed in a graphical form is that a graphical representation does not always help the reader to understand the information any better than a table.

Sometimes the same participants may be monitored prior to and following an intervention, or more than one group may be considered. If the data are still category type, a column (or bar) chart may be used (Figure 10.2).

A variety of **bar charts** (sometimes referred to as **histograms**) are found in the scientific literature (Figure 10.3). Bar charts do not differ substantially from the column charts described in Figure 10.2. Bar charts are often used if the same measurement is made on several occasions in a group of participants.

If the same measurement is taken from a number of participants on a number of occasions, and the participants are from two or more groups, it is often better to view the results as a **line graph** (Figure 10.4). However, care must be taken when joining data points by

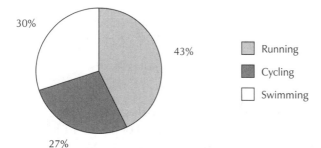

Figure 10.1 Proportion of participants who consider either the swimming, cycling or running event the most important in an Olympic distance triathlon (an example of a pie chart)

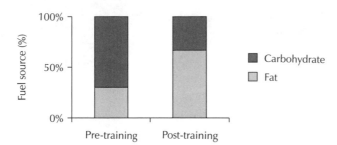

Figure 10.2 Proportion of carbohydrate and fat sources during exercise prior to and following a training intervention (an example of a column chart)

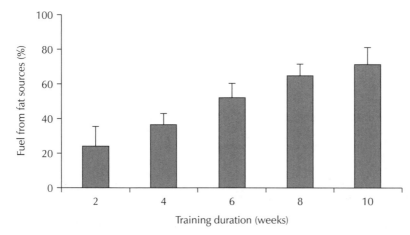

Figure 10.3 Proportion of fat used during exercise after 2, 4, 6, 8 and 10 weeks of training (mean and standard deviation) (an example of a bar chart, or histogram)

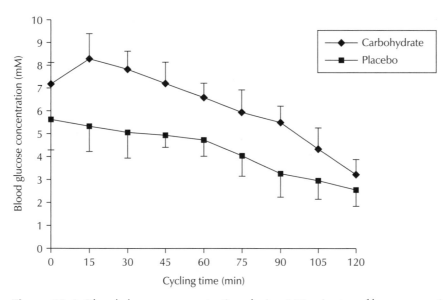

Figure 10.4 Blood glucose concentration during 120 minutes of heavy exercise following ingestion of either 100 g of carbohydrate (10 % solution) or placebo 1 hour prior to exercise (mean and standard deviation) (an example of a line graph)

scientific transferable skills

lines. It is only appropriate to join points by lines if points are related in some way; for example, the same measurement has been made repeatedly. Care must also be taken when selecting which variable forms the x-axis (abscissa) and which variable forms the y-axis (ordinate). The general rule is that the independent variable forms the x-axis and the dependent variable(s) forms the y-axis. The independent variable refers to the variable manipulated by the investigator in order to observe the change in the dependent variable.

If the points on a graph simply refer to individual participants and demonstrate the relationship between two variables, a **scatter plot** may be produced. Again, the same rules apply as is the case for the line graph when allocating variables to axes.

The text that accompanies the tables and figures should draw the readers' attention to important information and make reference to the overall findings. For example, if all participants except one responded in a certain way to an intervention, attention may be drawn to the unique result. The order of presentation of the main findings should be carefully considered. It is often appropriate to take the reader through the results as they emerged from the investigation.

The presentation of statistical results, whether descriptive or inferential in nature, should include an explanation of abbreviations used. For example, the first time that a sample mean average is mentioned, it is important to write the term in full with the abbreviation in brackets following, that is, mean ($\bar{X}$). When an inferential test has been performed to establish whether a difference exists between two data sets, the confidence level selected for the test is normally included after a statement, that is, a significant difference existed

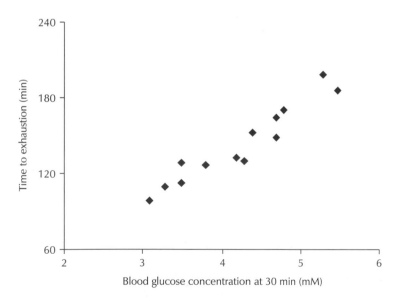

Figure 10.5 Relationship between time to exhaustion and blood glucose concentration after 30 min of exercise (an example of a scatter plot)

between group 1 and 2 ($p < 0.01$). In some situations it may be appropriate to provide the test statistic. For example, in a t-test, the test statistic would be given as $t = 4.54$, where 4.54 would refer to the t-value derived from the statistical test. For further information regarding data analysis, see Chapter 8.

WRITING THE DISCUSSION

Once the results have been presented, it is necessary to explain the results to the reader. The explanation should make reference to the information provided in the introduction and review of literature. Any interpretation of the results should refer to the findings of previous investigations in the area. It is often necessary to include further references, beyond those mentioned in the review of literature, to support points that you are attempting to make. Writing a good discussion is a difficult skill to learn, and looking at discussion sections of published articles in refereed journals may be helpful.

As with the other sections of the report, it is important to lead the reader through the discussion in a logical order. It is often useful to start by summarising the main findings. The hypotheses stated in the introduction (or after the review of literature) should be accepted or rejected in light of the findings of the study.

If inferential data analysis has been undertaken, it will be necessary to discuss the variables that changed significantly within the study. The changes in these variables in relation to changes in other variables that did not reach a significant level may also be of interest. The discussion should attempt to explain why any observed outcomes might have resulted from the investigation. Such a discussion may require consideration of potential mechanisms for the observed outcomes.

It is often important to discuss any potential reasons for discrepancies between the findings from the investigation in question and previous investigations. For example, similarities and differences in the participant groups recruited might be a useful area to explore. The implications of the trained status of the group, or whether the groups are female or male or mixed might be usefully discussed.

Finally, a discussion normally finishes by making the implications of the findings clear. For example, the outcomes might have implications for the practice of training athletes in the future. Alternatively, the findings might have implications for how future research should be conducted. It is quite common to see a discussion of further research areas that result from the findings of the investigation.

WRITING THE CONCLUSION

The main objective of the conclusion is to relate the main findings to the aims of the study and the hypotheses. Were the aims of the study realised, and if so, what were the main implications of these findings? It is quite common to end the conclusion section with a mention of future research which leads on from the present study. It is always useful to emphasise the implications of the findings, since this section highlights the justification for the study. However, it is worth exercising some caution at this stage. A common mistake is to make claims about the implications that are too ambitious, or not substantiated by the findings of the study.

PRODUCING THE REFERENCES

A common question from students of exercise and sport is: why is referencing so important? Most importantly, if the work of other investigators is not acknowledged, a serious academic offence has been committed. This offence is known as **plagiarism**. In many academic courses, the penalty for plagiarism is a complete loss of marks for the work, or more seriously a loss of marks for the whole module or semester. It is not unknown for students to fail their degree for plagiarism offences.

From the outset, it is important to develop a logical system for listing sources that have been consulted. In many cases the sources are numerous, so a method of listing the sources is essential. If a student learns a recognised style of referencing from early in their studies, the work of the student will benefit in the long term. Although the methods used in the most common referencing systems may not seem logical or simple initially, their long standing use by academics is evidence of their usefulness.

There are two components to a referencing system:

1. The provision of a reference in the main text of the report.
2. Production of a list of references at the end of a report.

The styles which are adopted by most institutions and refereed academic journals are the Harvard and Vancouver referencing systems. In the Harvard system, the references appear in the reference list in alphabetical order. In the Vancouver system, the references appear in the reference list in the order in which they were used within the text. For the Harvard system, the citations within the text are given as the author(s) name followed by the year of publication; for example, Williams and James (2000). When more than two authors are on the publication, the reference is given as Williams et al. (2000). For the Vancouver system, within the text a number is given to identify the reference in the reference list at the end of the report.

Both the Harvard and the Vancouver systems are widely used in peer-reviewed exercise and sport journals, and these journals should be consulted for examples. Both systems dictate a convention for reporting a journal or book in a reference list at the end of a report. The following examples include the appropriate method of referencing specific types of book (e.g. single or multiple author, or edited book).

An example of a reference to a journal article:

Atkinson, G. and Nevill, A.M. (1998) Statistical methods for assessing measurement error (reliability) in variables relevant to sports medicine. *Sports Medicine* 26 (4): 217–238.

An example of a reference to a book:

Hinton, P.R. (1996) *Statistics Explained: A Guide for Social Science Students*. London: Routledge.

An example of a reference to a chapter in an edited book:

Rowbottom, D.G., Keast, D. and Morton, A.R. (1998) Monitoring and preventing overreaching and overtraining in endurance athletes. In *Overtraining in Sport*. Kreider, R.B., Fry, A.C. and O'Toole, M.L. (eds) Leeds: Human Kinetics.

APPLICATION OF SCIENCE TO EXERCISE AND SPORT

APPLICATION ONE

When studying exercise and sport, many courses will expect students to perform a laboratory practical following a lecture. The aim of the practical will normally be to provide the student with a greater understanding of points covered in the lecture. A laboratory practical is usually planned by the lecturer, and the students are provided with a protocol to adhere to. Therefore, the main learning is taking place through the observation of and involvement in the practical, and through the comprehension and understanding of the experiment via the production of a report.

A student is encouraged to think through many issues covered in the practical when trying to express the main issues in a clear objective manner in a scientific report. By producing an introduction and review of literature section, the student will be required to visit some of the recommended reading. Through such reading, the student will learn about the basis for the practical, and the outcome of other attempts to perform the same type of investigation. When describing the methods used, the student will learn to outline the participants involved, protocol employed and the treatment of collected data clearly and objectively. Through production of the result section, the student will learn appropriate techniques to analyse and to present the results. The discussion and conclusion will provide experience of relating the findings to previous studies and explaining the practical implications.

APPLICATION TWO

The production of the method section is certainly complicated by the use of an apparatus that is formed from several pieces of equipment. An example would be the traditional

apparatus used for examining gas exchange (see Chapter 2 for further information). This apparatus is often used when studying exercise and sport, and consists of many pieces of equipment, so the description must be carefully written. It may be useful to structure the description of equipment in a chronological order, as is the case when other areas of the method section are described. For example, when examining pulmonary gas exchange, the equipment used could be described in order of where the gas moves after exhalation. You might start with the mouthpiece, then mention any connecting hoses, followed by collection or measurement equipment. Again, for the measurement equipment used for the expired gas, the numerous pieces of equipment should be treated in a logical order. Finally, it may also be important to describe calibration procedures for each piece of measurement equipment.

SELF-TEST

1. List the various sections normally included in a scientific report.
2. List five areas to be included in the abstract section of a scientific report.
3. List five areas to cover in the method section of a scientific report.
4. Describe the main objective of the conclusion section of a scientific report.
5. What referencing styles are normally used in the study of exercise and sport?
6. Show how a book and journal paper are referenced in the reference list.
7. Using the Harvard system, explain how a citation in the text of a report is organised with either two authors or more than two authors.
8. In which section of a scientific report does the author provide the context of the study?
9. In which sections of a scientific report does the author make reference to previous research in the area?

CONCLUSION

It is essential that scientific report writing skills are developed during the study of exercise and sport, since a scientific report is the most common form of communication of information in this area. Most undergraduate courses in exercise and sport related subjects have a final year dissertation based on an investigation performed by the student. The dissertation is arguably the most important single piece of work completed by the student during such courses. The development of scientific report writing skills throughout a course will enable the student to claim an extremely useful transferable skill, in addition to getting the best possible mark for the dissertation project report.

A scientific report does not differ greatly across the range of scientific disciplines. The writing style should be objective, and the writing should be in the third person. The presentation of information should enable the reader to extract the necessary information in the shortest time (see Table 10.2). The use of primarily factual material, presented in a logical order, will help the reader to extract the important information. The factual information should, however, be presented in relation to other previously published work in the area.

Table 10.2 A summary of the content of each section of a scientific report

Report section	Content
Abstract	Sentence to introduce the problem Aim of investigation Brief description of the methods Summary of results Conclusion in relation to aims
Introduction[a]	Narrows from general context to specific investigation rationale Contextual references provided Research question and/or hypotheses[b]
Review of literature	References provided for previous studies in the area Detail given on previous studies, including critical appraisal Research question and/or hypotheses[b]

Methods	Description of the study, including:
	    Participant details
	    Study design
	    Protocols
	    Measurement procedures
	    Data analysis procedures

Results	Description of participant characteristics Tables and figures of results with informative titles Objective written description of results with no attempt to interpret findings
Discussion	Explanation of results Comparison of results with findings from other studies Implications of results for practice and further research
Conclusions	Relate findings to research question/hypotheses Summary of implications for practice and further research
References	List of all references cited in the text Conform to Harvard or Vancouver systems

(a) The introduction may sometimes include the review of literature.
(b) Research questions and/or hypotheses may either be included within the introduction or the review of literature.

188

scientific transferable skills

The nature of scientific work is based upon the idea that a testable scientific theory is developed, which is then subjected to rigorous appraisal. The theory is then adapted if it is found to be inadequate. Therefore, any scientific investigation should set clear hypotheses, based on theoretical underpinnings, which can be tested. Once the results of the study are known, the hypotheses are either accepted or rejected. Since this approach underpins all scientific work, it is essential that any scientific reports present clear, testable hypotheses. The conclusion of a scientific report should always make reference to the hypotheses.

KEY POINTS

- Scientific reports are usually divided into sections to allow the reader to extract information quickly.
- The use of sections in scientific reports is helpful to the author when writing the report.
- Usual sections included in a scientific report include: abstract, introduction, review of literature, method, results, discussion, conclusion and references.
- An abstract normally includes an introductory sentence, a description of the method, and main findings, with a concluding sentence.
- An introduction normally places the investigation in context, and provides detail on the aims and testable hypotheses.
- A review of literature normally describes previous studies in the area in an order which helps the reader to follow a logical thought process.
- A method section normally includes a description of the investigation, including consideration of the participants, design, protocols, measurements, equipment and data analysis.
- Appropriate style of writing and use of terminology will make the description of the methods objective and unambiguous. As a consequence, it should be possible to repeat the experiment exactly.
- A results section will normally present the results in the most appropriate manner, with no form of interpretation.
- A discussion section will normally consider the results in relation to the hypotheses, and the results of previous studies in the area.
- A conclusion section will normally make reference to the aims of the study, and state whether the hypothesis was accepted or rejected.
- Referencing should normally conform to the Harvard or Vancouver systems.

BIBLIOGRAPHY

Day, R.A. (1998) *How to Write & Publish a Scientific Paper*, 5th edition. Cambridge: Cambridge University Press.

Gidlow, C., Johnston, L.H., Crone, D., Ellis, N. and James, D.V.B. (2006) A systematic review of evidence of the relationship between socio-economic position and physical activity. *Health Education Journal*, 65: 338–367.

Graziano, A.M. and Rawlin, M.L. (1993) *Research Methods: A Process of Enquiry*. New York: HarperCollins.

Hyllegard, R., Mood, D.P. and Morrow, J.R. (1996) *Interpreting Research in Sport and Exercise Science*. St Louis, MI: Mosby-Year Book.

Silverman, D. (1993) *Interpreting Qualitative Research*. London: Sage.

Thomas, J.R. and Nelson, J.K. (1996) *Research Methods in Physical Activity*. Champaign IL, Human Kinetics.

Williams, C. (1997) Children's and adolescents' anaerobic performance during cycle ergometry. *Sports Medicine*, 24 (4): 227–240.

FURTHER READING

Barrass, R. (2002). *Scientists Must Write. A Guide to Better Writing for Scientists, Engineers and Students*. London, Routledge.

Beynon, R.J. (1993) *Post Graduate Study in Biological Sciences: A Researchers Companion*. London: Portland Press.

Girden, E.R. (1996) *Evaluating Research Articles*. London: Sage.

Peck, J. and Coyle, M. (2005) *The Student's Guide to Writing. Grammar, Punctuation and Spelling*. New York: Palgrave MacMillan.

scientific transferable skills

APPENDIX 1

HEALTH QUESTIONNAIRE

UNIVERSITY OF
GLOUCESTERSHIRE
at Cheltenham and Gloucester

SPORT & EXERCISE LABORATORIES

Health Questionnaire

About this questionnaire

The purpose of this questionnaire is to gather information about your health and lifestyle. We will use this information to decide whether you are eligible to take part in the testing for which you have volunteered. It is important that you answer the questions truthfully. The information you give will be treated in confidence. Your completed form will be stored securely for 5 years and then destroyed.

Section 1, which has been completed by the tester, provides basic information about the testing for which you have volunteered. Sections 2 to 7 are for you to complete: please circle the appropriate response or write your answer in the space provided. Please also complete section 8. Sections 9 and 10 will be completed by the tester, after you have completed sections 2 to 8.

Section 1: The testing (completed by tester)

To complete the testing for which you have volunteered you will be required to undertake:

Moderate exercise (i.e. exercise that makes you breathe more heavily than you do at rest but not so heavily that you are unable to maintain a conversation)

Vigorous exercise (i.e. exercise that makes you breathe so heavily that you are unable to maintain a conversation)

The testing involves:

Walking	❏	Generating or absorbing high forces through your arms	❏
Running	❏	Generating or absorbing high forces through your shoulders	❏

Cycling ❑	Generating or absorbing high forces through your trunk	❑
Rowing ❑	Generating or absorbing high forces through your hips	❑
Swimming ❑	Generating or absorbing high forces through your legs	❑
Jumping ❑		

Section 2: General information

Name: .... Sex: M ❑ F ❑ Age: ....

Height (approx.): .... Weight (approx.): ....

Section 3: Initial considerations

1. Do any of the following apply to you?   No   Yes

    a) I have HIV, Hepatitis A, Hepatitis B or Hepatitis C
    b) I am pregnant
    c) I have a muscle or joint problem that could be aggravated
       by the testing described in section 1
    d) I am feeling unwell today
    e) I have had a fever in the last 7 days

(If you have answered "Yes" to question 1, go straight to section 8)

Section 4: Habitual physical activity

2a. Do you typically perform moderate exercise (as defined in   No   Yes
     section 1) for 20 minutes or longer at least twice a week?

2b. Have you performed this type of exercise within the last 10 days?   No   Yes

3a. Do you typically perform vigorous exercise (as defined in   No   Yes
     section 1) at least once a week?

3b. Have you performed this type of exercise within the last 10 days?   No   Yes

Section 5: Known medical conditions

4. Do **any** of the following apply to you?   No   Yes

    a) I have had Type 1 diabetes for more than 15 years
    b) I have Type 1 diabetes and am over 30 years old
    c) I have Type 2 diabetes and am over 35 years old

5. Have you ever had a stroke?   No   Yes

6. Has your doctor ever said you have heart trouble?　　　No　　Yes

7. Do **both** of the following apply to you?　　　No　　Yes
   a)　I take asthma medication
   b)　I have experienced shortness of breath or difficulty with
   breathing in the last 4 weeks?

8. Do you have any of the following: cancer, COPD, cystic fibrosis,　No　　Yes
   other lung disease, liver disease, kidney disease, mental illness,
   osteoporosis, severe arthritis, a thyroid problem?

(If you have answered "Yes" to any questions in section 5, go straight to section 8.)

Section 6: Signs and symptoms

9. Do you often have pains in your heart, chest, or the surrounding　No　　Yes
   areas?

10. Do you experience shortness of breath, either at rest or with　No　　Yes
    mild exertion?

11. Do you often feel faint or have spells of severe dizziness?　　No　　Yes

12. Have you, in the last 12 months, experienced difficulty with　No　　Yes
    breathing when lying down or been awakened at night by
    shortness of breath?

13. Do you experience swelling or a build up of fluid in or around　No　　Yes
    your ankles?

14. Do you often get the feeling that your heart is racing or skipping　No　　Yes
    beats, either at rest or during exercise?

15. Do you regularly get pains in your calves and lower legs during　No　　Yes
    exercise that are not due to soreness or stiffness?

16. Has your doctor ever told you that you have a heart murmur?　No　　Yes

17. Do you experience unusual fatigue or shortness of breath during　No　　Yes
    everyday activities?

(If you have answered "Yes" to any questions in section 6, go straight to section 8.)

Section 7: Risk factors

18. Does **either** of the following apply to you?　　　No　　Yes
    a)　I smoke cigarettes on a daily basis
    b)　I stopped smoking cigarettes on a daily basis less than
    6 months ago

19. Has your doctor ever told you that you have high blood pressure?   No   Yes

20. Has your doctor ever told you that you have high cholesterol?   No   Yes

21. Has your father or any of your brothers had a heart attack,   No   Yes
heart surgery, or a stroke before the age of 55?

22. Has your mother or any of your sisters had a heart attack,   No   Yes
heart surgery, or a stroke before the age of 65?

23. Do **any** of the following apply to you?   No   Yes
    a)   I have had Type 1 diabetes for less than 15 years
    b)   I have Type 1 diabetes and am 30 or younger
    c)   I have Type 2 diabetes and am 35 or younger

Section 8: Signatures

Participant: ....   Date: ....

Guardian*: ....   Date: ....

(*Required only if the participant is under 18 years of age.)

_____

Section 9: Additional risk factors (to be completed by the tester if relevant)

24. Is the participant's body mass index >30 kg/m²?   No   Yes

25. Has the participant answered no to questions 2a **and** 3a?   No   Yes

Section 10: Eligibility (to be completed by the tester)

26. Is the participant eligible for the testing?   No   Yes

Name (of tester): ....

Signature: ....   Date:...........................

APPENDIX 2

EXAMPLE CONSENT FORM

Royal Devon and Exeter
NHS Foundation Trust

Study Number [number issued by R&D Office]: ....

Patient Identification Number for this trial: ....

CONSENT FORM

Title of Project: ....

Name of Researcher: ....

Please initial box

1   I confirm that I have read and understand the information sheet [Version 1 dated] for the above study and have had the opportunity to ask questions. ☐

2   I understand that my participation is voluntary and that I am free to withdraw at any time, without giving any reason, without my medical care or legal rights being affected. ☐

3   I understand that sections of any of my medical notes may be looked at by researchers in the study where it is relevant to my records and that this information will be kept secure. ☐

4   I am aware of all tests and procedures involved in the research visits. ☐

5   I understand what each exercise test involves and the associated risks of exercise testing. ☐

6   I give consent for my personal data to be used as indicated in the patient information sheet [Version 1 dated]. I understand that my personal data file and computer used to store my data will be password protected. My data will be stored for 15 years after the end of the study. ☐

7   I agree to take part in the above study. ☐

_____	_____	_____
Name of participant	Date	Signature
_____	_____	_____
Name of parent or guardian	Date	Signature
_____	_____	_____
Researcher	Date	Signature

Version 1; date; 1 for patient; 1 for researcher; 1 to be kept with hospital notes

APPENDIX 3

THERMAL EQUIVALENTS OF OXYGEN

Thermal equivalents of oxygen for the non-protein respiratory quotient (RQ), including per cent kilocalories and grams derived from carbohydrate (CHO) and fat

Non-protein RQ	kcal per litre O_2	Per cent kcal derived from		Grams per litre O_2 derived from	
		CHO	Fat	CHO	Fat
0.707	4.686	0.0	100.0	0.000	0.495
0.71	4.690	1.0	99.0	0.012	0.490
0.72	4.702	4.4	95.6	0.054	0.473
0.73	4.714	7.8	92.2	0.095	0.456
0.74	4.727	11.3	88.7	0.136	0.439
0.75	4.739	14.7	85.3	0.177	0.423
0.76	4.751	18.1	81.9	0.218	0.406
0.77	4.764	21.5	78.5	0.259	0.389
0.78	4.776	24.9	75.1	0.301	0.372
0.79	4.788	28.3	71.7	0.342	0.355
0.80	4.801	31.7	68.3	0.383	0.338
0.81	4.813	35.2	64.8	0.424	0.321
0.82	4.825	38.6	61.4	0.465	0.304
0.83	4.838	42.0	58.0	0.507	0.287
0.84	4.850	45.4	54.6	0.548	0.270
0.85	4.862	48.8	51.2	0.589	0.254
0.86	4.875	52.2	47.8	0.630	0.237
0.87	4.887	55.6	44.4	0.671	0.220
0.88	4.899	59.0	41.0	0.712	0.203
0.89	4.911	62.5	37.5	0.754	0.186
0.90	4.924	65.9	34.1	0.795	0.169
0.91	4.936	69.3	30.7	0.836	0.152
0.92	4.948	72.7	27.3	0.877	0.135
0.93	4.961	76.1	23.9	0.918	0.118
0.94	4.973	79.5	20.5	0.959	0.101
0.95	4.985	82.9	17.1	1.001	0.085
0.96	4.998	86.3	13.7	1.042	0.068

0.97	5.010	89.8	10.2	1.083	0.051
0.98	5.022	93.2	6.8	1.124	0.034
0.99	5.035	96.6	3.4	1.165	0.017
1.00	5.047	100.0	0.0	1.207	0.000

Source: G. Lusk (1926), *Science of Nutrition*

APPENDIX 4

SCIENTIFIC JOURNALS IN EXERCISE AND SPORT

American Journal of Sports Medicine
Applied Psychophysiology and Biofeedback
Applied Physiology, Nutrition and Metabolism
Australian Journal of Science and Medicine in Sport
British Journal of Physical Education
British Journal of Sports Medicine
Culture Sport Society
European Journal of Applied Physiology
European Physical Education Review
Exercise and Sports Science Review
International Journal of Physical Education
International Journal of Sport Psychology
International Journal of Sport Nutrition
International Journal of Sports Medicine
International Journal of the History of Sport
International Review for the Sociology of Sport
Journal of Ageing and Physical Activity
Journal of Applied Biomechanics
Journal of Applied Physiology
Journal of Applied Sport Psychology
Journal of Human Movement Studies
Journal of Motor Behaviour
Journal of Physical Education Recreation and Dance
Journal of Physiology
Journal of Science and Medicine in Sport
Journal of Sport and Exercise Psychology
Journal of Sport and Social Issues
Journal of Sport Behaviour
Journal of Sport Rehabilitation
Journal of Sports Management
Journal of Sports Medicine and Physical Fitness

Journal of Sports Sciences
Journal of the Philosophy of Sport
Medicine and Science in Sport and Exercise
Motor Control
New Studies in Athletics
Pediatric Exercise Science
Perceptual and Motor Skills
Quest
Research Quarterly for Exercise and Sport
Sociology of Sport Journal
Sport History Review
Sport Psychologist
Sports Medicine
Women in Sport and Physical Activity Journal

APPENDIX 5

MEASUREMENT CONCEPTS

In exercise and sport work, either in the laboratory or in the field, it is often necessary to critically examine any data collected. Quite often it is desirable to know how similar the results would be were the same procedure repeated on more than one occasion. Such a concept may be given several terms depending on the type of measurement. If measurements are taken from a single piece of equipment, the appropriate term is 'precision'. If measurements are taken from more than one piece of equipment, and then used to determine a further value, the appropriate term is 'reliability'. If data are taken from a psychological inventory, the appropriate term is also 'reliability'.

It is also desirable to know whether measurements are giving the correct information. Again, such a concept may be given several terms depending on the type of measurement. When data are collected from a single measurement, the appropriate term is 'accuracy'. When data are derived from several measurements, the appropriate term is 'validity'. When data are derived from a psychological inventory, the appropriate term is also 'validity'.

When dealing with data from interviews, it is not possible to separate reliability from validity. A composite measure is that of trustworthiness. Saying data are trustworthy is similar to saying they are both valid and reliable.

An example of precision without accuracy

An example of accuracy and precision

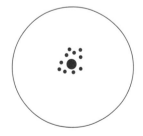

	Reliability		*Validity*
Single measurement	Precision		Accuracy
Compilation of measurements	Reliability		Validity
Psychological inventory	Reliability		Validity
Interview		Trustworthiness	

KEY TERMS

Abstract   An overview of a research paper or research report.

Acceleration   Increase in velocity with respect to time.

Acute   Short term or sudden.

Adenosine triphosphate   A high-energy compound essential for human energy transfer.

ATPS   Refers to gas volumes under specific conditions, which include **a**mbient **t**emperature (in kelvins), ambient **p**ressure (in mm of mercury) and saturated with water vapour (at 37°C water vapour pressure is 47.1 mmHg).

Bar chart   A graphical representation of data, in which bar height normally represents the magnitude of the dependent variable.

BMR   Basal metabolic rate (BMR) is reflected by the body's heat production during basal conditions under specific conditions, which include no food consumption in the previous 12 hours, no intense physical activity in the previous 24 hours, and a 30 minute period of rest in the supine position prior to data collection. The BMR is directly determined using a calorimeter or indirectly estimated by measuring whole body respiratory variables.

BTPS   Refers to gas volumes under specific conditions, which include **b**ody **t**emperature (in kelvins, usually 310 K), ambient **p**ressure (in mm of Mercury) and saturated with water vapour (at 37°C water vapour pressure is 47.1 mmHg). Pulmonary physiologists normally report ventilation and lung function data in a BTPS form.

Calibration   A procedure comparing known reference values against measured values to determine accuracy.

Capacity   A magnitude of the ability to do something.

Carbohydrate   A macronutrient comprised of carbon, hydrogen and oxygen, supplying energy that is particularly important during intense physical activity.

Case study   A study of a single instance or matter for discussion.

Categorical data   Data that may be arranged in categories, but the categories cannot be ranked (e.g. sport preference).

Chemical energy   Energy stored in a chemical form that may be converted into an alternative form (e.g. heat).

Chronic   Continuing for a long time or constantly recurring.

Coefficient of variation   A standardised measure of variance which is a ratio of the standard deviation and the mean average, usually expressed as a percentage.

Cohesion   The attractive forces which hold together atoms or molecules forming a solid or liquid.

Composition of forces   The sum of more than one force expressed as a magnitude and direction.

Concentration   The strength of a solution, often expressed as the amount of solute for a given volume unit of solvent. The concentration can be expressed as weight in grams or milligrams, number of ions in moles (mol) or number of solute ions in equivalents (equiv.).

Conclusion   The summing up at the end of an essay or report that outlines the key findings.

Conduction   The transfer of heat energy when two surfaces are in contact with one another or the transfer of electrical energy from one place to another.

Confidence interval   An interval calculated as a number of standard deviations from the mean average of a data set. Used to determine, with a degree of confidence, whether a sample comes from a population or an individual observation comes from a sample.

Control group   A group of participants in a study that does not receive any intervention or treatment.

Correlation coefficient   A standardised measure of the degree of linearity of the relationship between two variables.

Cross-over design   A study design where the control group becomes the experimental group and the experimental group becomes the control group.

Cycle ergometer   A device for quantifying the work done by a participant rotating a wheel against a known resistive force.

Data   Information, sometimes in a numerical form, that may be collated, organised and analysed.

Declaration of Helsinki   A written document summarising the outcomes of a meeting in Helsinki regarding the treatment of human participants in clinical research.

Density   Density is a function of the ratio of mass and volume. The unit is $g \cdot cm^{-3}$.

Descriptive data analysis   Collation, organisation and manipulation of data in order to describe it.

Differentiation   The operation used in calculus to obtain the differential coefficient. Commonly applied to find a maximum value.

Direct measurement   Observing and recording a phenomenon through direct means.

Discussion   In relation to a report or essay, a section which examines the results in relation to other work in the area.

Dissertation   An extensive report of original research often forming part of a programme of study in academia.

Drag   A force opposing movement.

Efficiency   A term relating to the effectiveness of transfer of energy. In exercise and sport, the term is often applied to the ratio of energy used to work done.

Elasticity   The property of a material which allows it to return to its original shape after deformation.

Energy   The capability to do work, expressed in units of joules (J) or kilocalories (kcal).

Energy expenditure   The energy expended by the body as a result of the basal metabolic rate and the thermic effects of food and physical activity.

Ethics committee   A group that has responsibility for examining the conduct of working practice to see that fair treatment of individuals takes place.

Experimental group   Participants in a study who receive the intervention.

Fat   A macronutrient composed of carbon, hydrogen and oxygen, which is an important source of energy for lower intensity physical activity.

Fatigue index   The reduction of power output (or speed) during all-out physical activity, expressed in a quantified form.

Force parallelogram   A diagrammatic representation of forces that is helpful when attempting to compose or resolve forces.

Force plate   A metal plate which is inserted into the ground so that its surface is level with the ground. The plate can determine force in one vertical and two horizontal directions through a series of strain gauges.

Force   A vector quantity which causes acceleration or deceleration of an object when acting upon it. Force is measured in newtons (N).

Friction   A resistive force when one object moves relative to another object and their surfaces are in contact.

Gravitational force   The force acting because of gravity. At the earth's surface, this force exerts $9.81 \text{ m}\cdot\text{s}^{-2}$.

Ground reaction force   The equal and opposite force acting on the body when it comes into contact with the ground surface.

Health questionnaire   A series of written questions which ask individuals about their health. The outcomes may allow a researcher to make decisions about safe exercise intensities for example.

Health screening   A process of systematically examining health status prior to treatment or intervention, often including completion of a health questionnaire and physical examination.

Histogram   A graphical representation of the frequency of observations within particular categories.

Human participants   Individuals who agree to take part in a study after being fully informed of the nature of the study and the risks and benefits involved.

Hyperbaria   Barometric pressure in excess of that normally found at the earth's surface.

Hypobaria   Barometric pressure less that that normally found at the earth's surface.

Hypotheses   Suggested explanations for a group of facts which are normally then tested through investigation. Often a null hypothesis and an alternative hypothesis are presented.

Ideal gas   A gas that behaves according to the ideal gas laws which specify the behaviour of gas under known conditions of volume, temperature and pressure.

Impact peak   The highest force exerted on the body as it comes into contact with the ground or another surface.

Impulse   A product of force (N) and time (s).

Indirect calorimetry   A method of estimating the metabolic rate by indirect means (e.g. respiratory gas exchange).

Inferential data analysis   Manipulation of data to determine, with a degree of confidence, relationships and differences in the populations under consideration. Relationship tests include Spearman's rank and Pearson's product moment correlation tests. Difference tests include *t*-test, analysis of variance, Mann-Whitney, Wilcoxon, Kruskal-Wallis, and Friedman.

Informed consent   An agreement to take part in an activity following a full explanation of the nature of the activity and the inherent risks and benefits. Normally it is good practice to obtain written consent.

Internal energy   The result of the movement of atoms within matter, often expressed as heat.

Interval   In relation to data, that which is continuous and may be subjected to parametric statistical analysis.

Introduction   The section of a scientific report which provides context and background.

Inverse   A function where the number in question is the denominator and the numerator is one.

Involuntary   An action which requires no conscious cognitive process.

Isokinetic   A change of joint angle as a result of muscle shortening or lengthening that takes place at a constant fixed velocity.

Isometric   A muscle contraction that does not result in muscle lengthening or shortening or a change in joint angle.

Isotonic   A change in joint angle as a result of muscle lengthening or shortening that takes place at a variable velocity.

Joule   A unit of energy or work defined as that required to displace a force of 1 N through 1 m in the line of action of the force.

Journals   Publications of peer-reviewed academic work, often including original research.

Kilogram calorie (Kilocalorie)   A unit of energy defined as that required to increase the temperature of 1 kg of water by 1°C under standard conditions.

Kinematics   The branch of mechanics concerned with motion without reference to mass or force.

Kinetic energy   The capability to do work as a result of movement.

Laminar   In relation to the flow of fluids, the situation with uniform velocity throughout a vessel.

Laws of motion   The fundamental laws upon which the dynamics branch of mechanics is based. Laws of motion are attributed to Sir Isaac Newton.

Lever   The application of a force pivoted about a fulcrum, which results in a mechanical advantage.

Limiting friction   The frictional force observed as the applied force is increased to a point where the object is about to start sliding.

Line graph   A graphical representation of data using an *x-y* coordinate system, with successive coordinate points joined by a line.

206

key terms

Mean absolute deviation A measure of variance of a sample of data, the calculation of which includes all observations within the sample of data.

Mean A measure of central tendency of a sample of data, the calculation of which includes all observations within the sample of data.

Mechanical stress The application of force, expressed in terms relative to the cross-sectional area of the object.

Median A measure of central tendency of a sample of data, the calculation of which includes all observations within the sample of data, but does not account for the magnitude of each observation.

Methods The section of a scientific report that describes the participants, study design, protocol, measurements and equipment included in a study. It should provide enough information for the study to be repeated.

Mode A measure of central tendency of a sample of data based on the most frequent observation.

Modulus of elasticity A constant value which is specific to a material and quantifies the elastic properties of that material.

Molarity The number of moles of solute per litre of solution.

Mole The amount of substance, defined as 6.02×10^{23} atoms, ions or molecules of a substance.

Newton The unit of measurement of force, abbreviated as N.

Nominal In relation to data, that which is discontinuous and may be organised into categories.

Normal distribution A bell-shaped frequency distribution that appears to underlie many human variables.

Ordinal In relation to data, that which is discontinuous, may be organised into ordered categories, and may be subjected to non-parametric statistical analysis.

Partial pressure In relation to gases, the pressure of a single gas within a mixed gas.

Pascal The standard international unit of pressure, abbreviated as Pa.

Performance The ability to undertake a clearly defined task.

Pie chart A graphical representation of data in the form of a circle, where the size of each sector of the circle reflects the magnitude of the category represented.

Plagiarism The use of ideas or work of another person, without giving appropriate credit.

Plastic A material which deforms under loading and does not return back to its original length.

Population In relation to statistics, the entire aggregate from which individuals or samples are drawn.

Potential energy The capability of an object to do work because of its position.

Power The unit of measurement for work done per unit time, or energy used per unit time, given the unit watt (W).

Pressure The unit of measurement for the force exerted per unit cross-sectional area, given the unit pascal (Pa).

Pressure gradient The difference in pressure between two points which results in the movement of a fluid (i.e. liquid or gas).

Principle of conservation of energy   The first law of thermodynamics states that energy cannot be created or destroyed, but can be changed from one form to another.

Protein   A nutrient composed of the chemical compounds nitrogen, carbon, hydrogen and oxygen, and which forms an essential part of the diet.

Pulmonary   A term used to describe something related to the lungs; for example, pulmonary circulation.

Radiation   A form of heat exchange which relies on electromagnetic waves.

Random errors   Errors that are not systematic and have no consistency during the measurement process.

Range   A measure of variation of data in a sample which simply takes into account the highest and lowest value of the sample.

Ratio   The highest level of data, which is continuous, and may be subjected to parametric statistical analysis.

Reaction force   An opposing force.

References   The section of a scientific report which includes the sources of the literature consulted in preparation of the report.

Repeated measures   Data which are collected from the same participants on more than one occasion.

Research ethics committee   A group of individuals whose job it is to review research proposals and provide ethical approval.

Research question   In a scientific study or report, the issue to be addressed expressed as a question.

Resolution of forces   Separation of a force into its component forces, all of which are allocated a magnitude and direction.

Results   The section of a scientific report which presents the findings, either in prose or in graphical form.

Review of literature   The section of a scientific report which makes reference to previous work published in the area.

Rigid body   A body which does not deform under conditions of moderate force application.

Sample   A group taken from a population which is representative of the population under investigation.

Scalar   A quantity which has a magnitude but no direction.

Scatter plot   A graphical representation of data by plotting x-y coordinates in two dimensions.

Scientific paradigm   In relation to scientific work, an investigative approach.

Solute   Substance that dissolves in a solvent, forming a solution.

Solution   A mixture of two or more substances, formed from a solute and a solvent.

Solvent   A liquid in which a solute dissolves.

Standard deviation   A measure of variation within a sample about a mean average value, which is numerically equal to the square root of the variance.

Standard error of the mean   A measure of variation of sample means about the mean average of the sample means.

208

key terms

Static electricity   A result of contact between two objects creating a net movement of positive and negative charges within each object.

Statistical error   An error in which an inappropriate conclusion about the population is drawn from an investigation caused by the criteria set for the data analysis. A type I statistical error occurs when no real difference exists but the data analysis shows a difference. A type II statistical error occurs when a real difference exists but the data analysis shows no difference.

STPD   Refers to gas volumes under specific standardised conditions, which include standard **t**emperature (in kelvins), ambient **p**ressure (in mm of mercury) and **d**ry (no water vapour).

Strain gauge   A device for determining the extent of deformation of a material as a result of stress placed upon it.

Surface tension   In water, the result of hydrogen bonding with oxygen.

Système Internationale (SI) units   A standardised system of units for reporting the magnitude of measurements, which is accepted internationally.

Tangent   In a right-angled triangle, the ratio of the side opposite the right angle and the side adjacent to the right angle.

Tensile limit   The maximum load that may be applied to a material before it fractures.

Theory   A explanation for observed events.

Thermal conductivity   The method of transfer of internal energy between atoms within a material.

Thermodynamics   The properties of a material which relate to the transfer of heat energy.

Third person   A style of writing which avoids the use of terms such as 'I', 'we', etc., and is used in scientific report writing.

Torque   The product of force and displacement of the application of the force from the pivotal fulcrum.

Trigonometry   A mathematical construct which is based on the properties of right-angled triangles.

Turbulent   The erratic pattern of flow of a fluid when the velocity of flow of the fluid is high or flow is obstructed.

Variance   A measure of variation within a sample of data, calculation of which is based on all the observations in the sample.

Vector   A quantity which has both magnitude and direction.

Viscosity   An internal friction of a fluid which provides resistance to motion.

Voluntary   An action involving a conscious cognitive process.

Watt   The unit of measurement of power, abbreviated as W.

Work   The transfer of energy, defined as the displacement of the application of the point of a force through 1 m in line with the direction of application of the force.

Yield point   The point in the deformation of a material at which the property of a material changes from elastic to plastic.

INDEX

eBooks – at www.eBookstore.tandf.co.uk

A library at your fingertips!

eBooks are electronic versions of printed books. You can store them on your PC/laptop or browse them online.

They have advantages for anyone needing rapid access to a wide variety of published, copyright information.

eBooks can help your research by enabling you to bookmark chapters, annotate text and use instant searches to find specific words or phrases. Several eBook files would fit on even a small laptop or PDA.

NEW: Save money by eSubscribing: cheap, online access to any eBook for as long as you need it.

Annual subscription packages

We now offer special low-cost bulk subscriptions to packages of eBooks in certain subject areas. These are available to libraries or to individuals.

For more information please contact webmaster.ebooks@tandf.co.uk

We're continually developing the eBook concept, so keep up to date by visiting the website.

www.eBookstore.tandf.co.uk